Study Guide

SURVEY OF
ECONOMICS

PRINCIPLES AND TOOLS

Study Guide

SURVEY OF
ECONOMICS

PRINCIPLES AND TOOLS

O'Sullivan/Sheffrin

Fernando Quijano
Yvonn Quijano
Janice Boucher Breuer

Upper Saddle River, New Jersey 07458

Executive editor: Rod Banister
Assistant editor: Marie McHale
Production editor: Wanda Rockwell
Manufacturer: Banta Book Group

ISBN 0-13-067066-9

10 9 8 7 6 5 4 3 2 1

TABLE OF CONTENTS

PREFACE

This study guide has been designed as a practicum; a place for you to practice the material that you have learned. The practicum is meant to promote comprehension of economic principles and your ability to apply these principles to different problems. This ability to apply the economic principles is the skill that you will be required to use when you take an economics exam and that will be further developed in future economics courses.

The study guide contains performance enhancing tips (PETS). These PETS are tips to help you through the rougher material in each chapter. They are also designed to reinforce some principles that are repeatedly used throughout the course.

The study guide also contains practice exam questions along with their answers. For the multiple-choice questions, the correct answer is explained in detail and explanations are provided for why the other options are incorrect. This will help you learn not only why an answer is right, but why other answers are wrong. Detailed answers for the essay questions are also provided. This practice will certainly help out when it comes time for an exam.

CHAPTER 1
PRINCIPLES OF ECONOMICS

I. OVERVIEW

In this chapter, you will be introduced to economics. You will also be introduced to basic graphing principles and the formula for a slope and for calculating a percentage change. You will learn about the basic economic problem of scarcity and see how it is represented with a graph. You will learn about the resources a society has that enable it to produce goods and services (output). You will learn what a market is. You will also learn about some of the terms and techniques used by economists use for thinking about problems that a society, an individual, or a firm faces.

You will also learn fundamental economic principles that will be used throughout this course. You will learn that decisions made by a household, business, or government generally involve an opportunity cost; choosing one option means that other options must be given up or sacrificed or foregone. You will learn about the marginal principle. The marginal principle can be used to guide decisions. It requires that the marginal benefit be compared to the marginal cost of undertaking an activity. You will learn about the principle of diminishing returns. The principle of diminishing returns means that more and more effort devoted to an activity leads to smaller and smaller increases (or improvements) in the activity. Diminishing returns arise when more and more effort is exerted but there is no change in other factors which affect the activity. You will learn about the spillover principle. The spillover principle means that the benefits and costs of an activity may "spillover" to other parties not directly involved in the activity. Lastly, you will learn about the reality principle. The reality principle requires that you think in "inflation-adjusted" terms. That is, you must always consider the effects of rising price (inflation) on your income, pay raises, and interest and dividend earnings from financial investments, as well as on your debt. A true picture of the national economy also requires that you think of its performance in inflation-adjusted terms.

II. CHECK LIST

By the end of this chapter, you should be able to do the following:

Explain the concept of scarcity.
√   Use the production possibilities curve to reflect scarcity.
√   List the resources or factors of production a society has that enable it to produce goods and services.
√   Describe what it means for a society to be producing at a point inside, along, and outside the production possibilities curve.
√   Define a market and explain why it exists.
√   Describe the usefulness of making assumptions.
√   Explain what is meant by "ceteris paribus."

√   Describe ways in which economic thinking can be used.

√   Distinguish between microeconomic and macroeconomic issues.

√   Draw a picture of a graph with a positive slope and a negative slope.

√   Compute the slope of a graph.

√   Determine what will cause a graph to shift and in what direction and what will cause a movement along a graph.

√   Compute a percentage change and use it to make other calculations.

√   Evaluate the opportunity cost that is encountered when choosing an activity (e.g. attending a party on Saturday night, furthering your education, opening up a new factory, building more schools, cutting tax rates).

√   Use the production possibilities curve to compute the opportunity cost of producing one good or bundles of goods instead of another.

√   Explain why opportunity costs increase in moving either up or down the production possibilities curve.

√   Use marginal analysis to decide the level at which an activity should be undertaken.

√   Explain why picking an activity level where "marginal benefit" = "marginal cost" is the best choice.

√   Explain why fixed costs are not relevant for marginal analysis, i.e. why it is that fixed costs do not matter in selecting an activity level.

√   Explain the circumstances under which diminishing returns occur and under what circumstances it does not occur.

√   Explain the spillover principle and give examples of spillover benefits and spillover costs.

√   Use the reality principle to assess how well off you are based on the income you earn, any pay raises you might get, or any interest earnings you might receive from financial investments.

√   Use the reality principle to get a true picture of the state of the economy.

√   Explain the difference between nominal and real variables.

III. KEY TERMS

Economics: the study of the choices made by people who are faced with scarcity.

Scarcity: a situation in which resources are limited and can be used in different ways, so we must sacrifice one thing for another.

Factors of production: the resources used to produce goods and services.

Natural resources: things created by acts of nature and used to produce goods and services.

Labor: human effort, including both physical and mental effort, used to produce goods and services.

Physical capital: objects made by humans used to produce goods and services.

Human capital: the knowledge and skills acquired by a worker through education and experience and used to produce goods and services.

Entrepreneurship: effort used to coordinate the production and sale of goods and services.

Production possibilities curve: a curve that shows the possible combinations of goods and services available to an economy, given that all productive resources are fully employed and efficiently used.

Microeconomics: the study of the choices made by consumers, firms, and government, how their decisions affect the market for a particular good or service.

Market: an arrangement that allows buyers and sellers to exchange things: a buyer exchanges money for a product, while a seller exchanges a product for money.

Macroeconomics: the study of the nation's economy as a whole.

Variable: a measure of something that can take on different values.

Ceteris paribus: Latin, meaning "other variables are held fixed."

Principle: a simple truth that most people understand and accept.

Opportunity cost: what you sacrifice to get something.

Marginal benefit: the extra benefit resulting from a small increase in some activity.

Marginal cost: the additional cost resulting from a small increase in some activity.

Fixed costs: costs that do not change as the level of an activity changes.

Explicit costs: costs in the form of actual cash payments.

Implicit costs: the opportunity cost of non-purchased inputs.

Diminishing returns: as one input increases while holding the other inputs are held fixed, output increases, but at a decreasing rate.

Total product curve: a curve showing the relationship between the quantity of labor and the quantity of output.

Marginal product of labor: the change in output from one additional worker.

Short Run: a period of time over which one or more factors of production is fixed; in most cases, a period of time over which a firm cannot modify an existing facility or build a new one.

Long run: a period of time long enough that a firm can change all the factors of production, meaning that a firm can modify its existing production facility or build a new one.

Spillover or externality: a cost or benefit experienced by people who are external to the decision about how much of a good to produce or consume.

Nominal value: the face value of an amount of money.

Real value: the value of an amount of money in terms of the quantity of goods the money can buy.

IV. PERFORMANCE ENHANCING TIPS (PETS)

PET #1

A graph of the relationship between X and Y (use whatever variables you like) will SHIFT when other variables, like Z, G, and J (use whatever variables you like) which are relevant to the relationship between X and Y change. Changes in the variables, X and Y, that are being graphed, will NOT cause a shift of the curve but instead will cause a MOVEMENT along the curve.

As your textbook discusses in the appendix to chapter 1, a graph shows the relationship between two variables while holding fixed or constant (i.e. the "ceteris paribus" condition) other variables that are relevant to the relationship being graphed.

Generically speaking, a graph of the relationship between X and Y holds other variables, like Z, G, J, etc. that are relevant to the relationship between X and Y fixed. That is, the relationship assumed to hold between X and Y is based on current state of other variables believed to be relevant to X and Y. The relationship between X and Y is drawn for today, and what the values of Z, G, and J are today, not, e.g. one year later. For example, a graph of the relationship between age and income earning potential holds other variables, like level of education, skills, and perhaps even whether the government administration is Republican or Democrat at the time the relationship is drawn.

Suppose the graph below labeled "A" was drawn for you during your senior year in high school when you had not yet decided whether or not you wanted to attend college.

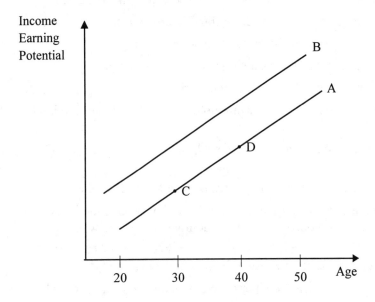

The graph shows that as you get older, your income earning potential will rise.

Now, draw the graph assuming you have graduated from college. You should expect your income earning potential, for any and every age, will be higher since you are now more educated. How could you represent this with the graph? Since your income earning potential will be higher after you have graduated from college than if you had not graduated from college, graph A would be shifted up, to the left. This is represented by the graph labeled B. Now, notice that when you compare your income earning potential at any and every age, it is higher, which is consistent with the assumption that more education leads to higher income earning potential, regardless of age. That is, the graph shows that at age 30, the income earning potential of the college graduate exceeds that of the high school graduate. The same is true at age 40, 50, and so on.

Suppose you are told that the earth's temperature had increased by 1 degree since the graph had been drawn. What would this do to the graph? Nothing. The change in the earth's temperature is not a variable that is relevant to the relationship between age and income earning potential. Therefore, its change will not cause a shift in the curve.

Suppose you are asked what happens to the curve when age increases? Since age is graphed on one of the axes, a change in age is simply represented by a movement along the curve, say from point C to D, as age increases. An increase in age should NOT be represented by a shift in the curve. A shift in the curve can only occur when some other variable, besides age or income earning potential, that is relevant to the relationship, changes.

PET #2

The numeric value computed from a slope can be a very informative piece of information, especially when debating economic policy. For example, a statement like "an increase in the budget deficit will raise interest rates" may be a given, but what is the magnitude (or numeric value) of this relationship? Is it big or small? If it is very small, perhaps policymakers needn't worry about the effects of the budget deficit on interest rates. Similarly, a statement like "an increase in the unemployment rate will bring inflation down" may be a given, but what is the magnitude (or numeric value) of this relationship? Is it big or small? If it is very big, then a country that has a high rate of inflation may be willing to sacrifice an increase in its unemployment rate in order to bring down inflation. Otherwise, maybe not.

An easy way to compare the slopes of two graphs of the same relationship is to draw them as below, where both of them start from the same value on the X or Y axis. Then, consider the same change in the value on either the X or Y axis:

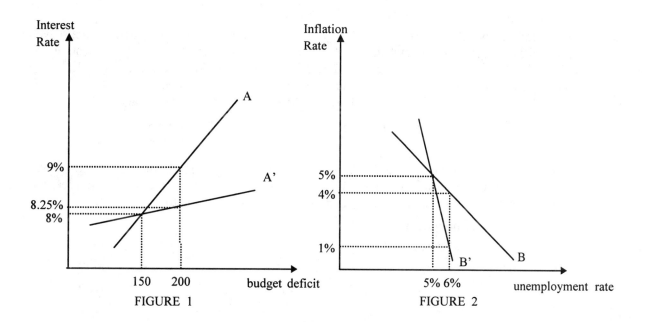

FIGURE 1

FIGURE 2

Is the slope of A or A' bigger in Figure 1? For the same $50 billion dollar increase in the budget deficit, the interest rate rises by 1% along graph A (slope = 1%/$50 billion) and by 0.25% along graph A' (slope = 0.25%/$50 billion). That is, a $50 billion dollar increase in the budget deficit will cause the interest rate to rise by 1% (and vice-versa for a decrease). Along graph A', a $50 billion dollar increase in the budget deficit will cause the interest rate to rise by 0.25% (and vice-versa for a decrease). Along graph A, the interest rate is more responsive (or sensitive) to the change in the budget deficit than along graph A'.

Is the slope of B or B' bigger in Figure 2? In this case, the slope of each graph is negative and so "bigger" means in "absolute" terms (i.e. ignore the negative sign). For the same 1% increase in the unemployment rate, along graph B', the reduction in inflation is bigger. Inflation falls by 4% compared to 1% along graph B. That is, the slope of graph B' is 4%/1% and along graph B is 1%/1%.

PET #3

Given a formula with three parts, knowing two parts will enable you to figure out what the third part is.

Let's illustrate this with an example. Suppose you are told that the percentage change in a stock price is 30%. Further, you know that the actual change in the stock price is $18. What is the initial or starting value of the stock price? You can use the formula for percentage changes in the Appendix to this chapter to figure out the answer by using the formula: percentage change = change in value/initial value.

$$30\% = +\$18/ \text{ initial value}$$

Then, using some algebra (see Appendix to practicum for details), you can solve for the initial value as:

$$\text{initial value} = \$18/0.30 = \$60 \ .$$

That is, the initial value of the stock was $60 and its price has gone up 30%, which is equal to $18 (0.3 X $60). You could also figure out that since the stock price was initially $60 and it has gone up $18, then the stock's price must now be $78.

Here's another example in which you can use a three-part formula given two other parts. Suppose you wanted to compute the average GPA in your classroom. Further, suppose that there are ten students in the class with the following GPAs: 2.0; 2.2; 2.3; 2.5; 2.5; 2.8; 2.8; 3.0; 3.2; 3.7. What is the average GPA? To figure out the average, you sum up all of the GPAs and divide by 10. The sum (or sum total) of the GPAs is 27. The average is 27 divided by 10, which is 2.7. The formula used to compute the average is:

$$\text{AVERAGE} = \text{SUM of observations/NUMBER of observations}$$

Now, if instead you were told that the average GPA in the class was 2.7 and that the sum of the GPAs was 27, you could figure out how many students there are in the class since you know two parts of a three-part formula. You could figure it by plugging in what you know and then doing the math:

$$2.7 = 27/\text{number of students}$$

So, $$\text{number of students} = 27/2.7 = 10$$

PET #4

Throughout this course, it is wise to always consider the best foregone alternative (option that is given up) when a household, firm, or government makes a decision. An understanding of what is being given up in order to have something else may alter your opinion about the proper course of action.

For example, suppose that a political candidate is proposing that household income tax rates be cut. What opportunity costs might arise if the proposal is adopted? On the surface, you might think that a tax cut is great because your take-home pay will be higher and allow you to buy more goods and services (assuming prices don't rise, remember the reality principle). However, as with most decisions, there is a cost -- something that is given up. In this case, a tax cut means that the government has less money to spend. So, the government may have to cut funding for space programs, or education, or highway repair, or police protection or whatever. These are opportunity costs of the tax cut. Which one of these government programs is the "best" foregone alternative depends on your viewpoint. If you value good schools, then the cut in education would be considered the opportunity cost associated with the tax cut. As you can see, debate over the opportunity costs of the proposal to cut taxes can lead to quite a lively discussion and may mean that not everybody agrees that a tax cut is such a good thing.

PET #5

*When you see the term "marginal," you should always think of computing the **change** in a variable. Computing the change requires that you have some numeric value before the change and some numeric value after the change. The difference between the two is the change in the variable.*

For example, suppose you have computed the revenue that your company earns from selling 5,000 jewelry boxes is $100,000. Furthermore, you have forecasted that if the company sells 6,000 jewelry boxes the revenue will be $108,000. What is the addition to revenue (marginal) revenue? It is $8,000 (for 1,000 more boxes). Suppose that the cost of producing 5,000 jewelry boxes is $90,000 and you forecast that the cost of producing 6,000 boxes will be $95,000. What is the addition to cost (marginal cost) associated with producing 1,000 more jewelry boxes? It is $5,000.

Now, use the marginal principle to answer whether your company would be better off by increasing production by 1,000 boxes. Since the marginal revenue (benefit to the company) is $8,000 and the marginal cost (cost to the company) is $5,000, the marginal principle dictates that production be increased since the marginal benefit exceeds the marginal cost. That is, the company will add more to its revenue than it will incur in costs by raising production. This means that the company's profits will increase.

PET #6

*The marginal cost or marginal benefit associated with **fixed** costs or fixed benefits is zero. When costs and/or benefits are fixed, the change in the costs or benefits must, by definition, be zero. This is why fixed costs and benefits are not considered when using the marginal principle to decide the best activity level.*

For example, suppose that the fixed costs of operating a factory are the rent and interest on loans (debt) that it must pay every month. Suppose these fixed costs total $3,400 per month. Consider the other monthly costs of operating a factory, including paying employees and paying for raw materials. Suppose these costs are $6,600. If the factory decides to increase production, it must hire more employees and purchase more raw materials. Suppose these costs rise to $8,900. What about rent and interest? Do they change when the company decided to produce more? No, they are fixed costs. So, what is the *marginal* cost associated with increasing production? All you have to do is compute the change in costs -- the cost of rent and interest on loans went from $3,400 to $3,400, which is a change of zero. There is no addition to fixed costs and thus no marginal cost associated with them. The costs of employees and raw materials have increased from $6,600 to $8,900 which is an increase of $2,300. The change in costs or marginal cost associated with increasing production is $0 + $2,300 = $2,300.

PET #7

*Diminishing marginal returns means that as an activity level (such as production) is **increased**, it increases but at a **decreasing** rate. Just because the term "diminishing" is used does NOT mean that an activity level (such as production) decreases or diminishes.*

For example, which table below illustrates the principle of diminishing returns?

Table A		Table B	
# of workers	Output	# of workers	Output
1	100	1	100
2	98	2	110
3	95	3	117
4	91	4	122

The correct answer is Table B. In Table B, output is increasing as more workers are hired. However, the rate at which output is increasing is decreasing. Output increases by 10 units (110-100) from hiring one additional worker, then by 7 units (117-110), and then by 5 (122-117). In Table A, output is decreasing as more workers are hired. This is not the definition of diminishing marginal returns.

PET #8

*Compare the inflation rate to the rate of change in any nominal variable to determine whether it has increased, decreased, or remained unchanged in **real** terms.*

For example, suppose your boss gives you a raise of 15% for the coming year. You may be quite happy about this until one of your economist friends points out that inflation is expected to be 18% this year. In this case, while your nominal income will grow by 15%, your real income (inflation-adjusted) will be expected to decrease by 3% (15%-18%). Maybe you should go back to your boss and ask for a bigger raise!

For another example, suppose that you invested $1,000 in the stock market at the beginning of this year. At the end of the year, your investment is now worth $1,200. What is the percent return on your investment? In nominal terms, it is 20% = [(1,200 - 1,000)/1,000] X 100. What is the percent increase in real terms? First, you'll need the inflation rate for that year. Suppose inflation was 4%. Then, in real terms, your investment has increased in value by 16% (20% - 4%).

V. PRACTICE EXAM: MULTIPLE CHOICE QUESTIONS

1. Which one of the following does NOT represent the concept of "scarcity"?

   a) a decision by your parents to put more of their savings to fund college expenses and less to life insurance.

   b) public policy in the state of Washington to reduce timber production so that more wildlife species will be preserved.

   c) a decision by a company to increase advertising expense for a new board game by decreasing its budget for telephone expense.

   d) a decision to commit more time to perfecting your volleyball serve and more time to perfecting your tennis serve.

   e) a decision by a student to spend more time studying and less time partying.

2. Which one of the following would NOT be considered a resource or factor of production?

   a) a conveyor belt.

   b) a financial analyst with a B.A. degree.

   c) tin.

   d) a new house.

   e) a computer.

3. Which one of the following is an example of "human capital"?

   a) money earned playing the stock market.

   b) skills by a medical technologist used in correctly identifying different types of a killer bacteria.

   c) a robot.

   d) a machine that must be operated by a human.

   e) the strength to lift 50 pounds on a continuous basis.

4. Which one of the following statements is true about point B below?

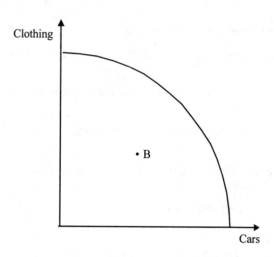

a) there may be over-employment of resources.
b) resources may not be efficiently used.
c) the economy could produce more of both goods.
d) the economy faces a tradeoff in moving from point B to point A.
e) (b) and (c).

5. Which one of the following would cause the production possibilities curve (PPC) to shift to the left?
a) a technological advancement.
b) an increase in the skill level of workers.
c) a deterioration in the interstate highway system.
d) a discovery of more oil.
e) an increase in the amount of plant and equipment.

6. Which one of the following would NOT cause a rightward shift in the production possibilities curve (PPC)?
a) an increase in the utilization of workers.
b) an increase in the pool of available labor.
c) a technological breakthrough.
d) a newer stock of physical capital.
e) all of the above will cause a shift to the right in the PPC.

7. Which one of the following statements is true?

   a) the production possibilities curve is positively sloped which shows that as society wants to produce more of one good, it must produce less of another.

   b) the production possibilities curve is negatively sloped because with a limited set of resources, society can only produce more of one good by taking resources out of producing another good.

   c) at a point outside the production possibilities curve, resources are fully employed.

   d) at a point inside the production possibilities curve, resources are efficiently used.

   e) a movement along the production possibilities curve shows that society can produce more of both goods.

8. Which one of the following could explain the picture below?

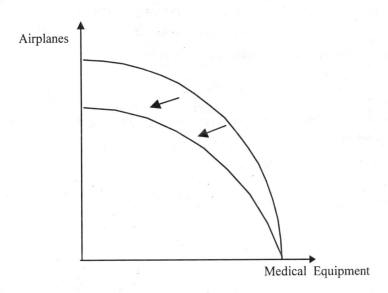

   a) a decline in human capital used in the airplane industry.

   b) a decline in technology.

   c) a technological breakthrough in the production of medical equipment.

   d) underutilization of workers in the medical equipment industry.

   e) none of the above.

9. Economic analysis is based on all of the following EXCEPT:

   a) simplifying assumptions.

   b) individuals acting in their self-interest.

   c) people making informed decisions.

   d) the need for government intervention.

   e) all of the above.

10. Which one of the following statements is the most accurate?

    a) "If I increase the amount of time spent reading my economics textbook and working through the study guide, my course grade in economics should improve."

    b) "If the U.S. budget deficit was reduced, then interest rates would be lower."

    c) "If the tax on cigarettes was increased, fewer packages of cigarettes would be sold."

    d) "If my company lowers the price of its product, it should sell more, assuming that our competitors don't do likewise."

    e) "Lower interest rates will lead to consumers taking out more car loans."

11. Which one of the following illustrates a negative (inverse) relationship between two variables?

    a) as auto insurance rates decrease, number of automobile purchases remains unchanged.

    b) as patrol cars out on the road increase, highway speeding decreases.

    c) as highway speeding decreases, highway fatalities decrease.

    d) as drunken driving increases, auto insurance rates increase.

    e) (b) and (c).

12. Consider a graph of grade point average versus hours studied. Which one of the following would be assumed held constant in such a graph?

    a) number of classes attended.

    b) grade point average.

    c) hours studied.

    d) phases of the moon.

    e) all of the above are held constant.

13. Which one of the following statements is true about the graph below? The graph shows the relationship between the average cost of production and the quantity of output produced.

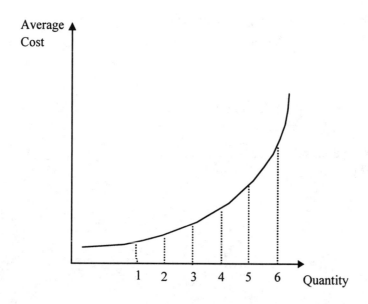

a) the average cost of production is increasing at a decreasing rate.

b) if the quantity of output produced increases, the curve will shift to the right.

c) the average cost of production is increasing at an increasing rate.

d) the slope of the average cost of production is constant.

e) the average cost of production curve is negatively sloped.

14. Suppose you volunteer at a local food bank and find that for every additional 100 brochures you send out seeking financial donations, the food bank sees an increase in the donations received of $1500. If you convince the executive director of the food bank to send out 200 more brochures this year than last year, by how much can you expect donations to increase by?

a) $3000.

b) $750.

c) $30.

d) $135.

e) cannot be determined from information given.

15. Suppose you go out to dinner with your friends and your bill comes to $12. You thought the service the waiter provided was adequate, so you decide to leave a tip of 15%. What would be the amount of your tip?

a) $1.25.

b) $1.80.

c) $2.40.

d) $1.50.

e) $0.18.

16. The "bowed out" shape of the production possibilities curve (PPC) arises because:

a) as we move farther inside the PPC, an economy loses increasing amounts of both goods.

b) the opportunity cost associated with a move from a point on the PPC to a point outside the PPC increases in terms of what must be given up to get there.

c) to continue to get the same increment in the production of a particular good requires that more and more of the other good be given up.

d) since resources are scarce, producing more of one good means we must produce less of another.

e) none of the above.

17. Based on the following diagram, which statement is correct?

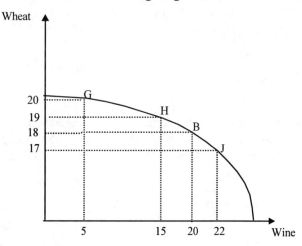

a) moving from G to H incurs an opportunity cost of 1 bushel of wheat.

b) as the economy moves along the PPC, more wheat can be obtained along with more wine.

c) the opportunity cost of moving from G to H to B increases while the opportunity cost of moving from B to H to G decreases.

d) moving from H to B incurs an opportunity cost of 5 barrels of wine.

e) moving from G to J entails no opportunity cost.

18. Which one of the statements is true of the graph below?

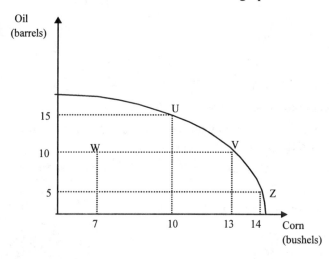

a) the opportunity cost of moving from U to V is 3 bushels of corn.

b) the opportunity cost of moving from Z to V is 5 barrels of oil.

c) the opportunity cost of moving from W to U is zero.

d) resources are not being efficiently used at point V.

e) all of the above are true.

19. You are deciding whether to stay at home and study from 3:00 p.m. - 8:00 p.m. or go to a park with friends. The park charges no admission fee. If you go to the park, which one of the following is not likely to be an opportunity cost associated with your decision?

    a) your time away from studying.

    b) the $1 you spent on a soda shortly after you arrived.

    c) time spent eating dinner at the park.

    d) cost of the gasoline used by your automobile to get to the park.

    e) all of the above.

20. Which one of the following is an example of a fixed cost?

    a) electricity.

    b) raw materials.

    c) telephone.

    d) supplies.

    e) rent.

21. Suppose you are debating whether to open up your own pet shop. Which one of the following is an example of an implicit cost?

    a) cost of fish tanks.

    b) cost of a computerized bookkeeping system.

    c) cost of your time spent setting up the shop and monitoring it.

    d) cost for sales clerks.

    e) cost of pet food.

22. Suppose Fred computes the marginal benefit of working one more hour as a salesclerk in an electronics store to be $7.75. However, by working one more hour, he must give up the opportunity to attend a free, one-hour workshop on how to start your own business. However, Fred believes he will learn a lot by attending the workshop. Based on this information, which one of the following statements is correct?

    a) Fred should work one more hour in the electronics shop since the workshop is free.

    b) Fred should not work that one more hour in the electronics shop if the implicit value of what he will learn by attending the workshop is $25.00.

    c) Fred should not work that one more hour in the electronics shop if the implicit value of what he will learn by attending the workshop is $5.00.

    d) Fred should work one more hour in the electronics shop if the implicit value of what he will earn by attending the workshop is $5.00.

    e) (b) and (d) are correct statements.

23. Use the table below to answer the following question.

# of workers	Output
1	5
2	15
3	30
4	37
5	40
6	38

Diminishing returns occurs:

a) between the first and second worker.

b) between the second and third worker.

c) between the third and fourth worker.

d) between the fourth and fifth worker.

e) between the fifth and sixth worker.

24. Which one of the following statements is true?

a) diminishing returns occur when a firm can change the amount of all of the factors of production it uses.

b) if Helena finds that the marginal benefit of eating an ice cream cone is equal to the marginal cost of eating an ice cream cone, then Helena would be better off to eat one more ice cream cone.

c) the short run is defined as a period during which some workers are idle.

d) the production possibilities curve is positively sloped.

e) none of the above are true statements.

25. Which one of the following activities is least likely to generate a spillover?

a) wearing perfume.

b) smoking a cigarette.

c) reading a comic book.

d) picking up trash from the roadside.

e) repainting the exterior of your house.

26. Which item list below is most likely to carry with it a positive spillover?

    a) riding a motorcycle.

    b) education.

    c) nuclear power production.

    d) reading *War and Peace*.

    e) eating doughnuts.

27. Suppose that your boss just informed you that you will be receiving a raise of 8% for this coming year. Suppose further that you have heard economic forecasts that the inflation rate for this coming year will be 9%. Based on this information, you might think to yourself:

    a) "Wow, they must really like me - I'm effectively getting a 17% pay raise! I need to call home and tell mom!"

    b) "Gee, thanks for the raise but the raise isn't actually a raise at all since my real income will decline by 1%."

    c) "This isn't much of a raise but at least my real income will increase by 1%."

    d) "Well, this isn't really a raise - my real income is going to decline by 0.72%."

    e) "This isn't really a raise - my real income is going to decline by 7.2%."

28. If your salary increases from $28,000 per year to $29,400, then the percentage increase in your salary is _____%. If inflation is 6% a year, then your "real" or "purchasing power" income has changed by _____%.

    a) 5%; 11%.

    b) 14%; 8%.

    c) 5%; -1%.

    d) 50%; 45%.

    e) 5%; 1%.

29. Suppose an old high school friend calls you up and desperately pleads to borrow $1,000 from you. You've been out working for a few years and have a little bundle in savings and decide that this is a good friend who really needs your help. So, you lend them $1,000 with the promise that they pay you the $1,000 back, without interest, at the end of the year. In one year after you are paid back:

    a) In real terms, the money you will be paid back will be worth less than $1,000 if inflation was greater than 0%.

    b) In real terms, the money you will be paid back will be worth more than $1,000 if inflation was greater than 0%.

    c) In real and nominal terms, you will be paid back $1,000.

    d) In nominal terms, the money you will be paid back will be worth less than $1,000 if inflation was greater than 0%.

    e) In nominal terms, the money you will be paid back will be worth more than $1,000 if inflation was greater than 0%.

VI. PRACTICE EXAM: ESSAY QUESTIONS

1. Consider a society that is producing two types of goods: birdhouses and pianos. Explain what happens in a society if a decision is made to produce more birdhouses.

2. Suppose you hear a commentator on the radio state that when interest rates fall, the stock market tends to rise. Draw a picture of such a relationship. Describe the slope. What factors would cause a movement along the graph? What factors might cause a shift in the graph?

3. Explain what happens when a country decides to move from one point on its production possibilities curve to another. Be sure to discuss opportunity cost and the allocation of scarce resources.

4. What advice would you give to a friend who has received two job offers both of which offer the same starting salary of $30,000 and the same benefits package? The jobs are basically the same. However, one job is located in Boston and the other job in Columbia, S.C.

VII. ANSWER KEY: MULTIPLE CHOICE QUESTIONS

1. Correct answer: d.

Discussion: This statement does not represent the concept of scarcity because it does not reflect any sacrifice or trade-off. That is, you have decided to commit more of your limited amount of time to both activities. Thus, you are not giving up anything. Of course, you will obviously have to cut back time on other activities, (perhaps to sleeping, studying, shopping, or whatever) but such trade-offs are not expressed in the answer.

Statements a, b, and c all represent the concept of scarcity. Statement a represents the concept of scarcity because it reflects a sacrifice or tradeoff made by your parents. Their decision to put more of their savings toward college expenses means that they will have less savings to devote to life insurance. That is, while your parents have to give up some funding of life insurance, in return, they are able to increase funding for college expenses. Statement b represents the concept of scarcity because it reflects a sacrifice or tradeoff made by legislators representing the state's interests. The sacrifice is that some timber companies will be put out of business. In return, more wildlife species will be preserved. Statement c represents the concept of scarcity because it reflects a sacrifice or tradeoff made by a business. The sacrifice is that its telephone budget will be reduced. In return, the company will be able to beef up its advertising expenses for the new board game.

Note: while there is a sacrifice, there is also something earned in return. Perhaps, another way to think of sacrifice is "trade-off" whereby something must be given up in order to obtain more of something else.

2. Correct answer: d.

Discussion: A resource or factor of production is any good, service, or talent that enables a society to produce output -- other goods and services. A new house does not enable society to increase production of other goods and services.

Statements a, b, c, and e are all examples of factors of production. A conveyor belt is physical capital. It may be used by a factory in its production process. A financial analyst is both labor and human capital. The financial analyst provides physical and mental effort on the job and also brings with him or her skills acquired through formal education. Tin is a natural resource. It may be used in many different production processes -- bottling, sheeting, etc. A computer may be used in the production process of a service like banking or in manufacturing.

3. Correct answer: b.

Discussion: Human capital is the skill and experience a worker brings to the job. So, statement (b) is correct.

Statement a is an example of "financial capital." Statements c and d are examples of physical capital. Statement e is an example of labor.

4. Correct answer: e.

Discussion: Point B is inside the production possibilities curves. Points inside the production possibilities curve represent either unemployment of resources and/or inefficient use of resources. Thus, at point B, the economy could produce more output – more of both goods. In fact, by moving to point A, it could produce more of both cameras and automobiles. Thus, statements b and c are both correct.

Statement a is not correct because at point B, resources are unemployed, not over-employed. Statement d is not correct because the economy does not have to sacrifice or give up cameras or automobiles in moving from point B to point A. It can have more of both goods. Opportunity cost arises when something must be given up in order to obtain something else. With unemployed or inefficiently used resources, there are slack resources that can be used to produce more of both goods at the same time.

5. Correct answer: c.

Discussion: A leftward shift in the PPC means that society can now produce *fewer* goods and services of all types. This occurs because its resources or factors of production have, for whatever reason, been depleted. A deterioration in the interstate highway system is a reduction in the physical capital resource that society uses to (indirectly) produce all types of goods and services.

Statements a, b, d, and e are all examples that would be represented by shifting the production possibilities curve to the right. A technological advancement makes it easier for society to produce more goods and services with its *existing* set of natural resources. An increase in the skill level of workers is an increase in the factor of production "human capital." More skilled workers tend to be more productive. That is, workers are able to produce more while on the job. A discovery of more oil is an increase in the factor of production "natural resources." With more natural resources available for production, more goods and services can be produced. An increase in the amount of plant and equipment is an increase in a society's capital stock, which enables it to produce more of all types of goods and services. All of these would be represented with a rightward shift in the PPC. A rightward shift shows that society is able to produce more of all types of goods and services.

6. Correct answer: a.

Discussion: An increase in the utilization of workers implies that workers must have been idle or underutilized prior to the increase. This is represented by a point inside the PPC. When the utilization of workers (or for that matter, production facilities) is increased, society moves from a point *inside* the PPC toward a point on the PPC. There is no shift in the PPC. Notice that society, in this case, does not face a trade-off. It can produce more of both types of goods.

Statements b, c, and d will all cause a rightward shift in the production possibilities curve, not a movement to the PPC. An increase in the pool of labor available to work is an increase in the factor of production labor. With more labor available to work, more goods and services can be produced. This would be represented by a rightward shift in the PPC. A technological breakthrough enables a society with its given set of resources (factors of production) to produce more goods and services. This would be represented by a rightward shift in the PPC. A newer stock of physical capital enables society to produce more than before because its physical capital (equipment, factories, etc.) is not as old and therefore as subject to breakdown. This would be represented by a rightward shift in the PPC. Statement e cannot be correct since answer a is correct.

7. Correct answer: b.

Discussion: Statement b is true. The production possibilities curve is negatively sloped which shows that in order to produce more of one good, less of another good must be produced. The reason this trade-off arises is because when society has a limited set of resources that are fully employed and efficiently used, the only way it can physically produce more of one good is to take resources out of the production of another good. Thus, production of the other good must necessarily decline.

Statements a, c, d, and e are all false. Statement a is false because the production possibilities curve is not positively sloped; it is negatively sloped. Statement c is false because a point outside the production possibilities curve represents a combination of goods and services that is unattainable given society's current set of resources and its current state of technology. Society does not currently have enough resources to produce at a point outside the production possibilities curve. Thus, the issue of full-employment is moot. Statement d is false because a point inside the production possibilities curve reflects a society that is either underutilizing its resources (there is some "idleness") or is not using its resources efficiently. If society was using its resources efficiently and the resources were fully employed, a point on the production possibilities curve would be attained. Statement e is false because a movement along the production possibilities curve reflects a trade-off which means that more of one good can be produced but only at the expense of reducing production of another good.

8. Correct answer: a.

Discussion: The decline in human capital in the airplane industry affects only the airplane industry and not the medical equipment industry. Thus, if all resources were devoted to airplane production, the decline in human capital would show up as a decrease in the amount of airplanes that could be produced were all resources devoted to airplane production or to a combination of airplanes and medical equipment. The easiest way to start off the new graph would be to consider how many airplanes the industry could produce given that human capital has declined. This event could be depicted by starting the production possibilities curve on a lower point on the airplane axis. Now, since the event does not affect the medical equipment industry, then it will continue to be able to produce as much medical equipment as before if all of the resources are devoted to medical equipment production. That is, for the medical equipment industry, the point on the axis that reflects all resources being devoted to the production of medical equipment will remain the same as before. By connecting these two extreme points, a graph that correctly shows what happens in both industries is drawn.

Statement b is not correct. A decline in technology, which affects both industries, will cause the entire production possibilities curve to shift in along both axes. Statement c is not correct because a technological breakthrough in the production of medical equipment would be depicted as a rightward shift in the production possibilities curve along the medical equipment axis with the graph anchored at the old point on the airplane industry axis. That is, since the technology does not affect the airplane industry, then even when all resources are devoted to airplane production, the same amount of airplanes as before will be produced despite the technological breakthrough in the medical equipment industry. Statement d is not correct because underutilization of workers would be represented as a point inside the production possibilities curve and not a shift of the curve.

9. Correct answer: d.

Discussion: Economic analysis is not based on the need for government intervention. In fact, in many cases, economic analysis proceeds under the assumption that government intervention is unnecessary.

Statements a, b, and c are all used in economic analysis.

10. Correct answer: d.

Discussion: Statement d is the most accurate because it is the only statement that qualifies the relationship between the two variables, price and amount sold. For example, without the qualifier, a company may lower its price but find that its sales do not increase. This situation may arise because the company's competitors may also lower their price making it harder for the company to sell more even though it has lowered its price. The qualifier, in effect, holds fixed other variables that may be relevant to the relationship between price and amount sold. The qualifier thus makes clearer what the expected relationship is between the two variables.

Statements a, b, and c are not as accurate as statement d because none of these answers adheres to the "ceteris paribus" condition of holding other variables fixed that might also be important to a relationship between two variables. Statement a would be more accurate if it was qualified with a clause like "assuming that I continue to attend class regularly and take and recopy my notes." That is, even if you spend more time reading the textbook and using the study guide, if you decide at the same time, to skip class and stop taking notes, you may not see any improvement in your grade at all. Statement b would be more accurate if it was qualified with a clause like "assuming that the central bank decides not to raise interest rates." That is, a lower budget deficit may not necessarily lead to lower interest rates if something else happens in the economy to change them. Statement c would be more accurate if it was qualified with a clause like "assuming tobacco companies do not increase their advertising and/or do not lower the price they charge for a pack of cigarettes." That is, an increased tax on cigarettes may not have the desired effect of reducing the packages of cigarettes sold if tobacco producers respond by, say, lowering the price they charge for a pack of cigarettes.

11. Correct answer: b.

Discussion: Statement b is the only response that shows a negative (or inverse) relationship. A negative relationship exists when one variable increases and the other decreases, or when one variable decreases and the other increases. In statement b, as patrol cars out on the road increase, highway speeding decreases.

Statements a, c, and d do not illustrate a negative relationship. Statement a indicates that there is no relationship between auto insurance rate decreases and automobile purchases. Statement c illustrates a positive relationship. Even though both variables are decreasing, they move in the same direction. That is, you could also say that as highway speeding increases, highway fatalities increase. In either case, there is a positive (or direct) relationship between both variables. Statement d, for the reasoning just mentioned, illustrates a positive relationship between drunken driving and auto insurance rates. Statement e cannot be correct because statement c is not correct.

12. Correct answer: a.

Discussion: Number of classes attended is the only variable being held constant in this example. Since the graph will show a picture of grade point average versus hours studied, these variables will be on the axes of the graph. Suppose that grade point average is graphed on the vertical axis and hours studied on the horizontal axis, you should expect the graph to have a positive slope. Suppose it is drawn assuming that the full number of classes is attended. Now, if the number of classes attended drops, what would happen to the position of the graph? It would shift down, to the right indicating that for a given number of hours studied, the grade point average will, in all cases, be lower.

Statements b and c are not correct because they are the variables being graphed and therefore are subject to change. Statement d is not correct because the phases of the moon are not relevant to the relationship between the two variables and so it doesn't matter whether it is assumed to be held constant or not. Statement e is not correct by virtue of the fact that number of classes attended is held constant, as stated in a. It is reasonable to assume that this variable is relevant to the relationship between grade point average and number of hours spent studying.

13. Correct answer: c.

Discussion: The average cost of production is rising at an increasing rate. You can figure this out by comparing several points on the graph. Compare the change in the average cost of production from an increase in output of one unit from 1 to 2 units to the change in the cost of production from an increase in output of 5 to 6 units. You will see, even without numbers, the change in the average cost of production will be greater when output increases by one unit from 5 to 6 than when output increases one unit from 1 to 2. Alternatively, you could look at the change in the average cost of production as you move from producing 1 unit to 2 units to 3 units, and so on. Again, you will see that the average cost of production increases by more when going from producing 2 to 3 units than from 1 to 2 units. Thus, the average cost of production is increasing at an increasing rate.

Statement a is not correct because the average cost of production is increasing at an increasing rate, as explained above. Statement b is not correct. As the quantity of output increases (or decreases), this would be represented by a movement along the curve, not a shift in it. Remember that a shift in a curve only occurs when a variable that is relevant to the relationship to the two being graphed changes. When a variable on the axis itself changes, this is represented by a movement along the curve. Statement d is not correct because the average cost of production is increasing at an increasing rate. If the slope was constant, then the change in the average cost of production from producing 1 to 2 units, compared to 5 to 6 units would be exactly the same (as it would from 2 to 3 units, as well). Statement e is not correct because the graph is positively sloped. The graph shows that as output increases, the average cost of production increases (and vice-versa).

14. Correct answer: a.

Discussion: The information in the question reveals that the change in donations received is $1500 for every 100 additional brochures mailed out. That is, every 1 additional brochure sent out returns $15 in donations. ($1500 donations/100 brochures = $15 donations/1 brochure). So, if the food bank mails out 200 more brochures, it can expect to raise $15 per brochure X 200 brochures = $3000.

Statements b, c, and d are not correct based on the explanation above. Statement e is not correct because there is enough information to figure out the answer.

15. Correct answer: b.

Discussion: You can use a few methods for calculating the tip. You could multiply $12 by 0.15 (15/100) which would yield $1.80. If you don't have a calculator or want to double check your answer, you could compute 10% of $12, which is $1.20. Since 10% of $12 is $1.20, 5% of $12 must be $0.60 (half of $1.20). Then, add $1.20 + $0.60 to get $1.80.

Statements a, c, d, and e are all incorrect. Statement a reflects a tip of just a nickel over a 10% tip. Statement c reflects a tip of 20% ($12 X 0.20 = $2.40). Statement d reflects a tip of [($1.50/$12)] X 100 = 12.5%. Statement e reflects a tip of 1.5% ($12 X 0.015 = $0.18).

16. Correct Answer: c.

Discussion: The bowed out shape of the PPC reflects increasing opportunity costs (which arise because resources are not equally-well adapted to producing one good as another). Statement ( )is the only one that expresses that opportunity costs are increasing, i.e. that more and more of one good must be given up in order to get back the same increment (say 1 unit) of the other good. For example, to produce 1 more motorboat may require that an economy give up producing 100 rolls of carpet; if the economy wants to produce another 1 more boat, the economy now has to give up producing 125 rolls of carpet; and if the economy wants to produce yet 1 more motorboat, the economy now has to give up producing 175 rolls of carpet.

The question asks about the bowed out shape of the PPC and so requires an answer that addresses a movement along the PPC, not to or from it. Statements a and b are incorrect because they address movements from a point not on the PPC to a point on it (or vice-versa), neither of which deals with a movement along the PPC. Statement d is incorrect because it only explains why the PPC has a negative slope, not why it has a bowed out shape. Statement e is incorrect because answer c is correct.

17. Correct answer: a.

Discussion: Opportunity cost is measured by how much is given up or sacrificed. In this case, the graph shows that in moving from G to H, the economy foregoes producing (reduces production by) 1 bushel of wheat. In return, however, the economy is able to produce 10 more barrels of wine.

Statement b is incorrect because it is not true that as the economy moves along the PPC more wheat can be obtained along with more wine. The concept of opportunity cost means that the economy can only have more wheat if it produces less wine (and vice-versa). Statement c is incorrect because increasing opportunity costs are encountered moving in both directions along the PPC. To see this, note that as the economy moves from G to H, it must give up producing 1 bushel of wheat but gets back 10 barrels of wine. As the economy moves from H to B, it must give up 1 bushel of wheat, but this time only gets back 5 barrels of wine. That is, it is more costly to produce wine because less is gotten back in return for the same 1 bushel of wheat. Thus, opportunity costs of producing more wine are increasing as the economy moves from G to H to B. If the economy moves from B to H to G, opportunity costs will also be increasing. To see this, note that as the economy moves from B to H, it must give up producing 5 barrels of wine, while it gets back 1 bushel of wheat. In moving from H to G, the economy must now give up 10 barrels of wine while still only getting back 1 bushel of wheat. This just means that producing wheat has become more costly (i.e. the opportunity cost has increased). Statement d is not correct. Opportunity cost is measured by how much is given up; in moving from H to B, the economy has gotten back (not given up) 5 barrels of wine. Statement e is not correct because there is an opportunity cost; the opportunity cost is 3 bushels of wheat.

18. Correct answer: c.

Discussion: Statement c is correct because at a point inside the production possibilities curve, resources are unemployed and/or not being efficiently used. This means that there are resources available to produce more of both corn and oil. That is, production in one commodity does not require sacrificing or giving up production of another commodity. Since there is no sacrifice in moving from W to U, there is no opportunity cost associated with the movement.

Statements a and b are not correct because opportunity cost is based on what is given up, not what is gained. Statement a is not correct because in moving from U to V, three bushels of corn are gained. In moving from U to V, the opportunity cost is the reduction in oil production, which in this case is five barrels of oil. Statement b is not correct because in moving from Z to V, five barrels of oil are gained. In moving from Z to V, the opportunity cost is the reduction in corn production, which in this case is one bushel of corn.

Statement d is not correct because at a point on the production possibilities curve all resources are fully-employed and efficiently used. Statement e is not correct because statements a, b, and d are not true.

19. Correct answer: c.

Discussion: Statement c is correct because regardless of whether you stayed at home and studied from 3:00 p.m.- 8:00 p.m. or stayed at the park, you would have had to take time to eat dinner.

Statement a is not correct because time spent away from studying is an opportunity cost. By being at the park with friends, you give up that time for studying. Statement b is not correct because that $1 spent could have been spent on something else. Statement d is not correct because the cost of the gasoline could have been saved had you stayed home and that used money on something else. Statement e is not correct because statement c is not an example of an opportunity cost.

20. Correct answer: e.

Discussion: Rent is the only example of a cost that will not change with a firm's production level. That is, whether a firm produces 0, 1, or 1,000,000 e.g. skateboards will not change the cost of the rent the firm pays for the production facility.

Electricity, raw materials, telephone, and supplies are all examples of costs that will change with a firm's production level. The more a firm produces, the more electricity it will need to operate the factory, the more raw materials it will need to produce the product, the more telephone calls it will have to make to coordinate distribution and sales, and the more supplies (packaging, etc.) it will need in production.

21. Correct answer: c.

Discussion: An implicit cost is a cost for which a check does not have to be written. The cost of your time spent setting up the shop and monitoring it is time that you, as owner, could have spent elsewhere, perhaps working for a company. While you will be compensated for your time as shop owner through any profits the pet shop makes, you are not explicitly paid for your time, i.e. there is not set salary or wage per hour.

Fish tanks, a computerized bookkeeping system, sales clerks, and pet food are all expenses that you must explicitly write a check for. They are explicit costs that arise from operating a pet shop.

22. Correct answer: e.

Discussion: Statement e is correct because statements b and d are both correct. Statement b is correct because the marginal cost of not working one more hour (or of attending the workshop) is $7.75, i.e. Fred will give up $7.75 by attending the workshop. However, Fred will benefit. The marginal benefit of using that one hour to attend the workshop has a value of $25.00. In this case, the marginal benefit of attending the workshop exceeds the marginal cost of attending the workshop so Fred would be better off by attending the workshop. Statement d is also correct but for the reverse reasons. In this case, if Fred assesses the marginal benefit of the one hour of attending the workshop at $5.00, the marginal benefit exceeds the marginal cost of attending the workshop ($7.75 loss in wages from not working that one hour). Here, Fred would be better off working and not attending the workshop.

Statement a is not correct. Even though the workshop is free, it does not mean that there is no benefit to attending it. Thus, it is not correct to compare the marginal cost of attending the workshop of $7.75 to a zero benefit. Statement c is not correct. If the marginal benefit of attending the one-hour workshop is $5.00 and the marginal cost of attending it is $7.75 (loss in wages from not working that one hour), then Fred would be better off working that one hour. Here, the marginal benefit of attending the workshop is less than the marginal cost of attending the workshop. So, the workshop should not be attended. Statements b and d are both correct; however, option e allows you to pick both statements so that it is the correct answer.

23. Correct answer: c.

Discussion: Diminishing returns occurs when the addition of one more input (a worker in this example) adds less to output than the previous worker. Between the third and fourth worker, output increases by 7 units but had previously increased by 15 units (from 15 to 30). Thus, diminishing returns has set in.

Statement a is incorrect. Output has increased by 10 units from hiring one more worker but diminishing returns cannot yet be inferred until you are able to make one more comparison. Statement b is incorrect because, in this case, output has increased by 15 units from hiring one more worker (2 to 3 workers) and had previously increased by 10 units. This is an example of output increasing at an increasing rate, not a decreasing rate as is true of diminishing returns. (See PET #4). Statement d is not correct because the point at which diminishing returns has set in is where the rate of increase in output slows down; this happens between the third and fourth worker, not the fourth and fifth worker. While statement d does show that the addition to output is decreasing (it had been 7 units from the previous worker and is now 3), it is not the point at which diminishing returns has set in. Statement e is not correct because output actually *decreases* by hiring one more worker. That is, output goes from 40 units to 38 units (-2) by hiring one more worker. This is not an example of diminishing returns (see PET #4).

24. Correct answer: e.

Discussion: Statements a, b, c, and d are not true.

Statement a is incorrect because diminishing returns occurs because a firm CANNOT change the amount of all of the factors of production it uses. Statement b is incorrect because if Helena found the marginal benefit to eating an ice cream cone just equal to the marginal cost, then she is as well-off (or happy) as she can be. She should neither eat one more ice cream cone nor one fewer. She is eating just the right amount. Statement c is incorrect by definition. The short run is a time period during which a firm is not able to change the level of all of the factors of production that it uses to produce output. Statement d is incorrect because the production possibilities curve is negatively sloped.

25. Correct answer: c.

Discussion: Statement c is correct because it is the only activity that does not generate any benefits or costs to those who are not reading the comic book. That is, reading a comic book does not impose a cost to those around you, nor does it create a benefit for those around you.

Wearing perfume can generate a spillover cost to others who are allergic to perfume or are bothered by the scent. The same is true for smoking a cigarette. Picking up trash from the roadside can generate a spillover benefit to others who use the road. They get to enjoy a more picturesque road trip. Repainting the exterior of your house can generate a spillover benefit for your neighbors. The benefit is that they don't have to look at a rundown-looking house. Also, by keeping up the appearance of your house, you may help to keep the property values in your neighborhood from declining.

26. Correct answer: b.

Discussion: Statement b is correct because education is a service that "consumers" (students) benefit from but it carries with it a positive spillover in the sense that educated citizens are more likely to be employed, less likely to need government assistance, and less likely to engage in criminal activities.

Statement a is not correct because only the motorcyclist enjoys the benefits of riding a motorcycle. Moreover, motorcycle riding actually can carry negative spillovers (externalities) since motorcycle accidents typically involve head or spinal injuries that can create long-term health care costs that must be picked up by taxpayers. Statement c is not correct because nuclear power production carries a potential negative externality associated with any malfunction of the reactor. Remember Chernobyl. Statement d is not correct because no one else is likely to benefit from another person reading *War and Peace*. Statement e is not correct because no one else is likely to benefit from another person's consumption of doughnuts.

27. Correct answer: b.

Discussion: Since your nominal income is going to grow by 8% but prices are expected to go up by 9%, then in real terms, your income will decline by 1% (8% - 9%). (See PET #5).

Statement a is not correct. This statement assumes that you have added the two numbers. It is not correct to add the growth rate of your nominal income and the inflation rate to determine the effect on your real income. Statement c is not correct. This statement assumes that you should take the inflation rate and subtract the growth rate of the nominal variable. This is not correct; it is the other way around. Statements d and e are not correct. These statements assume that you have multiplied the numbers, which is not the correct method for computing the real value of a variable.

28. Correct answer: d.

Discussion: You can calculate the percentage change in your nominal income by using the formula to calculate percentage change found in the Appendix to Chapter 1. The percentage change in your salary is calculated as [($29,400 - $28,000)/$28,000] X 100 = +5%. However, since inflation has increased by 6%, then the real or purchasing power value of your salary increase is 5% - 6% = -1%. Since the inflation rate has outpaced your salary increase, your real income has actually declined by 1%. Based on these calculations, none of the other options are correct. Do remember, however, that you must subtract the inflation rate from the increase in the nominal value to obtain the percentage change in the real value.

29. Correct answer: a.

Discussion: If you have agreed to be paid back $1,000 without interest and inflation is greater than 0%, then in real terms, your $1,000 will be worth less than $1,000. In other words, your $1,000 will not be able to buy as much as it had the year before if inflation was greater than 0%. You should note that in nominal terms, you are still getting back $1,000 but in real terms, you are getting back less than $1,000.

Statement b is incorrect. If inflation is greater than 0%, then the $1,000 you are paid back will not be able to buy as much as the year before. Thus, in real terms, the money you will be paid back is less than $1,000. Statement c is not correct. In nominal terms, you will be receiving $1,000. However, in real terms, you may be getting back more or less than $1,000 depending on whether prices have fallen (deflation) or risen (inflation). Statement d is not correct because in nominal terms, you will be getting back $1,000. Statement e is not correct because again, you will be getting back $1,000 in nominal terms. Inflation affects how much you earn in real terms, not nominal terms.

VIII. ANSWER KEY: ESSAY QUESTIONS

1. If the society decides it wants to produce more birdhouses, then it must give up (sacrifice) the production of some pianos. Since the resources that a society has available to help produce output are scarce (limited, fixed amount) at a point in time, the only way the society can produce more birdhouses would be to cut back piano production. By cutting back piano production, the society frees up resources from producing pianos and can then allocate those resources (labor, capital, etc.) into birdhouse production. However, if the amount of resources available to the society were to increase, then these new resources could be devoted to producing more birdhouses without having to cut back on piano production.

2. The commentator is pointing out a relationship between two variables -- the interest rates and stock prices. The stated relationship is negative since the two variables move in opposite directions. That is, when interest rates fall, stock prices rise and vice-versa. Thus, a graph of the relationship should have a negative slope. Factors that would cause a movement along the graph are the two variables that would be labeled on each axis which are the interest rate and stock prices. Of course, there are other factors that could affect interest rates and stock prices. Such factors are held constant (not permitted to change) when drawing the relationship between interest rates and stock prices. For example, one factor that might be held constant is whether the president is a republican or democrat. If the relationship is drawn based on the current party of the president (democrat), the graph may shift (be further to the right or left) when the party changes to republican (assuming the party of the president is relevant to the relationship between interest rates and stock prices). Another factor that might be held constant is the unemployment rate. That is, the relationship is drawn assuming a certain unemployment rate. If the unemployment rate were to change (assuming it is relevant to the relationship between interest rates and stock prices), the graph may shift.

3. When a country moves from one point on its production possibilities curve to another, it has made a decision to produce fewer units of one good (e.g. apparel) and more of another (e.g. electronics). The country faces an opportunity cost -- the opportunity cost is that the country must cut back on production of apparel goods if it wants to produce more electronics. This is because resources are scarce. In order

to produce more electronics, more resources -- land, labor, capital -- will have to be devoted to the electronics industry which means that there will be fewer resources available to produce apparel goods. That is, there will be a re-allocation of resources from the apparel industry to the electronics industry. With fewer resources available to the apparel industry, apparel production will contract; the opposite will happen in the electronics industry. While the movement along the production possibilities curve assumes that resources remain fully-employed (and efficiently used), there may be an adjustment phase (setting up new factory floors, training apparel workers to work in the electronics industry) during which some resources may become idle.

4. The advice I would give to my friend would be to consider the cost of living in Boston compared to that in Columbia, S.C. That is, I would have them consider the price of food, rent, clothing, etc. in the one city compared to the other in determining which job offer provides the higher "real" salary. Since Boston is known to be a very expensive city and Columbia is in the Southeast, where the cost of living is typically lower than in the Northeast, I would suggest to my friend that in real terms, the salary offer from the company in Columbia is better than the other offer. I would suggest to my friend that if they really want to live in Boston, she tell the company that they will have to offer a higher nominal salary to entice her to work for them.

Take It to the Net

We invite you to visit the O'Sullivan/Sheffrin page on the Prentice Hall Web site at:

http://www.prenhall.com/osullivan/

for this chapter's World Wide Web exercise.

CHAPTER 2
SUPPLY, DEMAND, AND MARKET EQUILIBRIUM

I. OVERVIEW

In this chapter, you will learn about two basic economic constructs: demand and supply. These two constructs can be used to answer questions like: what might happen to housing prices in a subdivision if a new mall is built near the subdivision? What might happen to the price of a share of a health services company when the government revamps the health care system? What might happen to the price of bread when former Soviet-block countries begin to trade with the U.S? What might happen to the price of tea when the price of coffee rises? Not only can demand and supply be used to guide your thinking about what will happen to prices, it can also be used to guide your thinking about whether more or less will be bought and sold. In this chapter, you will learn how to use graphs of demand and supply to determine what happens to a market price and the quantity bought and sold. Thus, in this chapter it is imperative that you familiarize yourself with shifts of a curve versus movements along a curve (see Chapter 1 of Practicum).

II. CHECKLIST

By the end of this chapter, you should be able to do the following:

√   Explain the Law of Demand and the Law of Supply (for both price increases and price decreases).

√   Understand what will cause a movement along a demand or supply curve and what will cause the curves to shift.

√   Explain what happens to equilibrium price and equilibrium quantity when:

√   demand increases (shifts right)

√   demand decreases (shifts left)

√   supply increases (shifts right)

√   supply decreases (shifts left)

√   List factors that will cause demand to shift (and in which direction).

√   List factors that will cause supply to shift (and in which direction).

√   Explain what happens to price, quantity demanded and quantity supplied when there is an excess demand and use a graph in your explanation.

√   Explain what happens to price, quantity demanded and quantity supplied when there is an excess supply and use a graph in your explanation.

√   Define a normal and inferior good and represent their response, using a demand curve, to an increase in income and to a decrease in income.

√   Explain whether or not you can determine for certain what happens to equilibrium price and equilibrium quantity when demand and/or supply both shift.

√ Infer whether demand or supply shifted and in which direction by having information on the direction in which the equilibrium price and quantity moved.

III. KEY TERMS

Perfectly competitive market: a market with a very large number of firms, each of which produces the same standardized product and is so small that it does not affect the market price of the good it produces.

Demand schedule: a table of numbers that shows the relationship between price and quantity demanded by a consumer, ceteris paribus (everything else held fixed).

Individual demand curve: a curve that shows the relationship between price and quantity demanded by a consumer, ceteris paribus (everything else held fixed).

Law of demand: the lower the price, the larger the quantity demanded.

Change in quantity demanded: a change in the amount of a good demanded resulting from a change in the price of the good; represented graphically by a movement along the demand curve.

Substitution Effect: the change in consumption resulting from a change in the price of one good relative to the price of other goods.

Income Effect: the change in consumption resulting from an increase in the consumer's real income.

Market demand curve: a curve showing the relationship between price and the quantity demanded by all together, ceteris paribus (everything else held fixed).

Supply schedule: a table of numbers that shows the relationship between price and quantity supplied, ceteris paribus (everything else held fixed).

Individual supply curve: a curve that shows the relationship between price and quantity supplied by a producer, ceteris paribus (everything else held fixed).

Law of supply: the higher the price, the larger the quantity supplied.

Change in quantity supplied: a change in the quantity supplied resulting from a change in the price of the good; represented graphically by a movement along the supply curve.

Market supply curve: a curve showing the relationship between price and the quantity supplied by all producers together, ceteris paribus (everything else held fixed).

Market equilibrium: a situation in which the quantity of a product demanded equals the quantity supplied, so there is no pressure for the price to change.

Excess demand: a situation in which, at the prevailing price, consumers are willing to buy more than producers are willing to sell.

Excess supply: a situation in which, at the prevailing price, producers are willing to sell more than consumers are willing to buy.

Change in demand: a change in the amount of a good demanded resulting from a change in something other than the price of the good; represented graphically by a shift of the demand curve.

Normal good: a good for which an increase in income increases demand.

Inferior good: a good for which an increase in income decreases demand.

Substitutes: two goods related in such a way that an increase in the price of one good increases the demand for the other good.

Complements: two goods related in such a way that an increase in the price of one good decreases the demand for the other good.

Change in supply: a change in the amount of a good supplied resulting from a change in something other than the price of the good; represented graphically by a shift of the supply curve.

IV. PERFORMANCE ENHANCING TIPS (PETS)

PET #1

Since price is a variable on the axis of a graph of the demand and supply of a particular good, a change in the price will NOT cause the demand or supply curve for that good to shift but will instead be represented by a movement along the demand and supply curves.

Remember from Chapter 1 of the Practicum that in a graph of Y and X where Y and X are drawn on either axis, changes in Y or X will not cause the curve(s) to shift but instead cause movements along the curve. It may be wise to review practice question 8 and PET #1 from Chapter 1 to reinforce your memory of this principle.

PET #2

When the price of good X rises (falls), the quantity demanded falls (rises). Do NOT say that the demand falls (rises) since this means the whole curve shifts left (right).

For example, suppose you read on the exam a statement that says, "What happens in the market for peanut butter when the price of peanut butter falls?" One of the test options might be "the demand for peanut butter increases." This is not the correct answer. A statement like "the demand for peanut butter increases" would be represented by shifting the whole demand curve out to the right. However, since the price of peanut butter has fallen and is a variable on the axis for which the demand and supply of peanut butter are drawn, the decline in the price of peanut butter will be represented by moving along the demand curve. As the price of peanut butter falls, the quantity of peanut butter demanded increases. This would be the correct answer.

PET #3

When the price of good X rises (falls), the quantity supplied rises (falls). Do NOT say that the supply rises (falls) since this means the whole supply curve shifts right (left).

For example, suppose you read on the exam a statement that says, "What happens in the market for jelly when the price of jelly falls?" One of the test options might be "the supply of jelly decreases." This is not the correct answer. A statement like "the supply of jelly decreases" would be represented by shifting the whole supply curve to the left. However, since the price of jelly has fallen and is a variable on the axis for which the demand and supply of jelly are drawn, the decline in the price of jelly will be represented by moving along the supply curve. As the price of jelly falls, the quantity of jelly supplied decreases. This would be the correct answer.

PET #4

A rightward shift in the demand curve can be expressed in the following ways:

a. *at every price, the quantity demanded that buyers want is now higher.*
b. *at every quantity demanded, the price buyers would be willing to pay is now higher.*

To see this, look at the two graphs below. Demand curve a corresponds to statement a because at every price, the quantity demand is now higher. Demand curve b corresponds to statement b because at every quantity demanded, the price buyers would be willing to pay is now higher. In both cases, the demand curve is further to the right after the shift than before.

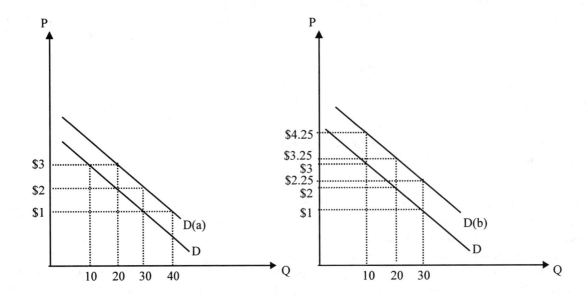

You should be able to re-write statements (a) and (b) for a leftward shift in demand.

PET #5

A rightward shift in the supply curve can be expressed in the following ways:

a. *at every price, the quantity that producers are willing to supply is now higher.*
b. *at every quantity supplied, the price at which producers would be willing to sell is now lower.*

To see this, look at the two graphs below. Supply curve a corresponds to statement a and supply curve b corresponds to statement b. In both cases, the supply curve is further to the right after the shift than before.

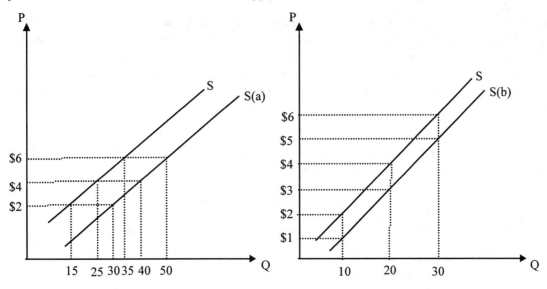

You should be able to re-write statements a and b for a leftward shift in supply.

PET #6

Factors other than a change in the price of good X may cause the demand and/or supply curves to shift to the right or left. These factors can be remembered with the simple mnemonic: P.I.N.T.E.O.

	For Demand	For Supply
P -	prices of related goods	prices of related goods
I -	income	input prices
N -	number of buyers (population)	number of producers
T -	tastes	technology
E -	expectations	expectations
O -	other (advertising, fads, etc.)	other (weather, strikes, taxes on producers, etc.)

While this mnemonic should help you if basic logic fails you during an exam (perhaps due to exam-induced stress), you should not simply memorize these lists. They should make sense to you. So, for example, if there is a technological improvement in producing computer chips, it should make sense that the technological improvement makes production of chips more efficient and less costly, which you would represent by shifting the supply curve for computer chips to the right. That is, supply increases. Likewise, it should make sense to you than when the price of peanut butter goes up, the demand for jelly (a complement) will decrease which you would represent by shifting the demand curve for jelly to the left. You should work through different examples of each to ensure that your logic is correct.

PET #7

When you are asked to consider the effects of a shift in demand together with a shift in supply, you should first consider the directional effects on price and quantity of each shift individually. Then, you should assess whether the combined shifts move price in the opposite or the same direction and whether the combined shifts move quantity in the opposite or same direction. If the shifts move price (or quantity) in opposite directions, you will be unable to determine (without further information) the ultimate effect on price (or quantity).

To see why this is so, look at the table below and read the discussion following it. You may want to draw a graph of each shift listed below to assure yourself that the table is correct.

Shift	Effect on Price	Effect on Quantity
Demand increases (shifts right)	Price rises	Quantity rises
Demand decreases (shifts left)	Price falls	Quantity falls
Supply increases (shifts right)	Price falls	Quantity rises
Supply decreases (shifts left)	Price rises	Quantity falls

Suppose you are given a test question that asks what happens in the market for bicycles when rollerblading becomes the rage and when the price of aluminum used in making bicycles increases.

First, you must categorize the rollerblading rage as one of the four shift factors above and the increased price of aluminum as one of the four shift factors above. The rollerblading rage would be categorized as a leftward shift in the demand for bicycles and the increased price of aluminum as a leftward shift in the supply of bicycles. Since rollerblading and bicycling are substitutes, the increased rollerblading rage might decrease the demand for bicycles (leftward shift), which is to say that at every price, the quantity of bicycles demanded would now be lower. Since aluminum is an input into bicycles, the increased price of aluminum makes bicycle production more costly which is to say that at every quantity supplied, the price that producers would be willing to accept would be higher (to cover their costs). That is, the supply of bicycles decreases (shifts left).

Now, the decrease in demand for bicycles will lower both the equilibrium price and quantity of bicycles. The decrease in the supply of bicycles will raise the equilibrium price and lower the equilibrium quantity of bicycles. In this case, the two shifts together move price in the opposite direction but have the same directional effect on the equilibrium quantity. Therefore, you can only answer for sure what happens to the equilibrium quantity. (It falls). If you knew the magnitudes of the shifts in demand and supply, you would be able to answer what happens to the equilibrium price.

PET #8

Maximum prices (price ceilings) that are set below the equilibrium price create an excess demand where quantity demanded exceeds quantity supplied. A price ceiling set above the equilibrium price is ineffective.

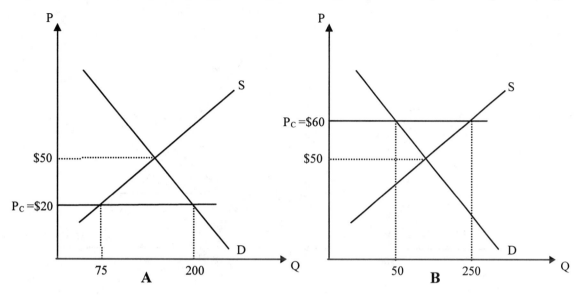

To see this, compare the two graphs above. Graph A illustrates a maximum price (or price ceiling) set below the equilibrium price and graph B a price ceiling set above the equilibrium price. A maximum price is typically a government-controlled price above which the equilibrium price may not rise.

In Graph A, at a price of $20, the quantity demanded is 200 units and the quantity supplied is 75 units. Thus, there is an excess demand (or shortage) of 125 units. If the maximum price was removed, the price would rise to $50 and the excess demand would be eliminated as quantity demanded would decline and quantity supplied would increase (movements along the curves).

In Graph B, at a maximum price (or price ceiling) of $60, the quantity demanded is 50 units and the quantity supplied is 250 units. However, the equilibrium (or market-determined) price is $50. Thus, there is no tendency for the price to rise above the imposed price of $60 and so the price ceiling, in this case, is not effective.

PET #9

Minimum prices (price floors or price supports) that are set above the equilibrium price create an excess supply (or surplus) where quantity supplied exceeds quantity demanded. A price floor set below the equilibrium price is ineffective.

To see this, compare the two graphs below. Graph A illustrates a minimum price (or price floor) set above the equilibrium price and graph B a minimum price set below the equilibrium price. A minimum price is typically a government-controlled price below which the equilibrium price may not fall.

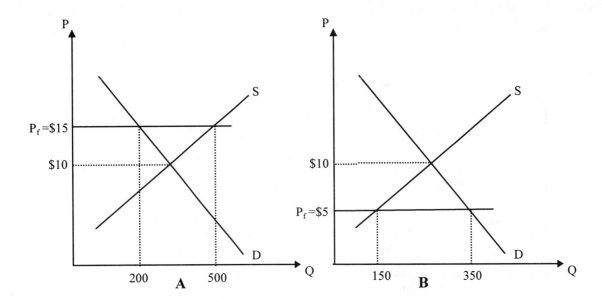

In Graph A, at a minimum price of $15, the quantity demanded is 200 units and the quantity supplied is 500 units. Thus, there is an excess supply (or surplus) of 300 units. If the minimum price was removed, the price would fall to $10 and the excess supply would be eliminated as quantity demanded would rise and quantity supplied would decrease (movements along the curves).

In Graph B, at a minimum price of $5, the quantity demanded is 350 units and the quantity supplied is 150 units. However, the equilibrium (or market-determined) price is $10. Thus, there is no tendency for the price to fall below $10 and so the minimum price of $5 is not effective.

V. PRACTICE EXAM: MULTIPLE CHOICE QUESTIONS

1. Which one of the following statements is correct about the Law of Demand?
   a) as the price of oranges decreases, the demand for oranges increases.
   b) as the price of oranges increases, the demand for oranges increases.
   c) as the price of oranges decreases, the quantity of oranges demanded increases.
   d) as the price of oranges increases, the quantity of oranges demanded increases.
   e) as the price of oranges decreases, the demand for oranges shifts left.

2. A decrease in the demand for product X will:
    a) cause the equilibrium price of product X to rise.
    b) cause the equilibrium price of product X to fall.
    c) cause the equilibrium quantity of product X to rise.
    d) cause the equilibrium quantity of product X to fall.
    e) (b) and (d).

3. Consider the market for flavored mineral water. If the price of soda (a substitute for flavored mineral water) increases, which one of the following might be an outcome?
    a) the demand for soda will decrease.
    b) the demand for mineral water will increase (shift right).
    c) the price of mineral water will fall.
    d) the equilibrium quantity of mineral water will fall.
    e) (b) and (c).

4. Which one of the following statements is correct about the Law of Supply?
    a) as the price of dog bones decreases, the supply of dog bones increases.
    b) as the price of dog bones increases, the supply of dog bones increases.
    c) as the price of dog bones decreases, the quantity of dog bones supplied decreases.
    d) as the price of dog bones increases, the quantity of dog bones supplied decreases.
    e) as the price of dog bones increases, the supply of dog bones shifts right.

5. Consider the market for mattresses. If the price of foam used in making mattresses declines, which one of the following might be an outcome?
    a) the supply of mattresses will increase (shift right).
    b) the demand for mattresses will increase.
    c) the price of mattresses will rise.
    d) there will be a shortage of mattresses.
    e) (a) and (b).

6. Which one of the following would NOT cause the supply of bananas to decrease?
    a) a technological advance in banana production.
    b) a decrease in the number of producers of bananas.
    c) an increase in the price of a fertilizer used in growing bananas.
    d) a severe rain shortage.
    e) a tax placed on banana producers.

7. Which one of the following would NOT cause the demand for walking shoes to increase?

    a) an advertising campaign that says walking is good for your health.

    b) an increase in income.

    c) a decrease in the price of rubber used in producing walking shoes.

    d) an increased preference for walking rather than running.

    e) all of the above will cause the demand for walking shoes to increase.

8. Consider the market for tulips depicted below.

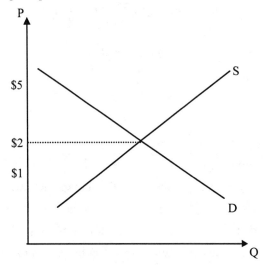

    Which one of the following statements is correct based on the graph above?

    a) if the price of tulips declines from $5 to $2, the demand for tulips will increase.

    b) at a price of $1, there would be an excess demand for tulips.

    c) at a price of $5, the quantity of tulips demanded exceeds the quantity supplied.

    d) if the price of tulips increases from $1 to $2, the quantity of tulips demanded would increase.

    e) none of the above.

9. Consider the market for chocolate candy. What is the effect on the equilibrium price and equilibrium quantity of a decrease in demand for and an increase in the supply of chocolate candy?

    a) equilibrium price rises; equilibrium quantity falls.

    b) equilibrium price falls; equilibrium quantity rises.

    c) equilibrium price = ?; equilibrium quantity falls.

    d) equilibrium price rises; equilibrium quantity rises.

    e) equilibrium price falls; equilibrium quantity = ?.

10. Use the graph below to answer the following question.

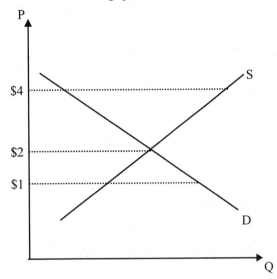

Which one of the following statements is true about the graph?

a) there is an excess demand at a price of $4.

b) there is an excess supply at a price of $4.

c) at a current price of $1, there is pressure for the equilibrium price to fall.

d) if the price fell from $4 to $2, quantity supplied would increase.

e) if the price fell from $4 to $2, demand would shift right.

11. Pretend that you are an economic detective and are given the following clues about the market for wine: the price of wine rose and the equilibrium quantity of wine declined. In writing up your investigative report, which one of the following would you conclude might be responsible for the outcome?

a) a decrease in the demand for wine.

b) a decrease in the supply of wine.

c) an increase in the demand for wine.

d) an increase in the supply of wine.

e) a decrease in the demand for wine and an increase in the supply of wine.

12. Suppose you hear reported in the news that the price of greeting cards declined at the same time the equilibrium quantity of greeting cards increased. Which one of the following would most likely be responsible?

a) a decrease in the price of paper used to make greeting cards.

b) a decrease in the demand for greeting cards.

c) a decrease in supply and an increase in demand for greeting cards.

d) an effective advertising campaign by the greeting card industry.

e) a decrease in the supply of greeting cards.

13. The U.S. imports a lot of cars from Japan. Suppose that the price of steel that Japan uses in making cars declines. What effect might this have in the U.S. market for cars?

    a) the supply of Japanese-made cars to the U.S. will decrease.

    b) the price of Japanese-made cars sold in the U.S. will decrease.

    c) the price of Japanese-made cars sold in the U.S. will increase.

    d) the demand for Japanese-made cars will increase.

    e) the quantity of Japanese-made cars sold in the U.S. will decrease.

14. Which one of the following statements would be true of an increase in demand for cameras?

    a) equilibrium price rises and the supply of cameras increases.

    b) equilibrium price rises and the supply of cameras decreases.

    c) equilibrium price falls and the quantity of cameras supplied decreases.

    d) equilibrium price rises and the quantity of cameras supplied increases.

    e) equilibrium price falls and the supply of cameras falls.

15. Suppose you are given the following information about tattoos. (1) the Center for Disease Control reports that tattoos can cause liver and kidney problems; and (2) the price of dye used in tattooing has increased. Given this information, what can you say about the equilibrium price and quantity of tattoos?

    a) equilibrium price will fall.

    b) equilibrium price will rise and equilibrium quantity will fall.

    c) equilibrium price will fall and equilibrium quantity will fall.

    d) equilibrium quantity will fall.

    e) equilibrium price will rise and effects on equilibrium quantity are uncertain.

16. Suppose income declines. What will be the effects on the equilibrium price and quantity of an inferior good like macaroni and cheese?

    a) demand will increase and the price of macaroni and cheese will increase.

    b) demand will decrease and the price of macaroni and cheese will decrease.

    c) demand will increase and the price of macaroni and cheese will decrease.

    d) demand will decrease and the price of macaroni and cheese will increase.

    e) uncertain price effects.

VI. PRACTICE EXAM: ESSAY QUESTIONS

1. Consider the market for athletic wear. Describe what happens to demand, supply, quantity demanded, quantity supplied, equilibrium price and equilibrium quantity when the price of spandex used in making athletic wear rises and at the same time a fitness craze sweeps the country, thanks in part, to Richard Simmons. Do not simply draw graphs. Write in complete sentences as you describe what happens.

2. Consider the market for American-made cheese. Suppose that the current equilibrium price is $1 per pound. Suppose that the French develop a preference for American-made cheese. Describe what would be true in the market if after this development, the price remained at $1. Would this be an equilibrium price? Why or why not? What would eventually happen in the market for American-made cheese?

VII. ANSWER KEY: MULTIPLE CHOICE QUESTIONS

1. Correct Answer: c.

Discussion: The law of demand expresses an inverse or negative relationship between the price of a good and the quantity demanded (holding other factors constant). Thus, when the price of X rises, the quantity of X demanded falls and when the price of X falls, the quantity of X demanded rises.

Statement a is incorrect because demand does not increase (which would be represented by the demand curve shifting right). The law of demand is about a movement along a demand curve, not a shift in the curve. Statement b and e are incorrect for similar reasons. Statement d is incorrect because it infers a positive relationship between price and quantity demanded.

2. Correct answer: e.

Discussion: A decrease in demand is represented by a leftward shift of the demand curve (which you may want to draw out using a demand and supply graph with price on the vertical axis and quantity on the horizontal axis). A decrease in demand has the result of lowering the equilibrium price of a product and reducing the equilibrium quantity. (We are assuming, as is most common, that product X is a normal good). Thus, statement e is correct since statements b and d are correct.

Statement a is not correct because a decrease in demand causes the equilibrium price to fall, not to rise. Statement c is not correct because a decrease in demand causes the equilibrium quantity to fall, not to rise.

3. Correct answer: b.

Discussion: Since mineral water and soda are substitutes, when the price of soda rises, consumers may switch to buying mineral water instead. Thus, the demand for mineral water increases, represented by a rightward shift in demand.

Statement a is incorrect because the price of soda is not a shift factor in the market for soda; a fall in the price of soda causes a movement along the demand curve for soda and thus causes the quantity of soda demanded (not the Demand) to decrease.

Statement c is not correct because when the demand for mineral water increases, the price of mineral water will rise. Statement d is not correct because when the demand for mineral water increases, the equilibrium quantity will rise. Statement e is not correct because statement a is not correct.

4. Correct answer: c.

Discussion: The Law of Supply states that there is a positive relationship between the price of X and the quantity of X supplied, holding other factors constant. This means that when the price of X increases, the quantity of X supplied increases and when the price of X decreases, the quantity of X supplied decreases. Statement c describes a positive relationship between the price of dog bones and the quantity of dog bones supplied.

Statements a, b and e are incorrect because a change in the price of dog bones will not cause the supply curve to shift in either direction but rather cause a movement along the supply curve (quantity supplied changes). Statement d is not correct because there is a positive relationship between the price and quantity supplied, not a negative relationship as implied in statement d.

5. Correct answer: a.

Discussion: Foam is an input into mattresses. When the price of foam decreases, it makes mattress production less costly. This would be represented by shifting the supply of mattresses to the right, i.e. supply increasing.

Statement b is not correct because the price of foam will not shift the demand for mattresses. What will happen, however, is that as the supply of mattresses increases, which will cause the price of mattresses to fall, the quantity of mattresses demanded will rise in response. Thus, b would have been correct if it had said "quantity demanded." Statement c is not correct because an increase in the supply of mattresses caused by the decrease in the price of foam will decrease the price of mattresses. Statement d is not correct because there is no reason given to think a shortage would occur. Statement e is not correct because statement b is not correct.

6. Correct answer: a.

Discussion: A technological advance in banana production would increase the supply of bananas, not decrease it.

Statements b, c, d, and e are all factors that would cause the supply of bananas to decrease. A decrease in the number of producers would obviously reduce the supply of bananas. An increase in the price of fertilizer raises the cost of producing bananas and would be represented by a leftward shift in supply, i.e. supply decreases. A severe rain shortage would obviously reduce the banana crop and thus decrease the supply of bananas. A tax on banana growers has the effect of raising the cost of doing business. This acts just like an increase in the price of fertilizer, i.e. the supply of bananas would shift left (decrease).

7. Correct answer: c.

Discussion: A decrease in the price of rubber used in producing walking shoes will lower the cost of producing walking shoes and cause the supply of walking shoes to increase, not the demand. However, quantity demanded would rise since the lower cost of production would translate to a lower price of walking shoes, which would raise the quantity of walking shoes demanded (movement along the demand curve).

Statements a, b, and d would lead to an increase in the demand for walking shoes. However, it may be worth noting that if walking shoes are considered inferior goods, then an increase in income would actually reduce the demand for walking shoes. Statement e is not correct because statement c should have been selected.

8. Correct answer: b.

Discussion: A price of $1 is below the equilibrium price of $2. As the price declines from $2 to $1, two things happen. First, quantity demanded increases based on the Law of Demand. Second, quantity supplied decreases based on the Law of Supply. Since quantity demanded has increased and quantity supplied has decreased, an excess demand (or shortage) is created at the $1 price. So, statement b is correct.

Statement a is not correct because it confuses what happens to quantity demanded with demand. A drop in the price of tulips will increase the quantity demanded, not demand. In other words, a decrease in the price of tulips will not shift the demand curve rightward. Statement c is not correct because at a price of $5, the quantity of tulips supplied will be greater than the quantity demanded. This happens because as the price of tulips rises, the quantity of tulips supplied increases (using the Law of Supply). Also, as the price of tulips rises, the quantity of tulips demanded decreases (using the Law of Demand). Thus, at a price of $5, which is above the equilibrium price, an excess supply will be created. Statement d is not correct, because as the price of tulips increases from $1 to $2 (or increases in general), the quantity of tulips demanded would decline, not increase. Statement e is not correct because statement b is a correct statement.

9. Correct answer: e.

Discussion: A decrease in demand for chocolate candy will lower the equilibrium price and lower the equilibrium quantity. An increase in the supply of chocolate candy will lower the equilibrium price and raise the equilibrium quantity. You can see these two cases by drawing graphs of them, separately. Since the demand and supply shift only push the price in the same direction, price will decline for sure. However, the demand and supply shifts push the equilibrium quantity in opposite directions so the effect is not known for certain.

10. Correct answer: a.

Discussion: A rightward shift in supply is a shift that will cause the price of a good to decline and the equilibrium quantity to rise. Thus, for the greeting card industry, there must have been an increase in supply. In this case, a decrease in the price of paper, which is an input into greeting cards, is the shift factor or cause for the increase in supply, and consequently for the decrease in equilibrium price and rise in equilibrium quantity.

Statement b is not correct because a decrease in demand for greeting cards (represented by a leftward shift in demand) will cause both the equilibrium price and equilibrium quantity to decline. Statement c is not correct because a decrease in supply and an increase in demand for greeting cards will raise the price of greeting cards and have uncertain effects on the equilibrium quantity. (See PET #7 for review). Statement d is not correct because an advertising campaign that is effective will increase the demand for greeting cards (represented by a rightward shift of demand) and thus raise the equilibrium price and quantity of greeting cards. Statement e is not correct because a decrease in the supply of greeting cards (represented by a leftward shift in supply) will cause the equilibrium price of greeting cards to rise and the equilibrium quantity to decline

11. Correct answer: b.

At a price of $4, the quantity supplied exceeds the quantity demanded which is the case of an excess supply or surplus. Just take the price of $4 and draw a line over to the demand and supply curves and then drop those points down to the quantity axis. You will see that the quantity supplied exceeds the quantity demanded.

Discussion: Statement a is not correct because there is not an excess demand (or shortage) but rather an excess supply (or surplus). Statement c is not correct because there would be pressure for the price to rise to the equilibrium price of $2. In fact, at a price of $1, there is a shortage. Statement d is not correct because if the price fell from $4 to $2, the quantity supplied would decrease. Statement e is not correct because if the price fell from $4 to $2, the quantity demanded would increase (not demand).

12. Correct answer: b.

Discussion: A decrease in the supply of wine is represented by shifting the supply curve to the left. A leftward shift in supply raises the equilibrium price and reduces the equilibrium quantity. You can see this by drawing a graph where supply shifts to the left and sketching out what happens to the equilibrium price and quantity.

Statement b is not correct because a decrease in demand would reduce the equilibrium price and reduce the equilibrium quantity. Statement c is not correct because an increase in demand would raise the equilibrium price and raise the equilibrium quantity. Statement d is not correct because an increase in supply would lower the equilibrium price and raise the equilibrium quantity. Statement e is not correct because the effects of these two shifts will have an uncertain effect on price but lower the equilibrium quantity for certain.

13. Correct answer: b.

Discussion: A decrease in the price of steel reduces the cost of manufacturing cars and thus increases the supply of Japanese-made cars. The increase in supply of Japanese-made cars will lower the price that American buyers pay for the cars. You can see this by drawing a graph where supply shifts to the right along the demand curve.

Statement a is not correct because the supply will increase, not decrease. Statement c is not correct because the price will decrease, not increase. Statement d is not correct because the event will not cause demand to shift; quantity demanded will however rise. Statement e is not correct because the quantity of cars sold in the U.S. will increase, not decrease.

14. Correct answer: d.

Discussion: An increase in the demand for cameras would be represented by shifting the demand curve to the right. The increase in demand raises the equilibrium price and quantity. As the equilibrium price rises, there is a movement along the supply curve which shows that the quantity supplied increases. You may wish to draw a graph to see this.

Statement a is not correct because the supply curve for cameras does not shift to the right; the quantity of cameras supplied increases. Statement b is not correct because the supply curve does not shift. Statement c is not correct because the equilibrium price rises, not falls, and the quantity of cameras increases not decreases. Statement e is not correct because the price of cameras rises and because the supply curve does not shift.

15. Correct answer: d.

Discussion: The report by the Center for Disease Control noting the health hazards associated with getting a tattoo should cause the demand for tattoos to decline. By itself, the decline in demand (represented by a leftward shift in demand) will cause the equilibrium price of tattoos to decline and the equilibrium quantity to decline, too. The effect of a rise in the price of dye used in tattooing causes the supply of tattoos to decline. This is represented by a leftward shift in the supply of tattoos. By itself, the reduction in supply of tattoos will raise the equilibrium price of tattoos and reduced the equilibrium quantity. When these two events are combined, you can see that the directional effect of the two events is the same on equilibrium quantity (it declines) but not on the equilibrium price. Therefore, without further information, you can only say that the equilibrium quantity of tattoos has fallen. Thus, statement d is correct and none of the other options can be correct.

16. Correct answer: a.

Discussion: An inferior good is a good for which demand increases when income decreases. Thus, a decline in income will have the effect of increasing the demand for macaroni and cheese. This would be represented by a rightward shift in demand. The increase in demand will have the effect of raising the equilibrium price of macaroni and cheese and increase the equilibrium quantity. Thus, statement a is correct.

Statements b and d are not correct since a decrease in income will increase the demand for an inferior good like macaroni and cheese. Statement c is not correct because while demand increases, the price of macaroni and cheese will increase, not decrease. Statement e is not correct since the directional effect on price is certain.

VIII. ANSWER KEY: ESSAY QUESTIONS

1. I will analyze the two events of an increase in the price of spandex and the fitness craze separately for their effect on the equilibrium price and quantity of athletic wear. Then, I will consider the combined effect of the two events on price and quantity. First, the increase in the price of spandex used in making athletic wear is an increase in an input price. As such, the increased input price raises the cost of producing athletic wear at every quantity supplied. This can be represented by shifting the supply curve of athletic wear to the left. The shift reflects that at every quantity supplied, the price that producers would be willing to accept in order to produce various amounts of athletic wear is now higher. By itself, this raises the equilibrium price of athletic wear and lowers the equilibrium quantity. (Notice that the price increase caused by supply shifting left will cause a movement along the demand curve which means that the quantity of athletic wear demanded will decrease). The fitness craze spawned in part by Richard Simmons will increase the demand for athletic wear. That is, at every price, the quantity demanded will now be higher than before. An increase in demand is represented by shifting the demand curve for athletic wear to the right. By itself, the rightward shift raises the price of athletic wear and increases the equilibrium quantity. (Notice that the price increase caused by demand shifting right will cause a movement along the supply curve which means that the quantity of athletic wear supplied will increase).

   When the effects of the shifts in demand and supply are combined, we know for certain that the equilibrium price will increase since both events cause price to increase. However, we do not know for sure what the effect is on the equilibrium quantity since in the first case, the equilibrium quantity declines but in the second case, the equilibrium quantity rises.

2. An increased preference by the French for American-made cheese would mean that there would be an increase in the demand for American-made cheese. This would be represented by shifting the demand curve for American-made cheese to the right, as Figure 2.1 shows. At every price, the quantity demanded is now higher (or at every quantity, the price that buyers would be willing to pay is now higher). If the price remained at $1 (rather than rising as it should), there would be a shortage of American-made cheese. That is, if the price remained at $1, the new quantity demanded would now exceed the quantity supplied at a price of $1. This would not be an equilibrium price any more. The shortage should not persist for too long because the shortage creates upward pressure on the price of cheese. Eventually, the price of cheese will rise to a new equilibrium price which is above $1. As the price rises, two things happen to eliminate the shortage. (1) As the price rises, the quantity supplied increases as the arrows along the supply curve indicate (Law of Supply; movement along supply curve); this helps eliminate the shortage. (2) As the price rises, the quantity demanded decreases as the arrows along the demand curve indicate (Law of Demand; movement along demand curve); this too helps eliminate the shortage. Eventually, a new equilibrium price will be reached where the new quantity supplied is equal to the new quantity demanded.

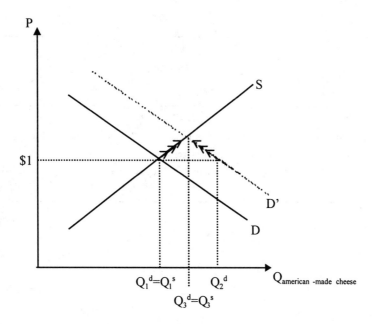

Figure 2.1

Take It to the Net

We invite you to visit the O'Sullivan/Sheffrin page on the Prentice Hall Web site at:

http://www.prenhall.com/osullivan/

for this chapter's World Wide Web exercise.

CHAPTER 3
ELASTICITY: A MEASURE OF RESPONSIVENESS

I. OVERVIEW

In this chapter, you will learn about the price elasticity of demand and the price elasticity of supply. Price elasticities can be used to compute by how much, in percentage terms, quantity demanded and quantity supplied of a good will change in response to an X% change in the price of that good. You will also learn that the elasticity of demand can be used to figure out what will happen to the total revenue of a firm when it lowers or raises the price of one of its products or services by X%. You will learn that the elasticity of demand and supply can be used to determine by what percentage the equilibrium price of a good will change when either demand or supply shifts. You will learn why the elasticity of demand for some products is very high and for others very low and you will learn what factors affect the elasticity of demand. You will learn that the concept of elasticity has important applications for business decision-making or policymaking. You will also learn about other elasticities. You will learn about income elasticity and cross elasticity. Since you will be using formulas that require that you compute percentage changes, you may wish to review appendix 1 of the text and the Basic Algebra chapter of the practicum.

II. CHECKLIST

By the end of this chapter, you should be able to:

√   Explain in words what the elasticity of demand and supply are.

√   Use formulas to compute the elasticity of demand and supply.

√   Explain in words the differences between inelastic, elastic, and unitary elastic demand.

√   Discuss factors that affect the price elasticity of demand.

√   Use formulas to compute the income elasticity of demand and the cross elasticity of demand.

√   Use the elasticity of demand and supply to figure out the percentage price change for a given percentage quantity change.

√   Use the elasticity of demand and supply to figure out the percentage quantity change for a given percentage price change.

√   Use the elasticity of demand to determine what happens to the total revenue of a firm when it raises or lowers the price of one of its products.

√   Use the elasticity of demand to determine whether a particular policy enacted by the government will have the desired effects.

√   Use the elasticity of demand and supply to determine what happens to the equilibrium price when demand or supply shifts.

III. KEY TERMS

Price elasticity of demand: a measure of the responsiveness of the quantity demanded to changes in price; computed by dividing the percentage change in quantity demanded by the percentage change in price.

Price elasticity of supply: a measure of the responsiveness of the quantity supplied to changes in price; computed by dividing the percentage change in quantity supplied by the percentage change in price.

Price-change formula: a formula that shows the percentage change in equilibrium price resulting from a change in demand or supply, given values for the price elasticity of supply and price elasticity of demand.

Income elasticity of demand: a measure of the responsiveness of the quantity demanded to changes in consumer income; computed by dividing the percentage change in the quantity demanded by the percentage change in income.

Cross elasticity of demand: a measure of the responsiveness of the quantity demanded to changes in the price of a related good; computed by dividing the percentage change in the quantity demanded of one good (X) by the percentage change in the price of another good (Y).

IV. PERFORMANCE ENHANCING TIPS (PETS)

PET #1

Elasticities are quoted on a "per unit basis."

Maybe this statement doesn't make sense quite yet, but it will after you look at the following example. Suppose you are told that the elasticity of demand is 2. What does that mean? You know that the elasticity of demand (E_d) for good X is given by the formula $\%\Delta Q^d_x / \%\Delta P_x$. You may think that when you are given the number 2, all you have is the number in the numerator. Since, 2 is equal to 2/1, you do have a number for the numerator and denominator of the elasticity of demand formula. The number in the denominator is 1. Thus, an elasticity of demand of 2 means that a 1% increase in the price of good X leads to a 2% decline in the quantity of good X demanded. Once you know the elasticity of demand on a per unit basis, you can also scale up or down the percentage changes in price and quantity but keeping the proportion equal to 2. For example, you could say that with an elasticity of demand of 2, a 10% increase in the price of good X leads to a 20% decline in the quantity of good X demanded.

PET #2

For any formula, if you are given two of three missing components, you can always figure out the third component. Likewise for three of four, four of five, and so on.

This performance enhancing tip will prove useful in this chapter as you apply it to elasticities and will also prove useful in other chapters of this textbook.

Let's see how this works by applying it to the elasticity of demand. Suppose you are told that the elasticity of demand is 0.5 and that a firm is considering reducing the price of one of its products by 10%. Can you determine by how much quantity demanded would change? All you have to do is plug the numbers that you are given into the formula:

$$E_d = \%\Delta Q^d_x / \%\Delta P_x$$
$$0.5 = \%\Delta Q^d_x / 10$$
$$0.5 \times 10 = \%\Delta Q^d_x$$
$$5 = \%\Delta Q^d_x$$

Thus, a 10% reduction in the price of the product will lead to a 5% increase in the quantity of the good demanded.

Let's try another example. Suppose you are told that the elasticity of demand is 4 and that a firm wants to increase the quantity it sells by 20%. By how much must it lower price in order to generate a 20% increase in the quantity it sells? The elasticity formula could be re-written to solve for $\%\Delta P_x$ as:

$$\%\Delta P_x = \%\Delta Q^d_x / E_d$$
$$\%\Delta P_x = 20/4$$
$$\%\Delta P_x = 5$$

Thus, the firm would have to lower the price of the product by 5% in order to generate a 20% increase in quantity demanded.

PET #3

Lowering the price of a good does not always lower the total revenue that a firm will earn nor does raising the price of a good always increase the total revenue that a firm will earn.

Let's see why the statement above is true. First, total revenue is computed as price X quantity demanded. In order to understand the effect on total revenue of a given percentage price change, you must also know by how much the quantity demanded will change in percentage terms. Obviously, a lower price will reduce total revenue but only if the quantity demanded does not increase but instead remains the same (no change). Likewise, a higher price will raise total revenue but only if the quantity demanded does not decrease but remains the same (no change).   However, it is usually the case that when the price of a good is lowered, the quantity demanded increases and when the price of a good is raised, the quantity demanded declines. In the case of a lower price, the lower price by itself reduces total revenue but since quantity demanded will increase, this will tend to raise total revenue. In the case of a price increase, the higher price will by itself raise total revenue but since quantity demanded will fall, this will tend to decrease total revenue. Thus, the combined effects on price and quantity must be determined.

Suppose you are told that the elasticity of demand is 2 and that a firm is going to raise the price of its product by 5%. What will be the effect on total revenue? With an elasticity of demand of 2, the percentage change in quantity demanded can be figured out. It will decrease by 10% (See PET #2). The net effect on revenue is based on a comparison of the percentage change in price to the percentage change in quantity demanded. A 5% increase in the price by itself would raise total revenue by 5%. A 10% decrease in the quantity demanded would by itself reduce total revenue by 10%. The combined effect depends on which one dominates. Since the 10% reduction is bigger in magnitude than the 5% increase, total revenue will decline.

PET #4

A unitary price elasticity of demand ($E_d = 1$) will occur when the percentage change in quantity demanded is equal to the percentage change in price. An "elastic" demand ($E_d > 1$) will occur when the percentage change in quantity demanded is greater than the percentage change in price. An "inelastic" demand ($E_d < 1$) will occur when the percentage change in quantity demanded is less than the percentage change in price.

You can best understand this PET by an example. Suppose the percentage change in quantity demanded = 4% and the percentage change in price = 4%. Obviously, the elasticity of demand would be 4%/4% = 1. Thus, you can infer that for a unitary elasticity, the percentage change in quantity demanded and price will be equal.

Now, suppose the percentage change in quantity demanded is 4% and the percentage change in price is 2%. Here, the elasticity of demand would be 2 (= 4%/2%) which is characterized as "elastic" since it is a number greater than 1. Notice that in this case, the percentage change in quantity demanded exceeds the percentage change in price. Thus, based on that information alone, without calculating a number for the elasticity, you could infer that the elasticity of demand would be greater than 1 and thus "elastic."

Now, suppose the percentage change in quantity demanded is 4% and the percentage change in price is 8%. Here, the elasticity of demand would be 0.5 (= 4%/8%), which is characterized as "inelastic" since it is a number less than 1. Notice that in this case, the percentage change in quantity demanded is less than the percentage change in price. Thus, based on that information alone, without calculating a number for the elasticity, you could infer that the elasticity of demand would be less than 1 and thus "inelastic."

V. PRACTICE EXAM: MULTIPLE CHOICE QUESTIONS

1. Which one of the following is the correct formula for the elasticity of demand?

   a) $\Delta P_X / \Delta Q^d_X$

   b) $\%\Delta Q^d_X / \%\Delta P_X$

   c) $\Delta Q^d_X / \Delta P_X$

   d) $\%\Delta P_X / \%\Delta Q^d_X + \%Q^s_X$

   e) $\%\Delta P_X / \%\Delta Q^d_X$

2. Suppose the elasticity of demand for bowling is 1.5 and the manager of the bowling alley decides to raise the price of a game by 5%. By what percentage will quantity demanded change?

   a) decline by 7.5%.

   b) rise by 7.5%.

   c) decline by 3%.

   d) rise by 3%.

   e) not enough information to answer the question.

3. Suppose the government wants to reduce teenage smoking by 50%. Suppose further that the government knows that the teenage elasticity of demand for a pack of cigarettes is 2. By what percentage would the government have to increase the price of a pack of cigarettes (through a tax) in order to cut teenage smoking by 50%?

   a) 100%.

   b) 25%.

   c) 50%.

   d) 250%.

   e) 20%.

4. Which one of the following defines an inelastic demand?

   a) $E_d > 1$

   b) $E_d = 1$

   c) $E_d < 1$

   d) $E_d > 0$

   e) $E_d < 0$

5. Which one of the following factors would reduce the elasticity of demand for a particular product?

   a) more time to shop around.

   b) no close substitutes.

   c) big part of budget.

   d) luxury item.

   e) all of the above reduce the elasticity of demand.

6. Which one of the following goods would you characterize as being the most elastic?

   a) insulin.

   b) coffee.

   c) cigarettes.

   d) gasoline.

   e) cookies.

7. Suppose product X's price is reduced by 5% and the quantity demanded increases by 2%. Based on this information, demand for product X would be:

a) unitary elastic.

b) inelastic.

c) elastic.

d) tertiary.

e) second-order elastic.

8. Suppose the elasticity of demand for flowers at a local florist is estimated to be 4, as computed by a savvy economics student. If the florist raises the price of flowers by 5%, then:

a) the revenue earned by the florist will decline.

b) the quantity of flowers sold by the florist will decline by 1.25%.

c) the quantity of flowers sold by the florist will decline by 0.2%.

d) the quantity of flowers sold by the florist will decline by 20%.

e) (a) and (d).

9. Suppose a dentist wants to increase her client base by 30%. Suppose further that the elasticity of demand for dental services is 5. By what percentage would the dentist have to reduce her dental fees in order to increase her client base by 30%?

a) 60%.

b) 6%.

c) 15%.

d) 150%.

e) 16.7%.

10. Total revenue _____ when the price of a good increases and its demand is inelastic. Total revenue _____ when the price of a good decreases and its demand is elastic.

a) increases/increases.

b) increases/decreases.

c) increases/does not change.

d) decreases/decreases.

e) decreases/increases.

11. What is the elasticity of the supply of cows if the price of a cow increases from $500 to $550 and the quantity supplied rises from 100,000 to 130,000? (Do not use the midpoint formula).

a) 3.33.

b) 3.0.

c) 5.0.

d) 6.0.

e) cannot be determined without information on percentages.

12. Suppose that the supply of tweed jackets increases by 20%. Further, suppose that the elasticity of demand for tweed jackets is 1 and the elasticity of supply is 4. What will happen to the equilibrium price of tweed jackets?

    a) rise by 8%.

    b) fall by 8%.

    c) rise by 4%.

    d) fall by 4%.

    e) fall by 5%.

13. Suppose a men's clothing store estimates that the income of its consumer base has increased by 24%. Further, suppose it has calculated the income elasticity of demand to be 1.2. By how much should the quantity of ties demanded change based on this information?

    a) increase by 12%.

    b) increase by 28.8%.

    c) increase by 20%.

    d) decrease by 28.8%.

    e) increase by 5%.

14. Suppose you observe an increase in the price of product J by 10%. At the same time, you observe a decrease in the quantity demanded of product L by 2%. Which one of the following statements is correct using this information?

    a) J and L are substitutes and the cross elasticity of demand is 5.

    b) J and L are complements and the cross elasticity of demand is 0.2.

    c) J and L are substitutes and the cross elasticity of demand is 0.2.

    d) J and L are complements and the cross elasticity of demand is 5.

    e) J and L are substitutes and more information is needed to calculate the cross elasticity.

15. Suppose you are given the following information:

    1999: average income = $50,000; quantity demanded = 20,000 units.
    2000: average income = $55,000; quantity demanded = 16,000 units.

All other factors over 1999-2000 are held constant. What is the income elasticity of demand and is the good a normal good or an inferior good?

    a) 10; inferior good.

    b) 2; normal good.

    c) 20; inferior good.

    d) 2; inferior good.

    e) 1/2; normal good.

VI. PRACTICE EXAM: ESSAY QUESTIONS

1. Discuss the short and long run effects of a government policy of imposing a tax that would raise the price of oil and gasoline by 20% assuming that the elasticity of demand for oil is currently estimated to be 0.5 and the elasticity of demand for gasoline to be 1.2. Be sure to address what factors might alter the elasticity numbers over time.

2. Suppose that you are an economic consultant for a large company that produces and sells lollipops that are shaped as the faces of Hollywood celebrities. The company has shops in the major cities around the country and also sells by mail order catalog. As an economic consultant, you have estimated the elasticity of demand for store-bought lollipops to be 0.75 and the elasticity of demand for mail order lollipops to be 3. What advice would you give to the president of the company if she wanted to increase revenue from the shops and through mail orders? Now, suppose that the price of sugar increases causing a 20% reduction in the supply of celebrity lollipops. What information would you need to compute the effect of the reduction in supply on the equilibrium price?

VII. ANSWER KEY: MULTIPLE CHOICE QUESTIONS

1. Correct answer: b.

Discussion: The elasticity of demand is the percentage change in the quantity of good X demanded by the percentage change in its price.

Statement a is not correct because it is not expressed in percentage changes (but rather absolute changes) and has the numerator and denominator reversed. Statement c is not correct because it is expressed in absolute changes. Statement d is not correct because the elasticity of supply does not enter the formula. Statement e is not correct because the numerator and denominator should be reversed.

2. Correct answer: a.

Discussion: A rise in the price will always reduce the quantity demanded so, first you must look for an answer that has quantity demanded declining. The percentage change in quantity demanded is computed by multiplying E_d times $\%\Delta P = 1.5 \times 5 = 7.5$.

Statement b is not correct because the quantity demanded will decline, not increase, when the price rises. Statements c and d are wrong based on the formula. Statement e is not correct because there is enough information to answer the question.

3. Correct answer: b.

Discussion: Since you are given the elasticity of demand and a desired percentage change in the quantity demanded, you can figure out the percentage change in price as $\%\Delta P_x = \%\Delta Q^d_x/E_d$. Thus, $\%\Delta P_x = 50\%/2 = 25\%$.

Statement a is not correct because the two numbers should not be multiplied. Statement c would only be correct if the elasticity of demand was 1. Statement d is not correct; it is off by a factor of 10. Statement e is also not correct.

4. Correct answer: c.

Discussion: An inelastic demand is defined as one for which E_d is less than 1 which means that a 1% increase in price reduces the quantity demanded by less than 1% (and vice-versa for a price decrease).

Statement a defines an elastic demand. Statement b defines a unitary elastic demand. Statements d and e are not correct because elasticity is defined with respect to 1, not zero.

5. Correct answer: b.

Discussion: When there are no close substitutes for a product that makes the demand for it more inelastic. That is, the price of the good can be raised by a big percentage but quantity demanded will not respond by very much because there are not close substitutes consumers could switch their purchases to. This describes a good that has an inelastic demand.

If consumers have more time to shop around, they are more likely to compare prices. This means that consumers will be more sensitive to price changes, i.e. demand will be more elastic. If a good is a big part of a consumer's budget, a small change in the price will have a bigger impact on their budget. Thus, consumers will be more likely to greatly reduce their purchases of the good even if its price goes up a little bit. This defines demand to be more elastic. (You may want to think about the effects on budget and spending if the price of a pen goes up by 10% to the price of housing going up by 10%). Luxury items, because they are not necessities, tend to have a more elastic demand. Since a, c, and d are likely to raise the elasticity of demand, (make it more elastic), statement e cannot be correct.

6. Correct answer: e.

Discussion: Cookies are the only good that are not a "necessity." Goods that are not a necessity tend to have a more elastic demand.

Insulin is a necessary good to a diabetic; no matter how much the price of insulin increases, the purchases of insulin will not drop. In this case, the elasticity of demand for insulin is likely to be zero. The same, to a lesser degree, is true of gasoline. People must have transportation to their jobs, the grocery store, etc. Thus, gasoline is more of a necessity than cookies. A similar story can be told for coffee. Most people cannot seem to get through the day without at least one cup of coffee, which makes coffee more of a necessity than cookies. Cigarettes have an addictive property, which means that price increases will have less of an effect of reducing consumption than for a non-addictive good. Thus, cookies are likely to have a higher elasticity of demand than cigarettes.

7. Correct answer: b.

Discussion: The elasticity of demand is calculated as the percentage change in quantity demanded divided by the percentage change in price. (See PET #2). Thus, the elasticity of demand would be 2/5 = 0.4. Since the elasticity of demand is less than 1.0, demand is said to be "inelastic." You should also be aware that if the percentage change in quantity demanded is less than the percentage change in price, demand for the product will be inelastic. In this case, the percentage change in quantity demanded is 2 while the percentage change in price is 5 and so demand must be inelastic.

Statement a is not correct. Unitary elasticity occurs when the elasticity of demand is 1.0. This happens when the percentage change in quantity demanded is exactly equal (in absolute value) to the percentage change in price. Statement c is not correct. An elastic demand occurs when the elasticity of demand is greater than 1.0. This will happen whenever the percentage change in quantity demanded (in absolute value) is greater than the percentage change in price. Statements d and e are made-up terms.

8. Correct answer: e.

Discussion: When the elasticity of demand is greater than 1, an X% price change will cause a greater than X% change in quantity demanded. In this case, the florist has chosen to raise, not lower, the price of flowers. With an elasticity of demand of 4, the 5% point increase in the price will lead to a 20% point decline in the quantity of flowers sold. Thus, statement d is correct. At the same time, since the percentage change in the price increase is swamped by the percentage reduction in the quantity of flowers sold, the revenue earned by the florist will drop. Thus, statement a is correct, too.

Statement b is not correct; the effect on quantity is not determined by dividing 5 by 4 but instead by multiplying the two numbers. Statement c is not correct because it is off by a factor of 10.

9. Correct answer: b.

Discussion: The percentage change in quantity demanded (i.e. client base) desired by the dentist is an increase of 30%. The dentist also knows the elasticity of demand for dental services to be 5. The formula for the elasticity of demand can be used to solve for the percentage change in the price of dental services that would generate the 30% increase in the client base. (See PET #2). Using the elasticity of demand formula: 5 = 30%/percentage change in price. So, percentage change in price = 30%/5 = 6%. Since the dentist wants the client base to increase (not decrease), dental fees must decline by 6%.

Based on the above, none of the other statements are correct.

10. Correct answer: a.

Discussion: With an inelastic demand, the percentage rise (in this case) in the price of the good is greater than the percentage reduction in the quantity demanded which means that on net, total revenue (p X q) will increase. With an elastic demand, the percentage drop (in this case) will be less than the percentage increase in the quantity of the good demanded. (Remember price and quantity demanded move in opposite directions). Thus, on net, total revenue will rise.

Statement b is not correct; it would have been correct if the second part of the question asked what happened to total revenue when the price of a good with an elastic demand was increased. Statement c is not correct; only a unitary elasticity of demand leads to no change in total revenue when price is raised or lowered. Statement d is not correct; it would have been correct if the question had asked what happens to total revenue when price is decreased and demand is inelastic and what happens to total revenue when price is increased and demand is elastic. Statement e is not correct; it would have been correct if the first part of the question had asked what happens to total revenue when price is decreased and demand is inelastic.

11. Correct answer: b.

Discussion: The percentage change in the price of a cow is 10% [($550-500)/500] X 100 and the percentage change in the quantity of cows supplied is 30% [(130,000-100,000)/100,000] X 100. The elasticity of supply is computed as the percentage change in the quantity supplied divided by the percentage change in the price which is 30%/10% = 3.

For the reasoning just mentioned, statements a, c, and d are not correct. Statement e is not correct because you are given information that allows you to compute percentage changes.

12. Correct answer: d.

Discussion: Since the supply of tweed jackets has increased, you should be looking for an answer that has the price of tweed jackets declining. The formula used to compute the percentage change in the equilibrium price is to take the percentage shift in supply (or demand, if that had been the question) and divide it by the sum of the elasticity of supply and demand. Thus, the percentage change in the equilibrium price will be 20%/(1 + 4) = 20%/5 = 4%.

Statements a and c cannot be correct because a supply increase causes a drop in the equilibrium price (see Chapter 4 for review if you don't remember this). Statements b and e are not correct because the formula gives an answer of 4%.

13. Correct answer: b.

Discussion: Since income has increased, you should be looking for an answer that says the quantity demand has increased. Thus, statement d can be ruled out right away. The income elasticity of demand formula is income elasticity of demand = percentage change in quantity demanded/percentage change in income. Since you know the income elasticity of demand is 1.2 and the percentage change in income is 24%, you can plug the numbers in and solve for the percentage change in quantity demanded. Thus, 1.2 = percentage change in quantity demanded/24%. Using a little algebra to solve for the answer gives (1.2 X 24%) = percentage change in quantity demanded. Thus, the correct answer is 28.8%. You may have incorrectly arrived at the answer of 20% if you had carelessly divided 24% by 1.2.

Based on the discussion above, none of the other options are correct.

14. Correct answer: b.

Discussion: Complements are goods for which the price change in one good leads to a change in quantity demanded of another good in the opposite direction of the price change. For example, when the price of peanut butter increases, the quantity of jelly demanded decreases because the two goods are complements. They are used together so that when the cost of one of the goods rises (peanut butter), it causes the price of the finished good (peanut butter and jelly sandwich) to rise and thus quantity of peanut butter and jelly sandwiches to decline which in turn indirectly reduces the quantity of jelly demanded. The cross-elasticity of demand is computed as the percentage change in quantity demanded of product Y/percentage change in the price of product X. Using the information from the question, the cross elasticity of demand is 2%/10% = 0.2. Thus, statement b is correct.

Since J and L are complements, statements a, c, and e are not correct. Statement d is not correct because the cross-elasticity is calculated as 2%/10% and not 10%/2%.

15. Correct answer: d.

Discussion: The income elasticity of demand is the percentage change in quantity demanded divided by the percentage change in price. In this case, the percentage change in quantity demanded is -20% = (16,000 - 20,000)/20,000. The percentage change in average income is +10% ($55,000 - $50,000)/$50,000. Thus, the income elasticity of demand, expressed in absolute terms (i.e. without the negative sign) is 20%/10% = 2. However, since you are told that quantity demanded has decreased while income has increased, you should infer (based on Chapter 4) that this is an inferior good. Inferior goods are goods for which increases in income cause demand to decline and so to, the equilibrium quantity. (vice-versa for decreases in income). Thus, statement d is correct.

Based on the discussion above, statements a, b, c, and e are incorrect.

VIII. ANSWER KEY: ESSAY QUESTIONS

1. Since the currently estimated elasticity of demand for oil is 0.5, a 20% increase in the price of oil will reduce the quantity demanded by 10% (0.5 X 20%), at least in the short run. The tax revenue collected by the government on oil will, however, increase. The tax revenue will increase because the percentage increase in the price of oil dominates the percentage decrease in the quantity demanded. For gasoline, a 20% increase in its price will reduce the quantity demanded by 24% (1.2 X 20%), at least in the short run. In the short run, the 20% increase in the price of gasoline is much more effective at reducing consumer use of gasoline than is the 20% increase in the price of oil at reducing consumer use of oil (compare 10% to 24%). However, the tax revenue collected on gasoline sales will actually decline because the percentage decrease in the quantity demanded outweighs the percentage increase in the price. Thus, on balance, tax revenue collected by the government on gasoline will decline. While in the short run, it may be difficult to find substitutes for oil or gasoline, in the long run, consumers may be

able to modify their spending behavior. They may find substitutes for oil or gasoline (perhaps because innovative companies will invent products like methanol or battery-run automobiles). Thus, in the long run, the estimated elasticities may increase. In fact, if the elasticity for oil increased above 1, then the tax increase of 20% would end up lowering the tax revenue collected by the government on oil consumption.

2. The advice I would give to the president of the celebrity lollipop company is this: raise the price of lollipops purchased in shops throughout the country and lower the price of lollipops purchased through mail order catalogs. However, be aware that eventually, when consumers become aware of the price difference, you may eventually see your revenue from the stores decline (rather than rise after you have raised the price) but your revenue from mail orders may eventually increase by more than originally estimated. This may happen because customers from the store-bought shops may begin to purchase by mail order. That is, they will have found an almost identical substitute for the store-bought lollipops.

If the price of sugar rises, the supply of celebrity lollipops will decrease (shift left). The decreased supply will raise the price of a store-bought and mail order lollipops. In order to know by how much the equilibrium prices would rise, you would need information on the elasticity of supply of store-bought and mail order lollipops (in addition to the elasticity of demand) as well as on the percentage reduction in the supply of each type of lollipop. For example, if the supply of mail order lollipops dropped by 40% and the elasticity of supply is 1 and you are given that the elasticity of demand is 3, then the equilibrium price will change by 40%/(1+3) = 40%/4 = 10%.

Take It to the Net

We invite you to visit the O'Sullivan/Sheffrin page on the Prentice Hall Web site at:

http://www.prenhall.com/osullivan/

for this chapter's World Wide Web exercise.

CHAPTER 4
PRODUCTION AND COST

I. OVERVIEW

In this chapter, you will learn about the costs a firm incurs when it produces output. You will learn that there are fixed costs and variable costs, and explicit and implicit costs of production. You will learn that a firm's marginal cost changes as it produces more and more (or less and less) output. You will learn that the productivity of a firm's workers affects its marginal cost of production. You will also learn about a firm's short and long run average costs. You will learn that the short and the long run are different time horizons that a firm considers when making decisions about how much to produce, whether to build another plant, hire more workers, or cut back production. You will re-encounter the concept of diminishing returns, which is a short run concept. You will learn about economies and diseconomies of scale, which are long run concepts.

II. CHECKLIST

By the end of this chapter, you should be able to:

√   Explain the difference between explicit and implicit costs.

√   Give some examples of explicit costs and implicit costs.

√   Explain the difference between accounting profit and economic profit.

√   Explain the difference between the short run and the long run.

√   Explain the difference between variable and fixed costs and why in the long run, all costs are variable.

√   Give some examples of variable costs and fixed costs.

√   Explain why diminishing returns causes marginal cost in the short run to increase.

√   Draw a short run average fixed cost curve and a short run average variable cost curve and explain their shape.

√   Draw a long run average cost curve and explain its shape.

√   Draw a short run marginal cost curve and explain its shape.

√   Explain the relationship between marginal cost and the average cost curves.

√   Explain what causes economies and diseconomies of scale.

√   Define a firm's minimum efficient scale and represent it with a graph.

III. KEY TERMS

Short run for microeconomics: a period of time over which the number of firms in an industry is fixed and existing firms cannot change their production facilities.

Long run for microeconomics: a period of time over which the number of firms in an industry can change and firms can change their production facility.

Short-run marginal cost (SMC): the change in total cost resulting from a one-unit increase in output from an existing production facility.

Short-run average total cost (SATC): short-run total cost divided by the quantity of output.

Fixed cost: costs that do not depend on the quantity produced.

Average fixed cost (AFC): fixed cost divided by the quantity produced.

Variable costs: costs that vary as the firm changes its output.

Short-run average variable cost (SAVC): variable cost divided by the quantity produced.

Indivisible input: an input that cannot be scaled down to produce a small quantity of output.

Long-run average cost (LAC): total cost divided by the quantity of output when the firm can choose a production facility of any size.

Economies of scale: a situation in which an increase in the quantity produced decreases the long-run average cost of production.

Minimum efficient scale: the output at which the long-run average cost curve becomes horizontal.

Diseconomies of scale: a situation in which an increase in the quantity produced increases the long-run average cost of production.

Explicit costs: the firm's actual cash payments for its inputs.

Implicit costs: the opportunity costs of non-purchased inputs.

Economic cost: the sum of explicit and implicit costs.

IV. PERFORMANCE ENHANCING TIPS (PETS)

PET #1

For any formula, if you are given two of three missing components, you can always figure out the third component. Likewise for three of four, four of five, and so on.

You encountered this PET in Chapter 5 where it was applied to the elasticity of demand. In this chapter, you can apply it to total, variable, and fixed costs, average total, average variable, and average fixed costs, and output. Let's see how.

Suppose you are told that the total cost of producing 100 units of output is $2,000. What is the average total cost? The average total cost (ATC) is computed using:

ATC = Total Cost/Output

Since you have two of the three missing components to the formula, you can figure out the third component. Thus, the average total cost would be $2,000/100 units = $20/unit.

Now, suppose you are told that the average total cost is $20/unit and that the output level is 100 units. What is the total cost (TC)? The formula above can be re-arranged as below to figure out the total cost:

TC = ATC X Output

Thus, the total cost would be $20/unit X 100 units = $2,000.

Next, suppose you are told that the average total cost is $20/unit and that the total cost is $2,000. How many units of output (Q) must the firm be producing? The formulas above can be re-arranged as below to figure out the output of the firm:

Q = Total Cost/Average Total Cost

Thus, the firm must be producing $2,000/($20/unit) = 100 units.

The same is true for computing variable costs (total or average) and fixed costs (total or average).

You can also apply this PET to the relationship between short run total cost, variable cost and fixed cost and to the relationship between short run average total cost, average variable cost and average fixed cost.

For example, suppose you are told that the variable cost of producing 100 units of output is $1,500 and the fixed cost of producing 100 units of output is $500. What is the short run total cost?

The short run total cost is the sum of the two:

Total Cost = variable cost + fixed cost

Thus, the total cost is $2,000.

Based on the information above, the average variable cost would be $1,500/100 units = $15/unit and the average fixed cost would be $500/100 units $5/unit. Thus, the average total cost would be:

Average Total Cost = average variable cost + average fixed cost

Thus, the average total cost would be $15/unit + $5/unit = $20/ unit.

PET #2

Short run marginal cost is computed by calculating the change in (or addition to) the short run total cost as output increases by one unit. Since the short run total cost is the sum of variable cost plus fixed cost, and since fixed costs do not change as the level of output changes, then marginal cost can also be computed by calculating the change in the short run variable cost as output increases by one unit.

Suppose you are told that the variable cost of producing 10 units of output is $250 and that the fixed cost of producing 10 units of output is $100. Further, you are told that the variable cost of producing 11 units of output is $275. Since fixed costs are fixed, the fixed cost of producing 11 units of output remains at $100. What is the total cost of producing 10 units of output? Of 11 units of output? What is the marginal cost of the 11th unit of output?

Total cost of producing 10 units of output is $250 + $100 = $350.

Total cost of producing 11 units of output is $275 + $100 = $375.

The marginal cost (addition to cost) of producing one more unit of output, the 11th unit is equal to the change in total cost, which is also equal to the change in the variable cost. Let's see why:

Marginal Cost of 11th unit = Change in total cost = change in variable cost + change in fixed cost.

The change in total cost is $375 - $350 = $25.

The change in variable cost is $275 - $250 = $25.

The change in fixed cost is $100 - $100 = $0.

Notice that the sum of the change in the variable cost plus the change in the fixed cost equals $25. This is because fixed costs do not change as output changes. That is, the marginal cost associated with fixed inputs is zero. Thus, in the short run, the marginal cost can also be computed as the change in the variable cost.

Remember that in the long run, all costs are variable costs. There are no "fixed" costs.

PET #3

When marginal cost is less than average total (or average variable) cost, average total (or average variable) cost will decrease. When marginal cost is greater than average total (or average variable) cost, average total (or average variable) cost will increase.

Suppose that you are told that the average total cost of producing 300 units of output is $60 and that the marginal cost of producing the 301st unit of output is $65. Will the average total cost of producing 301 units of output be greater or less than $60?

Since the marginal cost of increasing output by one unit to 301 units is greater than the average cost of producing the previous 300 units, then the average cost of producing 301 units will increase.

V. PRACTICE EXAM: MULTIPLE CHOICE QUESTIONS

1. Which one of the following would be considered an implicit cost by a firm?
   a) monthly electricity bill.
   b) monthly rent for use of a warehouse.
   c) weekly wages paid to workers.
   d) foregone interest income because an entrepreneur must use her own money to start up a business.
   e) payment for installation of a fax line.

2. In the long run, a firm can:
   a) alter the number of workers it hires.
   b) alter the amount of raw materials it uses.
   c) alter the size of the factory.
   d) open up new factories or close down factories.
   e) all of the above.

3. Use the table below to determine when diminishing marginal returns occurs.

Workers	Output (in units)
1	10
2	25
3	50
4	60
5	68
6	75

   a) after the first worker.
   b) after the second worker.
   c) after the third worker.
   d) after the fourth worker.
   e) after the fifth worker.

4. Use the table below to determine when diminishing marginal returns occurs.

Workers	Output (in units)
4	1
7	2
9	3
10	4
14	5
20	6

   a) after the first unit of output.

   b) between the first and second unit of output.

   c) after the third unit of output.

   d) after the fourth unit of output.

   e) after the fifth unit of output.

5. The short run production function (total product curve) is a graph showing the relationship between:

   a) output produced and the number of workers, holding everything else constant.

   b) the marginal product of a worker and output.

   c) output and average cost of production.

   d) number of workers and number of other inputs.

   e) the marginal cost of production and output.

6. Which one of the following statements is true?

   a) short run total cost = variable cost - fixed cost.

   b) short run total cost = variable cost + fixed cost.

   c) average total cost = average variable cost/average fixed cost.

   d) fixed cost = average fixed cost/output.

   e) average variable cost = variable cost X output.

7. Which one of the following statements is correct?

   a) a firm's average fixed costs increase as output increases.

   b) in the short run, a firm's marginal cost curve is negatively sloped because of diminishing marginal returns.

   c) in the long run, a firm's average total cost curve is U-shaped.

   d) if the marginal cost of production is less than the average total cost of production, then average total costs will be decreasing.

   e) average total costs = average fixed cost - average variable cost.

8. Which one of the following explains why a firm's short run marginal cost increases as it produces more and more output?

   a) diminishing returns.

   b) diseconomies of scale.

   c) increasing returns to scale.

   d) diminishing marginal utility.

   e) diseconomies of scope.

9. Which one of the following statements is true?

   a) a firm's short run average variable cost first increases and then decreases as output increases.

   b) a firm's short run average total cost curve is shaped like a "W."

   c) a firm's average fixed cost always decreases as output increases.

   d) average variable cost increases as output increases because each additional worker becomes less and less productive in the short run.

   e) (c) and (d).

10. Use the following information to answer the question below.

    output = 250 units.
    fixed cost = $1,000.
    average variable cost = $6 per unit.
    average total cost = $10 per unit.
    marginal cost = $12.

    Which one of the following statements is true based on the information above?

    a) average fixed cost = $4 per unit and total cost = $25,000.

    b) variable cost = $1,500 and average fixed cost = $4 per unit.

    c) variable cost = $2,500 and total cost = $1,500.

    d) average fixed cost = $4 per unit and total cost = $22.

    e) total cost = $1,006 and variable cost = $18.

11. Use the following information to answer the question below.

  output = 100 units

  average fixed cost = $3 per unit.

  short run total cost = $800.

  marginal cost = $60.

  The firm's total variable cost must be:

  a) $500.

  b) $770.

  c) $77.

  d) $7,700.

  e) cannot be calculated without more information.

12. Suppose you are told that the average total cost of producing 200,000 dartboards is $4 and that the total fixed costs of operation are $100,000. Based on this, you know that:

  a) total variable costs are $700,000.

  b) average fixed costs are $2.

  c) the marginal cost of production is $1.

  d) total costs are $900,000.

  e) total profits will be very low.

13. Use the graph below to answer the following question.

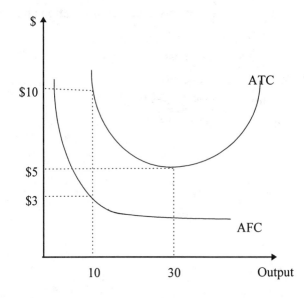

Which one of the following statements is true?

a) the average variable cost of producing 10 units of output is $13 per unit.

b) the total cost of producing 30 units of output is $5.

c) the variable cost of producing 10 units of output is $70.

d) the marginal cost of producing 30 units of output must be less than $5.

e) none of the above are true.

14. Which one of the following defines the long run average cost of production?

a) total cost divided by the quantity of output when the firm cannot alter the number of workers it hires.

b) total cost divided by the quantity of output when the firm can choose a production facility of any size.

c) total cost multiplied by the quantity of output when the firm can choose a production facility of any size.

d) total cost divided by the quantity of output when the firm cannot alter the size of its facilities.

e) total cost divided by the quantity of output when the firm cannot change the number of factories it operates.

15. Which one of the following is a reason for economies of scale?

a) specialization.

b) diminishing returns.

c) divisible inputs.

d) rising marginal costs.

e) comparative advantage.

16. Which one of the following is NOT an example of an indivisible input?

a) an industrial mold for a giant bowl of jello.

b) a large cargo ship.

c) "clean rooms" used by a computer-chip maker.

d) an expensive piece of medical equipment.

e) all of the above are examples of indivisible inputs.

17. Which one of the following statements is NOT true?

a) the minimum efficient scale for production is that output level where average costs are neither increasing nor decreasing, i.e. the long run average cost curve is horizontal.

b) diseconomies of scale may arise from the use of indivisible inputs.

c) diseconomies of scale may occur because of coordination problems that arise as more and more output is produced.

d) diseconomies of scale may occur because input costs increase as a firm produces more and more output.

e) in the long run, a firm does not encounter diminishing returns.

VI. PRACTICE EXAM: ESSAY QUESTIONS

1. Explain why specialization can lead to economies of scale.

2. Distinguish diminishing returns from diseconomies of scale.

VII. ANSWER KEY: MULTIPLE CHOICE QUESTIONS

1. Correct answer: d.

Discussion: An implicit cost is a cost for which there is not an explicit payment by check or money. The textbook lists two types of implicit costs -- the cost of a business owner's time and the cost of a business owner's use of his or her own funds (financial capital). Implicit costs should be included when figuring up economic profit. However, they are not included when figuring up accounting profit.

Statements a, b, c, and e are all examples of explicit costs.

2. Correct answer: e.

Discussion: The long run is defined as a period of time over which a firm is able to choose the combination of workers, raw materials, size of the factory, and number of factories to operate in order to produce output at the least per unit cost (average cost).

Statements a, b, c, and d are all factors of production that can be altered in the long run. In the short run, however, generally speaking, only the number of workers and the amount of raw material a firm uses can be altered. The size of the factory along with the number of factories currently in operation cannot simply be changed on short notice (say, one week).

3. Correct answer: c.

Discussion: Diminishing marginal returns is defined as when the change in output begins to decrease. Between the first and second worker, output increases by 15 units. Between the second and third worker, output increases even more by 25 units. So, for this range, the change in output is increasing. However, between the third and fourth worker, the change in output is 10 units. The change in output has decreased from 25 to 10. Between the fourth and fifth worker, the change in output is 8 units and between the fifth and sixth worker, the change in output is 7 units. Thus, after the third worker, the change in output begins to decline. This is one definition of diminishing marginal returns.

4. Correct answer: d.

Discussion: This table requires that you understand an alternative definition of diminishing marginal returns. Diminishing marginal returns can also be defined as when the addition to an input (labor) must be increased to get the same change in output, in this case one unit. As the table shows, from the first to the second unit of output, three additional workers must be hired. From the second to the third unit of output, two additional workers must be hired, from the third to fourth unit of output, one additional worker must be hired. So, for this range of output, less and less additional labor is needed to get the same increase in output. However, from the fourth to the fifth unit of output, four more workers must be hired to get a one unit increase in output. And, from the fifth to sixth unit of output, six more workers must be hired to produce one more unit of output. In this case, more and more additional labor is needed to get the same increase in output.

5. Correct answer: a.

Discussion: The short-run production function (total product curve) is a graph that shows the relationship between the amount of workers (labor) and the amount of output the workers can produce, assuming a given amount of capital, state of technology, plant size, etc.

6. Correct answer: b.

Discussion: Short run total cost is the sum of variable cost plus fixed cost. That's why it's referred to as "total."

Statement a is not correct because total cost is the sum of, not the difference between, variable cost and fixed cost. Statement c is not correct. It would have been correct if it had read "average total cost = average variable cost + average fixed cost." Statement d is not correct. It would have been correct if it had read "fixed cost = average fixed cost X output." Statement e is not correct. It would have been correct if it had read "average variable cost = variable cost/output." (See PET #2 for review).

7. Correct answer: d.

Discussion: When marginal cost, the addition to total cost, is less than average total cost, it will pull average total cost down. That is, average total cost will decline. See PET #4 for review.

Statement a is not correct because as output increases, a firm's average fixed costs decrease, not increase. Statement b is not correct because a firm's marginal cost curve will be positively, not negatively, sloped when there are diminishing returns. Statement c is not correct because in the long run, the firm's average total cost curve is declining and then has a flat portion to it. It is more L-shaped than U-shaped. Statement e is not correct since average total cost is equal to average fixed cost plus average variable cost.

8. Correct answer: a.

Discussion: Diminishing returns means that each additional worker that is hired to produce more output is less productive than the workers hired before him. Thus, it becomes more costly to the firm to get that worker to produce the same level of output as the previous workers. A way to think about it is that that worker would have to work more hours than the other workers (and therefore be paid overtime) in order to produce the same amount of output as the other workers are producing.

Diseconomies of scale is a long run concept. Increasing returns to scale is not a term you have encountered, nor is diseconomies of scope. Diminishing marginal utility is a concept related to consumer "satisfaction" not a firm's cost of production. Thus, statements b, c, d, and e are not correct.

9. Correct answer: e.

Discussion: Statement c is correct because fixed costs do not change with the level of output. Since average fixed cost is calculated as fixed cost/output, as output increases, average fixed cost must decline. (The number in the denominator gets bigger but the number in the numerator does not change). Statement d is also correct. It is another way of stating that diminishing returns gives rise to increasing average variable cost (as well as increasing marginal cost).

Statement a is not correct because average total cost first decreases and then increases as output increases. Statement b is not correct; a firm's average total cost curve is shaped like a "U." Statements c and d are both correct which is why statement e is the answer.

10. Correct answer: b.

Discussion: Variable cost is computed by multiplying average variable cost by the output level = $6 per unit X 250 units = $1,500. Average fixed cost is computed by dividing fixed cost by the output level = $1,000/250 units = $4/unit.

Statement a is not correct because total cost is $2,500, not $25,000. Total cost can be computed from figuring out variable cost (as above), which is $1,500, and adding to it the fixed cost of $1,000. Statement c is not correct based on the discussion. Statement d is not correct because total cost is not $22. (Total cost is not the sum of marginal cost plus average total cost). Statement e is not correct because total cost is not $1,006 and variable cost is not $18.

11. Correct answer: a.

Discussion: To arrive at the correct answer, you must compute fixed cost using average fixed cost and output. Fixed cost = $3 per unit X 100 units = $300. Then, you can compute variable cost from the difference between total cost and fixed cost = $800 - $300 = $500.

Statements b, c, and d are not correct based on the above discussion. Statement e is not correct because there is enough information (i.e. you don't need to know average variable cost) to compute total variable cost.

12. Correct answer: a.

Discussion: Based on the question, you can calculate the average total cost of production using PET #2. Total cost is equal to $4 X 200,000 units = $800,000. Since you also know that total fixed costs are $100,000, you can compute total variable cost as the difference between total cost and fixed cost. Thus, total variable cost is $800,000 - $100,000 = $700,000.

Statement b is not correct because average fixed costs are $0.50 ($100,000/200,000 units). Statement d is not correct since total costs are $800,000 ($4 X 200,000 units). Statement c cannot be an answer since you do not have enough information to compute marginal cost. You would need to have some information about change in cost and output. Statement e is not correct. You do not know anything about price or even what "very low" would be defined to mean.

13. Correct answer: c.

Discussion: The graph shows the average total cost and average fixed cost associated with different levels of production. Since the average total cost of 10 units of output is $10 per unit and the average fixed cost is $3 per unit, the average variable cost must be $7 per unit. Since the average variable cost is $7 per unit, the variable cost must be $7 per unit X 10 units = $70.

Statement a is not correct because the average variable cost is $7 per unit. Statement b is not correct. It would have been correct if it stated that the average total cost of production was $5. Statement d is not correct because average total cost is increasing beyond 30 units of output. If the average cost is increasing, the marginal cost must be greater than the average cost of $5, not less than $5. Statement e is not correct because statement c is correct.

14. Correct answer: b.

Discussion: Statement b is correct; it indicates a long run concept since the production facility's size can be changed and because an average cost is computed by dividing a total cost by an output level.

Statement a, d, and e are not correct because they imply short run concepts where the firm has some fixed factors of production that cannot be changed. Statement c is not correct because average cost is not computed by multiplying total cost by the output level.

15. Correct answer: a.

Discussion: When workers are able to specialize in the tasks that they do, they become more productive. They know how to do a task well and they don't have to spend time switching from task to task. Statement b is not correct; diminishing returns gives rise to increasing marginal (and variable and total) costs of production. Statement c is not correct; indivisible inputs give rise to economies of scale, not divisible inputs. Statement d is not correct because with economies of scale, marginal costs will be decreasing or not changing. Statement e is not a concept that is applied to economies of scale.

16. Correct answer: e.

Discussion: Indivisible inputs are those inputs that cannot be divided up to accommodate low levels of production. For example, a piece of medical equipment must be purchased by hospital regardless of whether they will use it for one patient, two patients, twenty patients, or one thousand patients. The same is true of an industrial mold, a large cargo ship, and clean rooms used by a computer chip maker. Can you think of other examples?

17. Correct answer: b.

Discussion: Statement b is the only statement that is not true. Indivisible inputs give rise to economies of scale, not diseconomies of scale. All of the other statements are true.

VIII. ANSWER KEY: ESSAY QUESTIONS

1. Specialization is a long run concept. In the long run, a firm is able to alter the amount of equipment each worker has to work with and the amount of space within which each worker works. Thus, in the long run, with more equipment and more space to work, workers can specialize at a task. This means that they can now spend more time on one task (rather than having to move between tasks). This makes workers more productive because time is not lost as workers move between tasks. Thus, each worker is able to produce more output per hour than before. Also, since workers spend more time on the same task, they learn to do the task more efficiently and thus can produce more output per hour than before. Since more output per hour is being produced by the workers and their wages have not changed, the average cost per unit of output will decline in the long run. Economies of scale is defined as a declining average cost as output increases.

2. Diminishing returns is a short run concept and arises because one (or more) of the factors of production with which a firm produces output is fixed, i.e. the amount is not able to be changed in the short run. Typically, plant and equipment are considered the fixed factors of production. Since the amount of plant and equipment is fixed, if a firm wants to produce more output, it must hire more workers but cannot alter the amount of plant and equipment. Consequently, more and more workers are jammed into factory floor space and may have to waste time waiting for a piece of equipment to use to finish their task. What this means is that each additional worker that is hired by the firm will produce less output per hour than the previous worker. This is the definition of diminishing returns.

Diseconomies of scale is a long run concept and arises because of coordination problems and increasing input costs when a firm gets bigger and bigger (produces more and more output). Diseconomies of scale is defined as an increase in long run average cost as output increases. This is the reverse of economies of scale. Coordination problems can contribute to the average cost of production increasing as output increases. Coordination problems may arise because of layers of bureaucracy or management that a business decision must pass through before actually being executed and/or because of personnel problems. Also, as a firm produces more and more output, it increases its demand for inputs, which can put upward pressure on the price of inputs. This can thereby contribute to an increase in the average cost of production.

Take It to the Net

We invite you to visit the O'Sullivan/Sheffrin page on the Prentice Hall Web site at:

http://www.prenhall.com/osullivan/

for this chapter's World Wide Web exercise.

CHAPTER 5
PERFECT COMPETITION:
SHORT RUN AND LONG RUN

I. OVERVIEW

In this chapter, you will learn about a perfectly competitive market structure and the characteristics that describe it. You will learn how a firm decides how much output to produce in a perfectly competitive market. You will use the cost concepts and cost curves that you learned about in the previous chapter together with a revenue and marginal revenue curve. You will re-encounter the marginal principle and apply it to determining the level of output that will maximize a firm's profit. You will learn about the factors that influence a firm's decision to either shut down its operation or to continue it even in the face of losses. You will learn what factors might contribute to entry to or exit from a perfectly competitive market. You will see how entry and exit affect the profit levels of the firms that are already operating in the market and how entry, exit, and the ability to alter facility size, in the long run, affect the market supply curve. You will learn about how changes in demand affect the price of a product differently in the short run than in the long run. You will also learn about increasing and constant cost industries which are determined by how productive inputs are as more firms enter (or exit) an industry and how the price of inputs changes as more firms enter (or exit) an industry. You will compare the slope of a short run supply curve to the slope of a long run supply curve.

II. CHECKLIST

By the end of this chapter, you should be able to:

√   List the characteristics of a perfectly competitive market structure.

√   Give some real world examples of a perfectly competitive market structure.

√   Define total and marginal revenue and represent them with a graph.

√   Explain why marginal revenue equals price in a perfectly competitive market.

√   Explain why the rule of picking an output level where price (marginal revenue) equals marginal cost maximizes a firm's profit.

√   Use a graph to pick the profit-maximizing output level and represent profit on the graph.

√   Explain when a firm would, in the short run, decide to shut down its operation and when in the long run, it would decide to shut down its operation.

√   Explain what would happen, in the short run, in a perfectly competitive market to the typical firm earning zero economic profit when there is an increase in market demand (and vice-versa).

√   Use graphs to show what would happen, in the short run, in a perfectly competitive market to the typical firm earning zero economic profit when there is an increase in market demand (and vice-versa).

√   Explain the difference between the short and the long run.

√ Explain what causes firms to enter and exit an industry in a perfectly competitive market structure.

√ Compare what happens to the quantity supplied by a market as demand (and thus price) of the product increases (or decreases), in the short and the long run, and compare the difference.

√ Explain what causes a supply curve to be positively sloped and explain what would cause it to be more steeply sloped.

√ Explain the difference between increasing and constant cost industries and illustrate the difference using a graph of the long run supply curve.

III. KEY TERMS

Perfectly competitive market: a market with a very large number of firms, each of which produces the same standardized product and takes the market price as given.

Total revenue: the money the firm gets by selling its product; equal to the price times the quantity sold.

Sunk cost: the cost a firm has already paid or has agreed to pay some time in the future.

Shut-down price: the price at which the firm is indifferent between operating and shutting down.

Short-run supply curve: a curve showing the relationship between price and the quantity of output supplied by a firm.

Short-run supply curve: a curve showing the relationship between price and quantity supplied in the short run (the number of firms is fixed and firms cannot change their production facilities).

Short-run marginal cost: the change in cost from producing just one more unit of output in an existing facility.

Economic profit: total revenue minus the total economic cost (the sum of explicit and implicit costs).

Long-run market supply curve: a curve showing the relationship between price and quantity supplied in the long run.

Increasing-cost industry: an industry in which the average cost of production increases as the industry grows, so the long-run supply curve is positively sloped.

Constant-cost industry: an industry in which the average cost of production is constant, so the long-run supply curve is horizontal.

IV. PERFORMANCE ENHANCING TIPS (PETS)

PET #1

Price and marginal revenue are the same number for a firm in a perfectly competitive market structure.

Let's explore why price and marginal revenue are the same number for a firm in a perfectly competitive market structure. In perfect competition, a firm is a price taker, which means that it does not have to lower the price of its product to sell more of it. It can sell all that it wants at the going price. This means that as a firm sells more and more units of its output, it continues to get the same price for its output.

For example, suppose the price of output was $2 per unit. If a firm sells one unit, the total revenue it receives is $2. If a firm sells two units, the total revenue it receives is $4. If a firm sells three units, the total revenue it receives is $6, and so on. Now, what is the marginal revenue (or addition to revenue) from selling one more unit? When the firm sells two units instead of one, it adds $2 to its total revenue ($4 - $2). When the firm sells three units instead of two, it adds $2 to its total revenue ($6 - $4), and so on. Thus, marginal revenue and price are the same for a firm in a perfectly competitive market structure.

PET #2

The rule of picking an output level where price is equal to marginal cost in order to maximize profit can also be expressed as picking an output level where marginal revenue is equal to marginal cost. This happens because in a perfectly competitive market structure, marginal revenue and price are the same number.

In the next few chapters, the rule for maximizing profits you will encounter is to pick an output level where marginal revenue is equal to marginal cost (instead of where price is equal to marginal cost). But, it is really the same rule you have learned in this chapter and the same rationale for why the rule maximizes a firm's profit applies. It may be better to remember the rule as marginal revenue = marginal cost instead of price = marginal cost as long as you understand that price and marginal revenue are the same for a firm operating in a perfectly competitive market.

PET #3

Firms that earn zero economic profit can continue to operate. This is because a firm earning zero economic profit can be earning a positive accounting profit. The positive accounting profit is what a firm may use to fund projects that will allow it to continue to operate in the future. Accounting profit is total revenue minus explicit costs whereas economic profit is total revenue minus explicit and implicit costs.

PET #4

The long run supply curve is flatter than the short run supply curve. This means that quantity supplied is more responsive to a given price change in the long run than is quantity supplied in the short run.

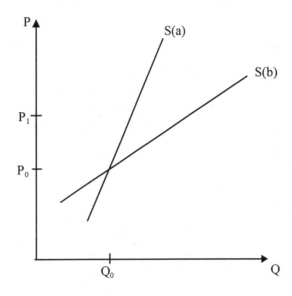

Compare the slope of supply curve (a) to supply curve (b) in the diagram above.

Supply curve (b) is flatter than supply curve (a). What does this mean in practical terms? Let's examine the response of quantity supplied to the same change in price along the two different supply curves. Draw a line from price P_0 across to the supply curves. Where the price line intersects the supply curves, draw a vertical line down to the quantity axis and mark this as the quantity supplied at price P_0 along graph (a) and (b). You will notice that at this price, the quantity supplied in the short and long run is the same amount.

Now, draw a line from price P_1 across to the supply curves. Where the price line intersects the supply curves, draw vertical lines down to the quantity axis and mark these as the quantity supplied at price P_1 along graph (a) and (b). Compare the changes in the quantity supplied along supply curve (a) and (b). You will see that as the price increases, the quantity supplied increases more along supply curve (b) than along supply curve (a). That means that quantity supplied is more responsive to price in the long run than in the short run. Why does this occur? It occurs because in the long run, as the price of a good increases, more firms enter the industry (attracted by profits due to the higher price) and existing firms may have expanded the size of their facility thus enabling them to produce more. Thus, for any given price increase, more is willingly supplied by firms.

PET #5

An increase in demand raises the price of a good by less in the long run than in the short run. A decrease in demand lowers the price of a good by less in the long run than in the short run.

To see this, draw an increase in demand (rightward shift in the demand curve) in the graph below.

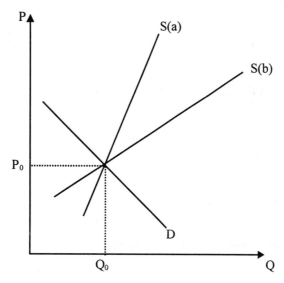

Now, mark the new equilibrium prices along the short run supply curve (a) and along the long run supply curve (b). Compare the change in the price from the initial price of P_0 along the two supply curves. What do you see? You should see that the price has increased by less along supply curve (b) -- the flat, long run supply curve than it has increased along supply curve (a).

Why does this occur? In the long run, remember that in response to a price increase, more firms enter the industry and existing firms will expand the size of their facility; the higher price creates economic profits, which motivate entry and expansion in the industry. Thus, in the long run, the industry is better able to satisfy the increased demand for their product. Buyers do not have to bid as fiercely against each other for the ability to purchase the product and thus the price of the product does not rise by as much.

You should work through a decrease in demand on your own.

V. PRACTICE EXAM: MULTIPLE CHOICE QUESTIONS

1. Which one of the following is NOT a characteristic of a perfectly competitive market structure?
    a) very large number of firms.
    b) standardized (or homogeneous) product.
    c) barriers to entry.
    d) no control over price.
    e) all of the above are characteristics of a perfectly competitive market structure.

2. Which one of the following would be an example of a perfectly competitive industry?
    a) restaurants.
    b) hog farmers.
    c) aircraft industry.
    d) auto dealerships.
    e) patented sheet-working tools.

3. Use the information below to answer the following question.

    quantity sold = 500,000 units
    price = $1.00 per unit
    explicit costs = $400,000
    implicit costs = $150,000

    Based on this information, the firm is:
    a) earning positive economic profit of $100,000.
    b) earning zero economic profit.
    c) earning positive accounting profit of $100,000.
    d) making an economic loss (negative economic profit) of $50,000.
    e) (c) and (d).

4. A firm can maximize its profits by picking an output level where:
    a) price > average variable costs.
    b) price > average total costs.
    c) marginal revenue = marginal cost.
    d) price = average variable cost.
    e) (b) and (c).

5. Which one of the following statements is always true of a firm in a perfectly competitive market?

   a) price = marginal revenue.

   b) price = marginal cost.

   c) price = total revenue.

   d) average total cost = average variable cost.

   e) economic profit is positive.

6. Use the graph below to answer the following question.

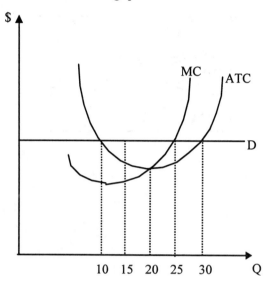

The output level that will maximize the firm's profit is:

   a) 10 units.

   b) 15 units.

   c) 20 units.

   d) 25 units.

   e) 30 units.

7. Use the diagram below to compute the profit that the firm is earning.

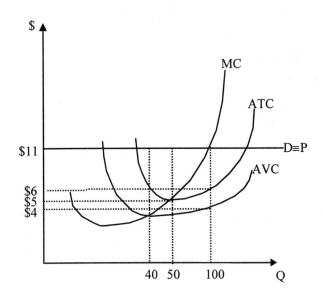

The firm's profit is:
a) $0.
b) $500.
c) $300.
d) $200.
e) $700.

8. Which one of the following statements is correct based on the following information?

price = $5.00 per unit
quantity = 200 units
total variable cost = $400
total fixed cost = $800
marginal cost = $5.00

a) the firm is making a loss but should, in the short run, continue to operate.
b) the firm is making a loss and should shut down its operation.
c) the firm is making a profit of $600.
d) the firm is making zero profit.
e) price is greater than average total cost.

9. Which one of the following statements is correct based on the graph below?

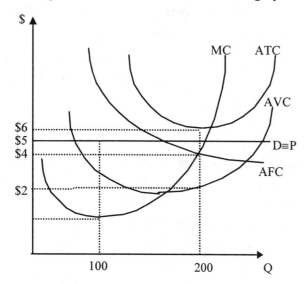

a) the firm is making a loss but should, in the short run, continue to operate.

b) the firm is making a loss and should shut down its operation in the short run.

c) the firm is making a profit of $600.

d) the firm is making zero profit.

e) price is greater than average total cost.

10. Which one of the following statements is true?

a) in the short run, if a firm shuts down it will have zero revenue and zero costs.

b) a firm should shut down if price is greater than average variable cost but less than average total cost.

c) a firm can maximize its profits by producing an output level where price equals marginal revenue.

d) in the short run, if a firm shuts down, it will have a loss equal to the amount of its sunk (or fixed) costs.

e) none of the above.

11. Suppose all firms in a perfectly competitive industry are currently earning zero economic profit. Assume the price of output is $10 per unit. Now, suppose that consumer demand for the industry's product declines. Which one of the following would be least likely to occur?

a) firms may begin to earn a negative economic profit in the short run.

b) price will decline.

c) marginal costs will rise.

d) some firms will exit the industry.

e) producer surplus will decrease in the short run.

12. Which one of the following is the definition of the long run?

    a) a period of time over which the demand for a product can increase or decrease.

    b) a period of time over which firms can enter and exit an industry.

    c) a period of time over which firms can alter the size of their production facility.

    d) a period of time over which the price of inputs used by an industry remains constant.

    e) (b) and (c).

13. Suppose the average cost of producing a set of golf clubs is $225. Suppose the price at which producers can sell a set of golf clubs is $230. Based on the information you are given, which one of the following best describes the industry response?

    a) firms will exit the industry because the economic profit per set of golf clubs is so small.

    b) firms will enter the industry because there are positive economic profits to be earned.

    c) the quantity of golf clubs supplied by the industry will remain unchanged.

    d) demand for golf clubs will increase.

    e) the cost of graphite used in making golf clubs will increase.

14. Which one of the following explains why, in the long run, the average cost of production may increase as an industry expands (produces more output)?

    a) rising input prices.

    b) rising productivity of inputs.

    c) falling input prices.

    d) increasing fixed costs.

    e) (a) and (b).

15. Suppose that a typical farmer sells 10,000 bushels of peaches each season and that the total revenue he earns is $100,000. Further, suppose that the average cost of producing 10,000 bushels is $12 per bushel. Based on this information, which one of the following statements is correct?

    a) there are positive economic profits and farmers will enter the industry.

    b) there are negative economic profits and some farmers will leave the industry.

    c) the average cost of production is rising.

    d) the elasticity of supply is 1.2.

    e) cannot be answered without information on price per bushel.

16. Which one of the following statements is NOT true?

    a) an increasing cost industry has a positively sloped long run supply curve.

    b) the long run average cost of production depends, in part, on how productive inputs are.

    c) a constant cost industry has a horizontal long run supply curve.

    d) diminishing returns explains why the average cost of production decreases in the long run.

    e) all of the above statements are true.

17. Consider the taxi industry, which is assumed to be a constant cost industry. If the demand for taxi services decreases, in the short run, the price for taxi services will _____ and in the long run, the price for taxi services will _____.

    a) increase; decrease.

    b) decrease; decrease.

    c) decrease; remain unchanged.

    d) remain unchanged; decrease.

    e) none of the above.

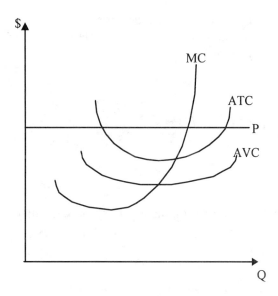

18. The graph above depicts the situation for a typical firm in a perfectly competitive market structure. Based on the graph, which would be the most likely industry response? Assume the industry is an increasing cost industry.

    a) there will be entry into the industry.

    b) existing firms will expand their production facilities.

    c) the prices of inputs will rise.

    d) the skill level of the workforce will decline.

    e) all of the above.

VI. PRACTICE EXAM: ESSAY QUESTIONS

1. Briefly explain why it is profit-maximizing for a firm to produce output up until the point at which marginal revenue equals marginal cost.

2. Suppose, after graduation, you take a job in a factory in Chile that produces faux leather shoes. One day, your boss comes in and says, "this factory isn't operating at a profit and so we can minimize our losses by closing up shop." Yikes! You didn't think you'd lose your job that quickly. Your boss continues talking and states that the company is having to pay 300,000 pesos a month for rent, interest on debt, and other non-avoidable costs. He also says that it costs 150,000 pesos a month just to pay you and all the other workers, including paying for the raw materials, to produce the shoes. He states that at current production of 5000 boxes of shoes a month, the company can only expect to get 40 pesos per box of shoes. Do you agree with your boss that the company should close up shop? Why or why not?

3. Explain why the long run supply curve is flatter than the short run supply curve.

4. Consider the market for beef. Suppose that the demand for beef declines because of health concerns. Explain what will happen to the price and quantity of beef supplied in the short and long run assuming the industry is an increasing cost industry.

VII. ANSWER KEY: MULTIPLE CHOICE

1. Correct answer: c.

Discussion: Barriers to entry characterize an oligopolistic and monopolist market structure, which you will learn about in later chapters.

A perfectly competitive market structure is one in which there are a very large number of firms each producing a very small portion of overall industry output. The product produced is said to be "standardized" or "homogeneous" which means that consumers don't perceive very much of a difference in buying from one producer than any other. Since there are so many firms providing such a small portion of industry output, the firms have no control over price; it is dictated by the market forces of supply and demand. Firms are said to be "price takers."

2. Correct answer: b.

Discussion: Hog farmers are many and produce a fairly standardized product, the hog.

Pizzerias are an example of a monopolistically competitive market structure since they produce a slightly differentiated product. The same may be true of auto dealerships (although auto manufacturers are considered to be an oligopoly). The aircraft industry is an example of an oligopolistic market structure since there are few firms in the industry that typically operate with economies of scale. A firm that has a patent typically has a monopoly. Thus, patented sheet-working tools are an example of a monopoly.

3. Correct answer: e.

Discussion: The total revenue that the firm is earning is $500,000 ($5 X 100,000 units). The economic cost is $550,000 (= $400,000 + $150,000). Thus, economic profit is -$50,000. That is, the firm is earning a loss.

The accounting profit that the firm is earning is equal to $100,000 ($500,000 - $400,000). Thus statements c and d are both correct. Statement a and b are not correct because the firm is making negative economic profit.

4. Correct answer: c.

Discussion: The rule for maximizing profits is to pick an output level where marginal revenue equals marginal cost. There is only one output level where this is true. When a firm follows this principle, it may make positive profit, zero profit, or even a negative profit (in which case we'd say that the firm would be minimizing its losses) but this is the best the firm can do. To assure yourself that this condition will maximize a firm's profit, consider the two other possibilities: (1) marginal revenue > marginal cost and (2) marginal revenue < marginal cost. If condition (1) is true, then a firm could add more to its revenue than to its costs by producing one more unit of output. This means that the firm's profits would increase if it produced more output. Thus, the firm could not be maximizing profits yet. If condition (2) is true, then a firm is adding more to its costs than to its revenue by producing the additional output. By producing this output level, the firm would be cutting into its profits and would be better off reducing production.

Statement a is not correct because there are a number of output levels where this would be true and thus the rule would offer no guidance about which output level to pick. The same is true of statement b. Statement d is not correct but it is the condition that would say that a firm is indifferent between shutting down and remaining open in the short run. Statement e is not correct because statement b is not correct.

5. Correct answer: a.

Discussion: For a perfectly competitive firm, which is a price taker, the firm's revenue from selling each additional unit of output, its marginal revenue, will always equal price.

Statement b is not correct since firms can, in the short run, earn positive or negative economic profit. Statement c is not correct; total revenue is equal to price X quantity. Statement d is not correct since a firm also has fixed costs. Statement e is not correct because a firm does not always earn positive economic profit.

6. Correct answer: d.

Discussion: The output level that a profit-maximizing firm will choose is the output level where marginal revenue (price) equals marginal cost. This occurs at an output level of 25 units (where the price and marginal cost curves intersect).

Statements a, b, c, and e are all incorrect based on the above method for finding a firm's profit maximizing level of output.

7. Correct answer: b.

Discussion: The profit is determined by first selecting the output level that a profit maximizing firm will choose. The profit-maximizing output level is where marginal revenue (price) equals marginal cost. This occurs at an output level of 100 units. Given that output level, the average total cost of 100 units of output is $6 and the price is $11. Thus, profit is equal to ($11 X 100) - ($6 X 100) = $500.

Statements a, c, d, and e are all incorrect based on the above method for finding and calculating a firm's profit.

8. Correct answer: a.

The firm's total revenue from operating would be $1,000 ($5 X 200 units). The firm's total cost would be $400 + $800 = $1,200. If the firm operates, it will make a loss of $200. This is less than the firm would lose if it shut down its operation.

If the firm shut down its operation it would not earn any revenue but would still have to pay for its fixed costs. Thus, the firm would lose $800. Thus, statement b is not correct. Statement c and d are not correct because the firm is not earning a profit. Statement e is not correct because average total cost is $1,200/200 units = $6. Thus, price is less than average total cost, which is why the firm is making a loss. Notice that since price is equal to marginal cost, the firm is doing the best it can, i.e. minimizing its losses.

9. Correct answer: a.

Discussion: This question is a graphical representation of question (8). To answer this question, you must first establish what the profit-maximizing output level of the firm is. It is found where price and marginal cost are equal (intersect) which is at an output level of 200 units. The average total cost of producing 200 units is $6. The average variable cost of producing 200 units is $2. The average fixed cost is $4. Since price exceeds average variable cost, the firm should continue to operate even though it will earn a loss of $200.

In order to answer the question, you could also calculate the total cost of producing 200 units of output as $1,200 and the revenue as $1,000. Thus, the firm will lose $200. Then, you could calculate how much the firm will lose if it shuts down. If it shuts down, it will have to pay its fixed costs, which can be read off the graph by taking the average fixed cost of $4 and multiplying it, by the output level of 200 units. Thus, the firm's loss would be $800.

Statements b, c, d, and e are all incorrect for the same reasons mentioned in the answer to question (8).

10. Correct answer: d.

Discussion: If a firm shuts down in the short run, it will have no revenue to offset the sunk or fixed costs that it must continue to pay. Thus, the firm will lose an amount equal to its sunk or fixed costs.

Statement a is not correct because if a firm shuts down in the short run, it will still have some costs to pay. Statement b is not correct. It would have been correct if it had said that a firm should remain open if price is greater than average variable cost but less than average total cost. Statement c is not correct because a perfectly competitive firm maximizes its profits by producing an output level where price (or marginal revenue) equals marginal cost. Statement e is not correct because statement d is correct.

11. Correct answer: c.

Discussion: If demand declines, you learned in Chapter 4 that this would cause price to decline. Thus, statement b is likely to occur. As the price of the product declines, firms that were initially earning zero economic profit will see price drop below their average total cost. This will cause them to make a loss (negative economic profit) in the short run. Thus, statement a is likely to occur. As firms earn negative economic profit, there will be exit from the industry. Thus statement d is likely to occur. As price declines, the profit-maximizing output level for firms will change -- it will decrease. That is, firms will produce less output. Since both price and output have declined, producer surplus must necessarily decline. (The effect on consumer surplus would be ambiguous since the price decline would raise consumer surplus but the quantity decline would reduce it). Thus, statement e is likely to occur. Statement c is least likely to occur because as a firm produces less output, its marginal cost of production will decline.

12. Correct answer: e.

Discussion: The long run is a period of time over which new firms can enter the industry (to capture positive economic profits) or exit the industry (to cut their losses). Over a longer period of time, firms already in the industry can also alter the size of their production facilities; they may wish to expand their operation if economic profits increase or they may wish to shut down some of their operation if they begin to incur losses.

Statements a and d are not correct because the long run is not defined with respect to changes in demand or changes in input prices. Statements b and c are both correct which is why statement e is the correct answer. Thus, statements b and c are both correct

13. Correct answer: b.

Discussion: Since the price that producers can get for a set of golf clubs exceeds the average cost of production by $5, firms will earn $5 of economic profit per set of golf clubs. That is, they will be earning positive economic profit. The positive economic profit will attract other firms into the industry. Entry will stop when economic profit is driven to zero.

Statement a is not correct; any positive economic profit is considered to motivate entry into an industry. Statement c is not correct because the positive economic profit will prompt entry into the industry and thus lead to an increase in the quantity supplied. Statement d is not correct because there is nothing in the information given that gives a reason for why the demand for golf clubs will increase. Statement e is not necessarily correct; it depends on whether the golf club industry is an increasing, decreasing or constant cost industry. If the industry is an increasing cost industry, then the price of graphite will likely increase. However, if the industry is a decreasing or constant cost industry, the price of graphite may actually decrease or not change at all as more golf club producers demand more graphite.

14. Correct answer: a.

Discussion: As an industry expands (produces more output), the demand for inputs increases. This increase in demand for inputs can put upward pressure on the price of inputs and thereby lead to a rise in the cost of the price of inputs. This, in turn, would raise a firm's average cost of production. Thus, statement a is correct.

Statement b is not correct. Rising productivity would actually decrease the average cost of production, not increase it. Statement c is not correct since falling input prices would actually decrease the average cost of production. Statement d is not correct because in the long run, there are no costs that are considered as fixed costs. Statement e is not correct because statement b is not correct.

15. Correct answer: b.

Discussion: In this question, you must determine whether the typical farmer is making a positive, zero, or negative economic profit. You can determine the profit situation of the farmer by either calculating the price per bushel that the typical farmer receives for his peaches or the total cost of producing 10,000 bushels. Once you have made either one of these calculations, you can determine whether there is entry or exit into the industry. The price per bushel can be calculated by dividing total revenue by the number of bushels sold. Since the total revenue is $100,000 and the number of bushels sold is 10,000, the price per bushel is $10. With the average cost of production being $12, the typical farmer will lose $2 on every bushel sold. Alternatively, you could have calculated the total cost of producing 10,000 bushels as $120,000 ($12 X 10,000). In this case, the farmer will lose $20,000 for the lot of 10,000 bushels sold (i.e. $2 for every bushel sold). With either calculation, you should see that the farmer will not be making a positive economic profit. The long run industry response to negative economic profits is for firms (farmers, in this case) to leave the industry.

Statement a is not correct based on the reasoning above. Statement c is not necessarily correct; it depends on whether the industry is an increasing, decreasing or constant cost industry. If the industry is an increasing cost industry, as firms exit, there will be less demand for inputs and the price of inputs would drop. This would mean that the average cost of production would decrease. If the industry is a constant cost industry, the exit of firms will have no effect on the input prices and the average cost of production would remain constant. If the industry is a decreasing cost industry, as firms exit, the cost of inputs will rise which will raise the average cost of production. Statement d is not correct because you are not given enough information to calculate an elasticity of supply. In order to calculate an elasticity, you would need changes in prices and quantity supplied from which you could compute percentage changes. Statement e is not correct because you are given enough information to answer the question.

16. Correct answer: d.

Discussion: Statement d is correct because it is the only statement that is NOT true. Remember that diminishing returns is a short run phenomenon. It arises because a firm, in the short run, cannot alter the size of the capital stock (plant and equipment) that it uses to produce output. On the other hand, average costs of production that decrease in the long run is a long run phenomenon and is a result of entry/exit and alteration of plant size.

Statement a, b, and c are all true. Since statement d is not true, statement e cannot be the correct answer.

17. Correct answer: c.

Discussion: The key to answering this question correctly is to know what the shape of the long run supply curve is when the industry is a constant cost industry. A constant cost industry has a horizontal supply curve. Thus, when demand decreases (shifts left) and moves along a horizontal supply curve, the price of the good will not change from its initial price. However, in the short run, the supply curve is positively sloped. Thus, a decrease in demand will lead to a lower price for the good in the short run.

Statement a and d should be ruled out. From chapter 4 and 5, you should know that a decrease in demand will lower the price of a good, not increase it or leave it unchanged. Statement b is not correct because in the long run, the price of the good will remain unchanged, not decrease. Statement e is not correct because statement c is correct.

18. Correct answer: e.

Discussion: The graph for this question shows that the typical firm is earning positive economic profit. In order to determine this, you must first choose the profit-maximizing output level of the firm. Remember that the profit-maximizing rule is to produce at an output level where marginal revenue equals marginal cost. For a perfectly competitive firm, price and marginal revenue are identical numerically. Thus, the profit-maximizing output level is found where the price (marginal revenue) and marginal cost curves intersect. Find this point on the graph and then draw a vertical line down to the quantity axis. This quantity is the profit-maximizing output level. You may wish to label it q*.

Now, you must determine whether the firm is earning a positive, zero, or negative economic profit. To do this, find the average cost of production for producing q* and compare it to the price. The average cost of production is found by drawing a vertical line up from q* to the average cost curve and then over to the $ axis. As you can see, the average cost is less than the price, which means the typical firm is making positive economic profit.

Now that you have determined that the typical firm is making a positive economic profit, you should know that this will attract entry into the industry, lead to expansion of existing firms, put upward pressure on the price of inputs as more are demanded as the industry grows (in an increasing cost industry) and also lead to a decline in the skill level of workers. As the industry grows and produces more output, it will have to hire more workers. However, the firms will not be able to hire the cream of the crop as these workers are already employed in the industry. Thus, firms will end up hiring less skilled (and therefore less productive) workers.

Since statements a - d are all true of an increasing cost industry earning positive economic profit, statement e is the correct answer.

VIII. ANSWER KEY: ESSAY QUESTIONS

1. Note: P = price, MR = marginal revenue, MC = marginal cost.

    When a firm produces output up to that level at which MR = MC, it is always adding more to revenue than it is to costs, and thus adding something (however small) to its profits. If a firm produced at an output level at which MR < MC, the firm is actually taking away from its profits because some of the output costs more to produce than it can be sold for. If a firm produces output where MR > MC, it could continue to expand production and though adding more to cost, could add even more to revenue, thereby adding to its profits. Thus, a firm maximizes profits where MR = MC.

2. Based on short run analysis, you should disagree with your boss:

    The costs of closing up shop in the short run are 300,000 pesos (due to fixed costs). That is, 300,000 pesos must be paid regardless of whether the factory produces no shoes or some shoes. This is the loss the firm would sustain in the short run if it were to close up shop. If the factory were to continue current operation, it could produce 5,000 boxes of shoes and earn revenue of 200,000 pesos, which could offset some of the fixed costs. However, by producing, the company would incur another cost -- variable costs in the amount of 150,000 pesos. On net, there is a positive difference of 50,000 pesos between revenue and variable costs. This positive difference can help pay for fixed costs so that if the firm continues to operate, its losses will be 250,000 pesos (Revenue - Fixed Costs - Variable Costs) instead of 300,000 (fixed costs).

    You might also point out that if the company is planning on closing the factory temporarily, it might make customers mad which can have deleterious effects on future sales. Moreover, if the company temporarily lays off workers, they may go find work elsewhere, and thus the company might face some retraining and re-hiring (or search) costs when they re-open the factory.

    On the other hand, if the company is planning on closing the factory permanently, i.e. in the long run, perhaps because of a perceived permanent downturn in demand for faux leather shoes, then your advice may be different. You may advise the company to close the factory and sell its assets (to cover some of its fixed costs, like interest on debt). Also, by closing the factory, the company may be able to avoid fixed costs like rent, as well.

3. The long run supply curve and the short run supply curve both show the relationship between the price of a good and the quantity supplied. However, the time period considered for the relationship is different. In the short run, the number of firms producing for the industry is fixed as is the current size of each firm's facility. In the long run, the number of firms producing for the industry can change as firms enter or exit the industry and the size of the facilities of existing firms can be altered. This means that in the long run, the total industry output can be much more responsive to a price change than in the short run. For example, when the price of a good increases (because of an increase in demand), the short run output response of the industry is constrained by how many firms are already producing for the industry and the current size of their operation. A given amount of firms with a given plant size can only produce so much more in response to a higher price for the output they produce. However, in the long run, a higher price may lure more firms into the industry as well as motivate some firms to alter the size of their operation. Thus, a higher price may elicit a bigger increase in output in the long run than in

the short run. Graphically, this would be represented by a supply curve that is flatter for the long run (and thus steeper for the short run). You may want to take a look at PET #4 of this chapter to inspect the difference between the long and short run supply curves.

4. An increasing cost industry has a long run supply curve that is positively sloped. Of course, the short run supply curve is also positively sloped. However, the long run supply curve is flatter (more elastic) than the short run supply curve as the graph below illustrates. A decline in the demand for beef would be represented by a leftward shift in the supply curve. The reduced demand for beef will in the short and long run lead to a lower price of beef as the graph shows. However, in the short run, the price drop will be bigger than in the long run. The graph also shows that the equilibrium quantity of beef will decline. It will decline by more in the long run than in the short run.

The drop in demand for beef will in the short run cause some firms to shut down their operation altogether. Other firms will continue to operate but they cannot change the size of the capital stock (and thus their fixed costs) that they operate with. In the long run, some firms will make a decision to exit the industry as they sustain losses whereas other firms that remain will likely reduce the size of their operation (lay off workers, shut down some factories, etc). In the long run, the number of firms in the industry will decline and the size of their facility will likely decrease.

Take It to the Net

We invite you to visit the O'Sullivan/Sheffrin page on the Prentice Hall Web site at:

http://www.prenhall.com/osullivan/

for this chapter's World Wide Web exercise.

CHAPTER 6
MONOPOLY

I. OVERVIEW

In this chapter, you will learn about the market structure of monopoly in which there is a single supplier of output to a market. You will learn about barriers to market entry that might give rise to a monopoly. You will learn how a monopolist chooses the profit-maximizing level of output and determines the price at which it will sell the output. You will learn that in contrast to a perfectly competitive market structure, price and marginal revenue are different for a monopolist and that a monopolist typically earns positive economic profit. You will learn about the costs and benefits to society of a monopoly. You will learn why some types of monopolies are regulated by the government. You will learn that in the case of natural monopolies, government regulation comes in the form of an "average cost pricing policy" which is aimed at achieving a more socially efficient outcome than would arise under an unregulated situation. You will learn that an average cost pricing policy ensures a natural monopoly a guaranteed profit but reduces the incentive for the monopoly to keep its costs of production low.

II. CHECKLIST

By the end of this chapter, you should be able to:

√   Describe the characteristics of a monopoly.

√   List factors that would give rise to a monopoly.

√   List some real world examples of a monopoly.

√   Explain why marginal revenue is less than price for a monopolist but equal to price for a perfectly competitive firm.

√   Use a graph to depict the profit-maximizing output level a monopolist would produce, the price that would be charged for the product, and the profit the monopolist would earn.

√   Discuss and compare the relationship of price, marginal revenue, marginal cost, and average cost for a profit-maximizing monopolist.

√   Compare the price and output decisions of a monopolist to a perfectly competitive firm.

√   Explain rent seeking.

√   Discuss the tradeoffs that occur when a patent is granted to a firm which gives the firm monopoly power.

√   Explain what gives rise to a natural monopoly.

√   List some real world examples of natural monopolies.

√   Explain why natural monopolies are often regulated.

√   Explain a natural monopoly's reaction to regulation.

√   Describe the objective and policy used in regulating natural monopolies.

√   Use a graph to show how an average cost pricing policy works.

III. KEY TERMS

Monopoly: a market in which a single firm serves the entire market.

Patent: the exclusive right to sell a particular good for some period of time.

Franchise or licensing scheme: a policy under which the government picks a single firm to sell a particular product.

Rent seeking: the process under which a firm spends money to persuade the government to erect barriers to entry and pick the firm as the monopolist.

Natural monopoly: a market in which there are large economies of scale, so single firm will be profitable but a pair of firms would lose money.

Average-cost pricing policy: a regulatory policy under which the government picks the point on the demand curve at which price equals average cost.

IV. PERFORMANCE ENHANCING TIPS (PETS)

PET #1

The profit-maximizing rule for a monopolist (as for any firm) is to produce an output level where marginal revenue equals marginal cost.

Remember that marginal revenue is the addition to revenue from selling one more unit of output and marginal cost is the addition to cost from producing one more unit of output. As long as the addition to revenue (marginal revenue) exceeds the addition to cost (marginal cost), the monopolist will add to its profits. Thus, the monopolist will maximize its profits by continuing to produce and sell output until marginal revenue is just equal to marginal cost. Beyond that output level, profits will actually be smaller (not maximized).

PET #2

For a profit-maximizing monopolist, the price of its output will be greater than the marginal cost.

This performance enhancing tip is based on two principles: (1) the addition to revenue (marginal revenue) that a monopolist earns from selling one more unit of output is less than the price it receives for selling that one more unit of output, (see your textbook for a good explanation); and (2) a profit-maximizing firm produces an output level where marginal revenue equals marginal cost. Statement (1) says that price > marginal revenue. Statement (2) says that marginal revenue equals marginal cost. Thus, it must be the case that for a monopolist, price > marginal cost.

PET #3

A monopolist produces an output level that is less than a perfectly competitive industry would produce and charges a price that is higher than would prevail under perfect competition.

Under perfect competition, a profit-maximizing firm produces an output level where marginal revenue equals marginal cost, just as does a monopolist. However, for a perfectly competitive firm, marginal revenue and price are identical. This means that a profit-maximizing firm in a perfectly competitive market also ends up producing an output level where price is equal to marginal cost. This is not true of a monopolist as PET #2 discusses. This is the reason that a monopolist will produce a lower output level and charge a higher price for its output than it would if it were a perfectly competitive firm.

To see this, look at the graph below

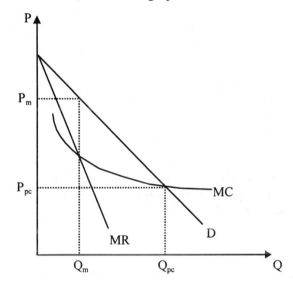

The monopolist will produce output level Q_m which is where marginal revenue and marginal cost are equal. The monopolist will decide on a price for output level Q_m by using the demand curve. At output level Q_m, the demand curve dictates that the price be P_m. Now, suppose the monopolist were to behave as a perfectly competitive firm. It would produce an output level where price equals marginal cost and charge a price dictated by the demand curve for that output level. Price equals marginal cost where the demand and marginal cost curves intersect. The output level in this case would be Q_{pc}. The price charged would be read off the demand curve corresponding to output level Q_{pc} which is P_{pc}. As the graph shows, the monopolist's price exceeds what would be charged by a perfectly competitive firm and produces an output level that is less than would be produced under perfect competition.

PET #4

An average cost pricing policy lowers the price that consumers would pay compared to an unregulated situation and increases the output produced compared to an unregulated situation.

To see this, look at the graph below.

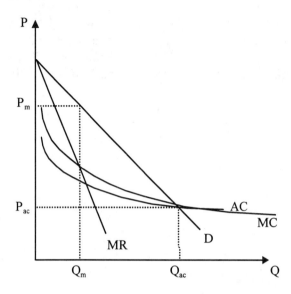

An unregulated natural monopoly would produce an output level where marginal revenue equals marginal cost and charge a price based on what the demand curve would support for that output level. In the graph below, the unregulated natural monopoly would produce an output level Q_m and charge a price P_m.

An average cost pricing policy dictates that the price of output equal the average cost to produce it. This occurs at the intersection of the demand (price) and average cost curves. The graph shows that the output level corresponding to price = average cost is Q_{ac}. Of course, the price associated with this output level (read off of the demand curve) is P_{ac}.

Since $P_{ac} < P_m$ and $Q_{ac} > Q_m$, the average cost pricing policy moves closer to a socially efficient outcome.

V. PRACTICE EXAM: MULTIPLE CHOICE QUESTIONS

1. Which one of the following characteristics is true of a monopoly?
    a) a large number of firms in the industry.
    b) barriers to entry into the industry.
    c) firm acts as a price taker.
    d) price equals marginal revenue.
    e) all of the above.

2. Which one of the following would NOT be an example of a monopoly?
   a) a patent granted to a computer company.
   b) a franchise awarded to a food service on campus.
   c) American Medical Association.
   d) Major League Baseball.
   e) all of the above.

3. A monopolist maximizes profit by picking the output level where:
   a) marginal revenue = marginal cost.
   b) price = marginal revenue.
   c) price = marginal cost.
   d) price > average cost.
   e) price = average cost.

4. Which one of the following is true for a monopolist?
   a) freedom of entry.
   b) price > marginal revenue.
   c) produces a socially efficient output level.
   d) is unable to price discriminate.
   e) earns zero economic profit in the long run.

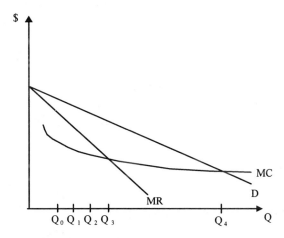

5. Use the diagram above to select the profit-maximizing output level that a monopolist would choose.
   a) Q_0
   b) Q_1
   c) Q_2
   d) Q_3
   e) Q_4

6. If the average cost curve is horizontal, say at $2 per unit of output, then:

   a) marginal cost = $2.

   b) marginal cost = $0.

   c) marginal cost > $2.

   d) marginal cost = $1.

   e) cannot be determined with information given.

7. Suppose the price at which a monopolist is selling its output is $12 and the marginal revenue associated with selling the last unit of output is $9. Further, suppose the marginal cost of the last unit of output sold is $10. Which one of the following best describes what the monopolist should do?

   a) increase output and raise price.

   b) increase output and lower price.

   c) decrease output and lower price.

   d) decrease output and raise price.

   e) shut down.

8. Which one of the following is a cost of a monopoly?

   a) price consumers pay is higher than they would under perfect competition.

   b) output is less than under perfect competition.

   c) rent seeking leads to loss in output in other industries.

   d) consumer surplus is less than under perfect competition.

   e) all of the above.

9. Which one of the following is a benefit to consumers of a patent-generated monopoly?

   a) rent seeking.

   b) innovation.

   c) price fixing.

   d) monopoly profits.

   e) price discrimination.

10. Which one of the following gives rise to a natural monopoly?

   a) patents.

   b) increasing average costs of production.

   c) economies of scale.

   d) inelastic market demand.

   e) competition.

11. Which one of the following would be the best example of a natural monopoly?

    a) video rental stores.

    b) wheat farming.

    c) oil refineries.

    d) sewerage treatment.

    e) auto dealerships.

12. The average cost curve of a natural monopoly is best described as:

    a) L-shaped.

    b) J-shaped.

    c) U-shaped.

    d) W-shaped.

    e) S-shaped.

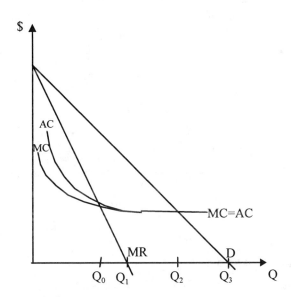

13. Based on the graph above, the output level a profit-maximizing natural monopoly would produce is _____ and the output level a regulated natural monopoly would produce is _____.

    a) Q_0; Q_1.

    b) Q_1; Q_2.

    c) Q_0; Q_2.

    d) Q_1; Q_3.

    e) Q_2; Q_3.

14. Based on the diagram below, the price a profit-maximizing natural monopoly would charge for its output is _____ and the price a regulated natural monopoly would charge is _____.

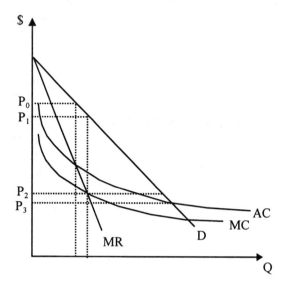

a) P_0; P_1.

b) P_1; P_2.

c) P_0; P_2.

d) P_1; P_3.

e) P_2; P_3.

15. Which one of the following statements is NOT true of an average-cost pricing policy:

a) it will create zero economic profit.

b) it is established where the demand curve intersects the average cost curve.

c) it creates little incentive for the monopolist to control costs.

d) it leads to a higher price than would be charged by an unregulated monopolist.

e) it leads to more output being produced than would arise if the monopoly was not regulated.

VI. PRACTICE EXAM: ESSAY QUESTIONS

1. Discuss the cost and benefits to society of a monopoly that is created because a patent is granted for the product the firm produces.

2. Public utilities such as electricity are referred to as natural monopolies and are often subject to regulation by a state authority (the "Public Regulatory Commission"). Explain why a public utility such as electricity is referred to as a "natural monopoly." Explain how and why an average cost pricing policy is applied to public utility. Discuss the effects of the policy on the price and output the utility sells at and produces. Discuss how the policy affects the utility's profits and costs.

VII. ANSWER KEY: MULTIPLE CHOICE QUESTIONS

1. Correct answer: b.

Discussion: A monopolistic market structure is characterized by barriers to entry — some barriers are artificial (or government created) and others arise naturally.

Statements a, c, and d are all characteristics of a perfectly competitive market structure.

2. Correct answer: e.

Discussion: Monopolies can be created by patents (which in the U.S. are awarded for 20 years without an annual renewal fee), franchise and licensing schemes, industrial, sports, and other associations that restrict the number of firms in the market.

3. Correct answer: a.

Discussion: A monopolist (or any type of firm) will maximize profits by producing an output level where marginal revenue = marginal cost (see PET #1 of this chapter for review).

Statement b describes the relationship between price and marginal revenue for a perfectly competitive firm. Statement c is another version of the profit-maximizing condition for a perfectly competitive firm. Statement d would ensure profit greater than zero but not necessarily the biggest (maximized) profit. Statement e would ensure zero economic profit.

4. Correct answer: b.

Discussion: A monopolist (unlike for a perfectly competitive firm), must lower the price of its output to all of its customers in order to sell more to a few more customers. This means that the price the monopolist receives from selling the last unit of output is not the addition to revenue (marginal revenue) from selling the last unit of output. The marginal revenue from selling the last unit will be less than the price the firm receives on that last unit because while the firm gets paid $X for the last unit of output, it loses revenue from lowering the price to the previous customers who were paying the higher price. The sum of these two effects makes the marginal revenue earned on the last unit of output sold less than the price received on the last unit of output sold.

Statement a is not correct because a monopolist does not face freedom of entry but rather barriers to entry. Statement c is not correct because a monopolist produces a socially inefficient output level (it produces too little output). Statement d is not correct because a monopolist may be able to price discriminate.   Statement e is not correct because a monopolist earns positive economic profit in the long run.

5. Correct answer: d.

Discussion: A profit-maximizing monopolist picks an output level where marginal revenue equals marginal cost (which occurs where these two curves intersect). The output level at the intersection of these two curves is Q_3. Thus, statement d is correct.

Statements a, b, c, and e are all output levels corresponding to other intersection points. The output level where the demand and marginal cost curves intersect, Q_4, is the output level that would be set if price = marginal cost was the rule the monopolist followed. This would be a socially efficient output level.

6. Correct answer: a.

Discussion: When the average cost curve is horizontal, it means that the average cost per unit of output is not changing as more and more output is produced. If the average cost is not changing, it must be the case that the marginal cost is equal to the average cost. (Your book gives an example using your GPA which is an average of the grades you made in the courses you've already taken. If your GPA is 3.0 and you get a B (= 3.0) on a course you take in the summer (the marginal course), your GPA (average) will remain at 3.0).

Statements b and d are for a marginal cost that is less than the average cost. If this were the case, then the average cost would be "pulled down" or decline and thus not remain constant. Statement c is for a marginal cost that exceeds the average cost; in this case, the average cost would be "pulled up" or increase and thus not remain constant. Statement e is not correct because you are given enough information to get an answer.

7. Correct answer: d.

Discussion: Since marginal cost > marginal revenue, the monopolist is not maximizing its profits and in fact, is producing too much output. If the monopolist is producing too much output, then based on the demand curve, he is charging a price below the profit-maximizing price. Thus, the monopolist should reduce his output level until marginal revenue = marginal cost. By reducing the output level, the monopolist moves back along the demand curve to a higher price for his output.

Statements a and b are not correct because if the monopolist increased his output level, he would continue adding more to his costs than to his revenue and thus profits would decline. Statement c is not correct because the monopolist should not lower price but raise it instead. Statement e is not correct because there is no information that tells you whether the monopolist should shut down.

8. Correct answer: e.

Discussion: A monopolist charges a higher price and produces less output than would arise under perfect competition. This is costly to consumers (see your textbook, PET #3, and essay #1 for further discussion). This also means that consumer surplus (a measure of the benefits to consumers from their purchases) is smaller under a monopolistic market structure than a perfectly competitive one. Monopolies, which often arise as a result of rent seeking undertaken by lobbyists, also entails an opportunity cost to society in that the lobbyists could be employed elsewhere thereby adding to output in other industries which consumers could in turn purchase.

9. Correct answer: b.

Discussion: The awarding of a patent to a firm grants the firm monopoly status (at least for 20 years). The monopoly status means the firm is assured of making positive economic profit. The profit incentive then motivates the firm to actually produce and market the product thereby making it available to consumers. Without the assurance of profit, the firm may not undertake production of the product and thus consumers would lose out on innovative new products.

Statements a and c are costs of a monopoly. Statement d is a benefit to the monopolist but not to consumers. Statement e is not necessarily a benefit to consumers; price discrimination by a monopolist might lead the monopolist to charge some groups of customers a higher price than other groups.

10. Correct answer: c.

Discussion: Economies of scale (average cost declining over large ranges of output) arise because of the fixed costs of starting up a business are very high. This typically occurs if the business requires the use of indivisible inputs.

Statement a is not correct because a patent creates an unnatural or artificial monopoly. Statement b is not correct; decreasing average costs over a large range of output characterize a natural monopoly. Statement d is not correct because the elasticity of demand does not define the market structure. Statement e is not correct; monopolies are characterized by barriers to entry and hence the absence of competition.

11. Correct answer: d.

Discussion: Natural monopolies typically arise because of the use of indivisible inputs and high fixed costs of start up. A natural monopoly is where there is a single supplier of a good or service. Sewerage treatment is a good example of a natural monopoly.

Since there are typically more than one video rental store per town and because the costs of start up are low, video rental stores are best characterized as monopolistically competitive firms. Wheat farmers produce a homogeneous product and serve a very small portion of the overall market. They also have little control over the price at which they can sell their wheat. Wheat farmers are thus best characterized as perfectly competitive firms. Auto dealerships have a lot in common with video rental stores and are thus characterized as monopolistically competitive firms. While oil refineries may have a high fixed cost of start up and require the use of indivisible inputs, there is typically more than one oil refining company that services a country. In chapter 12, you will see that an oil refinery is best characterized as an oligopolistic firm.

12. Correct answer: a.

Discussion: The average cost of production of a natural monopoly is very high at low levels of output. As output expands, average costs drop and continue to decline over large ranges of output. In fact, average costs typically are constant over large ranges of output. Thus, an average cost curve would be L-shaped.

A J-shaped average cost curve would indicate that average costs of production are low at low levels of output and then increase as output expands. A U-shaped average cost curve is typical of short run analysis. W and S-shaped cost curves have not been addressed in your textbook.

13. Correct answer: a.

Discussion: An unregulated natural monopoly produces where marginal revenue = marginal cost (the two curves intersect). This occurs at output level Q_0. A regulated natural monopoly produces where price = average cost (demand and average cost curves intersect). This occurs at output level Q_2. Thus, statement a is the only correct answer.

14. Correct answer: d.

Discussion: To arrive at the correct answer, you must first establish at what output level a profit-maximizing natural monopoly will produce. Once you have determined that output level, you read up to the demand curve and over to the price line to establish the price the natural monopolist would charge. In this case, the profit-maximizing output level occurs where marginal revenue = marginal cost (they intersect) and the price is P_1. For a regulated natural monopoly, price is set equal to average cost. This occurs where the demand and average cost curves intersect. At this point, read over to the vertical axis and that will be the price the regulator sets. In this case, it is P_3. Thus, statement d is the only correct option.

15. Correct answer: d.

Discussion: One of the aims of an average cost pricing policy is to lower the price that customers must pay for the product or service. Thus, an average cost pricing policy leads to a lower price, not a higher price than would be charged by an unregulated monopolist.

Statements a, b, c, and e are all true of an average cost pricing policy. Since the policy sets price = average cost, the monopoly earns zero economic profit. This price setting policy can be depicted where demand and the average cost curves intersect. Since the regulated monopolist's price will always be set equal to average costs, it has no incentive to hold down its costs. The monopolist knows that whatever costs they incur, they will always be covered by the pricing policy. Another aim of the average cost pricing policy is to force the monopolist to serve as many customers as possible. Thus, the policy will increase the output of the monopolist.

VIII. ANSWER KEY: ESSAY QUESTIONS

1. The costs to society of a monopoly are that consumers are charged a higher price for the product than they would if entry into the industry could occur as in perfect competition. Also, the industry output under a monopolist is less than would occur if the industry operated as a perfectly competitive one. Thus, society loses on two accounts — they pay a higher price for the output and there are some customers who don't get to purchase the output because not enough is produced. This means that consumer surplus is lower under a monopolistic market structure than under a perfectly competitive

market structure. Also, rent-seeking behavior is likely to occur and this entails an opportunity cost to society. Rent seeking occurs because, in general, firms prefer to be protected from competition so that they can thereby earn positive economic profits indefinitely. Thus, a firm might hire lobbyists to go to Washington, DC in the hopes that the lobbyists will be able to get the firm some form of protection from competition, i.e. status as a monopoly. The time and effort of the lobbyists, however, entails an opportunity cost in that the lobbyists could be employed in other industries thereby increasing output elsewhere that consumers could purchase.

Of course, there are benefits to the monopolist (a member of society, too). The monopolist earns positive economic profit (at least for the life of the patent). Also, with patent-generated monopolies, a society at least gets the benefit that new products will be produced instead of none at all. That is, innovation benefits society. For example, a new drug that benefits cancer may not be produced unless a patent which ensures the innovating firm positive economic profits is granted. That is, a firm with the technology to produce a new drug may choose not to if they know that as soon as they produce it, other firms will enter the market and drive economic profits to zero.

The problem with patent-granting is that the government does not always know which products will be produced even without a patent. Thus, the government may inadvertently grant monopoly status and thus monopoly profits to a firm that does not otherwise truly need the assurance of monopoly profits to produce the product. In this way, society loses for the reasons mentioned above.

2. A public utility, such as an electric company, is an example of a natural monopoly. A natural monopoly occurs when there is a single supplier of the output to the market because any more than one firm in the industry would not be profitable. The reason that more than one firm would not be profitable is that a natural monopoly is characterized by very high fixed start up costs and thus very high average costs at low levels of output. This means that with more than one firm in the market, each firm would have only a portion of the overall market and thus will produce for a smaller portion of the market. However, since average costs of production are very high at low levels of output and since each firm is producing for only a portion of the market, each firm will face a very high average cost of production. The firms may not be able to extract a price from their customers that is high enough to cover the costs of providing a service to them and thus each firm will earn negative economic profit. Faced with this prospect, firms typically choose not to enter an industry with high fixed costs of start up where one firm is already present. In other words, the market supports only one firm in the industry. Since this type of monopoly arises naturally, i.e. without the government offering franchises, patents, etc, it is referred to as a natural monopoly.

An average cost pricing policy is often used in the interest of creating a more socially efficient outcome — that is where price is lower and output higher than would arise if the monopolist were unregulated. Under an average cost pricing policy, the regulatory commission effectively sets a price equal to the monopolist's average cost of production and requires that the electric company serve all customers willing to pay the price. In terms of a graph, the regulatory commission forces the utility to produce an output level where the demand and average cost curves intersect. Since price is set equal to average cost, the electric company earns zero economic profit (but positive accounting profit). The average cost pricing policy creates a disincentive for the utility to minimize its costs of production. The reason the disincentive is created is that the utility knows that the regulated price will be set based on the utility's average cost of production; the utility's average cost of production will always be covered and so the utility is always assured of at least zero economic profit, no less. Thus, the utility does not have an incentive to keep costs of production low, as would an unregulated firm that desires to maximize profits.

Take It to the Net

We invite you to visit the O'Sullivan/Sheffrin page on the Prentice Hall Web site at:

http://www.prenhall.com/osullivan/

for this chapter's World Wide Web exercise.

CHAPTER 7
MONOPOLISTIC COMPETITION, OLIGOPOLY, AND ANTITRUST

I. OVERVIEW

In this chapter, you will learn what entrepreneurs must consider before deciding to enter a particular industry. You will learn that in the case of industries with small economies of scale, there is often a great deal of entry and thus competition amongst firms. This is the case of monopolistic competition. You will learn about some of the characteristics that define a monopolistically competitive market structure and see how it differs from a perfectly competitive market structure and a monopoly. You will learn that in contrast to a monopoly, prices and profits tend to be lower and average costs of production higher in a monopolistically competitive industry. You will also learn that a monopolistically competitive market structure brings with it product variety. You will learn how firms already in an industry are affected by the entry of new firms into the industry.

You will learn about the market structure of oligopoly. You will learn about the characteristics of an oligopoly and what gives rise to an oligopoly.   You will also learn how oligopolists make pricing decisions. You will learn that oligopolists act strategically, anticipating the actions of their competitors in response to their own pricing decisions. You will learn that oligopolists may enter into price fixing schemes, price matching schemes, mergers and trusts in an attempt to avoid the consequences of competition. You will use a game tree to analyze the choices and probable strategic outcomes of oligopolists. You will also learn about an "insecure" monopolist and the steps they may take to deter entry by other firms.

You will also learn about antitrust policies, which are designed to promote competition in markets dominated by a few large firms. You will also learn about deregulation as a policy aimed at promoting competition. You will briefly review the history of antitrust legislation and learn that antitrust legislation is aimed at breaking up monopolies, preventing corporate mergers, and regulating business practices in instances where competition in the marketplace is threatened. You will learn about some of the strategies used by firms to reduce or eliminate competition. You will learn about a lot of different real world cases in which antitrust legislation and/or regulation has been used to thwart the efforts of firms that engage in anti-competitive behavior.

II. CHECKLIST

By the end of this chapter, you should be able to:

√   Describe what happens to the price, average costs, output, and profits of firms after a second firm enters a market previously served by only one firm.

√   Explain why profit for a monopolist declines after a second firm enters the market.

√   List the characteristics of a monopolistically competitive market structure.

√   List some real world examples of firms that operate under monopolistic competition.

√   Discuss the elasticity of demand for products in a monopolistically competitive market.

√   Describe how monopolistically competitive firms might differentiate their products from other firms in the industry.

√   Explain the profit-maximizing rule for a monopolistically competitive firm and depict it with a graph for both the short and the long run.

√   Explain what motivates firms to enter a monopolistically competitive market structure.

√   Describe what happens to the price, average costs, output, and profits of firms in a monopolistically competitive market structure in the long run.

√   Discuss the costs and benefits to a monopolistically competitive market structure.

√   Describe the characteristics of an oligopoly.

√   Explain what gives rise to an oligopoly.

√   List some real world examples of an oligopolistic market structure.

√   Discuss the duopolist's (2-firm oligopoly) dilemma.

√   Discuss and explain the rationale for price-fixing schemes, price matching schemes, predatory pricing, and mergers and trusts. Discuss why such schemes are often likely to breakdown.

√   Use a game tree to determine what the likely pricing outcome will be between duopolists.

√   Explain the behavior of an insecure monopolist.

√   Define a concentration ratio and discuss how it might be used to establish whether an oligopoly exists.

√   Discuss the purpose of antitrust legislation.

√   Discuss the purpose of government regulation of business practices.

√   Discuss the circumstances under which the government would permit a merger.

√   Discuss the major pieces of antitrust legislation.

√   Discuss why the government may prevent a merger between two (or more) rival firms.

√   Discuss a firm's motives for attempting to reduce competition.

√   Discuss some of the major anti-competitive cases that have been ruled on by the Federal Trade Commission.

III. KEY TERMS

Entrepreneur: a person who has an idea for a business and then coordinates the production and sale of goods and services, taking risks in the process.

Monopolistic competition: a situation in which each firm has a monopoly in selling its own differentiated product, but competes with other firms selling similar products.

Oligopoly: a market served by a few firms.

Concentration ratio: a measure of the degree of concentration in a market; the four-firm concentration ratio is the percentage of output produced by the four largest firms.

Cartel: a group of firms that coordinate their pricing decisions, often by charging the same price.

Price fixing: an arrangement in which two firms coordinate their pricing decisions.

Game tree: a visual representation of the consequences of different strategies.

Dominant strategy: an action that is the best choice under all circumstances.

Duopolists' dilemma: a situation in which both firms would be better off if they picked the high price, each one picks the low price.

Guaranteed price matching: a scheme under which a firm guarantees that it will match a lower price by a competitor; also known as a "meet-the-competition" policy.

Grim-trigger: a strategy under which a firm responds to underpricing by picking a price so low that each firm makes zero economic profit.

Tit-for-tat: a strategy under which the one firm starts out with the cartel price, and then picks whatever price the other firm picked in the previous period.

Insecure monopoly: a monopoly that faces the possibility that a second firm will enter the market.

Limit pricing: a scheme under which a monopolist accepts a price below the normal monopoly price to deter other firms from entering the market.

Contestable market: a market in which the costs of entering and leaving are very low, so the firms in the market are constantly threatened by the entry of new firms.

Trust: an arrangement under which the owners of several companies transfer their decision-making powers to a small group of trustees, who then make decisions for all the firms in the trust.

Merger: a process in which two or more firms combine their operations.

Tying: a business practice under which a consumer of one product is required to purchase another product.

IV. PERFORMANCE ENHANCING TIPS (PETS)

PET #1

A monopolistically competitive firm maximizes its profit by producing at an output level where marginal revenue equals marginal cost.

The same reasoning discussed in PET #1 of Chapter 10 applies to a monopolistically competitive firm as well. You may want to review it if you are not comfortable with the principle.

PET #2

The entry of firms into a monopolistically competitive market structure causes the demand curves of all firms to shift to the left since each firm now gets a smaller piece of the consumer market. Since the demand curves shift to the left, the marginal revenue curves also shift to the left.

Since the demand and marginal revenue curves of monopolistically competitive firms shift as entry occurs in the industry, the profit-maximizing output level and corresponding price the firms will charge will also change.

PET #3

The oligopolist's (or duopolist's) dilemma is that each firm knows that by choosing to sell its output at a high price, the competition will sell at a lower price and thus undercut the high-priced firm's profits. Thus, each firm chooses to sell at the low price but in so doing, each firm ends up with a profit below what they could earn if they collectively agreed to the high price.

The dilemma thus creates an incentive for the oligopolists to collude -- devise pricing schemes that lead to the high price outcome for all firms. However, such schemes are often illegal under anti-trust policy.

PET #4

Cartels and other price-fixing schemes create the incentive for one or more of the participating firms to cheat (undercut the agreed upon price). The cheater is tempted to cheat because his firm's profits will increase at the expense of the other cartel members.

Because of the temptation to cheat, cartels and other price-fixing schemes are often hard to sustain unless there is some enforcement mechanism or punishment that deters the cheater(s) from cheating.

PET #5

Antitrust legislation does permit mergers as long as they would not threaten competition.

V. PRACTICE EXAM: MULTIPLE CHOICE QUESTIONS

1. Entry of firms into a market typically occurs if:
   a) there are not large economies of scale in production.
   b) there are currently economic profits being earned by other firms in the market.
   c) price is greater than marginal revenue.
   d) (a) and (b).
   e) (a), (b), and (c).

2. As entry into a market previously served by a single firm (monopolist) occurs:
   a) the demand curve facing the original firm shifts to the right.
   b) the market price remains at the level set by the original firm.
   c) the output produced by the original firm decreases.
   d) the average cost of production of the original firm declines.
   e) all of the above.

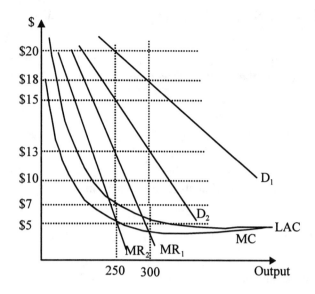

3. Use the graph above to calculate the firm's profit assuming entry has occurred.

   a) $5,000.

   b) $2,000.

   c) $2,500.

   d) $5,400.

   e) $3,300.

4. Which one of the following statements is NOT true?

   a) empirical studies show that market entry reduces price.

   b) The Motor Carrier Act of 1980 caused a decrease in the market value of a firm's trucking license.

   c) deregulation of markets creates competition.

   d) a firm may attempt to differentiate its product from others in the industry by creating a certain image for it.

   e) in a monopolistically competitive market, the demand for products is price inelastic.

5. Which one of the following would NOT be a characteristic of a monopolistically competitive market structure?

   a) a homogeneous (or standardized) product.

   b) many firms in the industry.

   c) elastic demand.

   d) no artificial barriers to entry.

   e) all of the above are characteristics of a monopolistically competitive market structure.

6. Which one of the following would NOT differentiate one product from another under monopolistic competition?

    a) location.

    b) special services that go along with the purchase of a product.

    c) economies of scale.

    d) physical characteristics.

    e) product image.

7. Entry into a monopolistically competitive market structure occurs until:

    a) demand is zero.

    b) economic profits are zero.

    c) marginal revenue is zero.

    d) marginal revenue equals marginal cost.

    e) average cost is minimized.

8. In the long run, firms in a monopolistically competitive market structure:

    a) earn zero economic profit.

    b) produce an output level where price = marginal cost.

    c) do not produce output at minimum average cost.

    d) produce an output level where marginal revenue = marginal cost.

    e) a, c, and d are true.

9. Under monopolistic competition, entry typically causes price to _____ and profits to _____.

    a) decrease; decrease.

    b) decrease; increase.

    c) increase; increase.

    d) increase; decrease.

    e) decrease; remain unchanged.

10. Which one of the following would be the best example of a monopolistically competitive firm?

    a) sugar farmer.

    b) railway transportation.

    c) Italian restaurants.

    d) drug company.

    e) food service at a national park.

11. Which one of the following is NOT a benefit associated with monopolistic competition?
    a) lower price.
    b) more variety.
    c) more locations.
    d) lower average cost of production.
    e) all of the above are benefits.

12. Which one of the following is an example of an oligopolistic industry?
    a) aircraft and parts.
    b) video rental stores.
    c) apple growers.
    d) sewerage and water treatment.
    e) clothing stores.

13. Which one of the following would NOT be true of an oligopolistic market structure?
    a) each firm sells a similar product or service.
    b) each firm is a price-taker.
    c) economies of scale in production.
    d) a firm may carry out a big advertising campaign.
    e) a few firms serve the market.

14. A cartel is:
    a) an industrial association in which research and development is shared.
    b) the firm in the industry that sets the going price.
    c) a policy designed to prevent mergers that produce a concentration ratio greater than 40%.
    d) a group of firms that coordinate their pricing decisions, often by charging the same price.
    e) an industry watchdog group that monitors the price of output to ensure that consumers are not being ripped off.

15. Which one of the following statements is true?
    a) cartels and price-fixing are legal in the U.S.
    b) a four-firm concentration ratio is the percentage of industry profits earned by the four biggest firms.
    c) a kinked demand curve is flatter (more elastic) below the kink than above.
    d) a grim trigger strategy is when a firm prices its output so low that the competition makes losses and thus is driven out of the market.
    e) free trade policy promotes competition.

16. Suppose you are given the following information on a two-firm oligopoly (duopoly).

    Firm A will earn $5,000 in profit if it charges a price of $10 and Firm B charges a price of $10; Firm B will earn $5,000 in profit.

    Firm A will earn $2,000 in profit if it charges a price of $10 and Firm B charges a price of $7; Firm B will earn $6,000 in profit.

    Firm A will earn $6,000 in profit if it charges a price of $7 and Firm B charges a price of $10; Firm B will earn B will earn $2,000 in profit.

    Firm A will earn $3,000 in profit if it charges a price of $7 and Firm B charges a price of $7; Firm B will earn $2,000 in profit.

    If firm A must pick the price at which it sells its output without knowing what price Firm B will pick and firm B must pick the price at which it sell its output without knowing what price Firm A will pick, what price combination will firms A and B ultimately sell at?
    a) $10; $10.
    b) $10; $7.
    c) $7; $10.
    d) $7; $7.
    e) cannot be determined without further information.

17. The rational outcome of a guaranteed price matching or "meet-the-competition" policy is that:
    a) both firms will sell at the low price.
    b) one firm will sell at a high price until the competition sells at a low price; then it will sell at the low price.
    c) both firms will sell at the high price.
    d) consumers are fooled into thinking the price matching scheme will protect them from high prices.
    e) (c) and (d).

18. Which one of the following is NOT a retaliation strategy that firms would apply to one that cheated on a price-fixing scheme by selling at a price below the agreed-upon fixed price?
    a) all other firms sell at the same low price as the cheating firm.
    b) all other firms sell at a price that ensures zero economic profit for all firms.
    c) each period, all other firms sell at the price picked by the cheater in the previous period.
    d) all other firms collect a penalty fee from the cheater.
    e) all of the above are retaliation schemes used by oligopolists.

19. Which one of the following statements is NOT true?

    a) a firm that chooses to cheat on a price-fixing scheme should consider the short-term gain in profits from cheating versus the long-term loss in profits from being punished.

    b) the duopoly-pricing strategy leads to negative economic profits.

    c) cartels may break down because of the incentive to cheat.

    d) price leadership arrangements are an implicit price-fixing scheme.

    e) all of the above are true statements.

20. Which one of the following statements is NOT true?

    a) a monopolist may act like a firm in a market with many firms, picking a low price and earning a small profit so as to deter entry and thereby guarantee profits for the longer term.

    b) a contestable market is one in which firms can enter and leave the market without incurring large costs.

    c) government licensing schemes can give rise to oligopolies.

    d) price fixing schemes are illegal under antitrust laws.

    e) a limit pricing scheme is a decision by a firm to limit the amount by which it lowers its price in response to price cuts by competitors.

21. Which one of the following statements is true?

    a) The Sherman Act made it illegal to monopolize a market or to engage in practices that resulted in a "restraint of trade."

    b) Airlines used an advanced price listing system to avoid the appearance of explicitly fixing prices.

    c) price leadership agreements often lead to garbled signals when the price leader initiates a price cut.

    d) in order for price fixing schemes to last, punishment to the price cutter must be enforced.

    e) all of the above are true.

22. The purpose of antitrust policies is:

    a) to promote competition in markets dominated by a few large firms.

    b) to ensure that consumers pay the lowest price possible.

    c) to prevent price discrimination by firms.

    d) to make sure that firms produce an output level where marginal revenue equals marginal cost.

    e) to prevent banks and trust companies from merging.

23. The Sherman Act of 1890:

    a) outlawed asset-purchase mergers that substantially reduce competition.

    b) extended antitrust legislation to proprietorships and partnerships.

    c) made it illegal to monopolize a market or to engage in practices that result in a restraint of trade.

    d) outlawed price discrimination.

    e) placed a duty (tax) on industries served by fewer than four firms.

24. Which one of the following statements is NOT true of antitrust legislation?

    a) the Federal Trade Commission was established to enforce antitrust laws.

    b) the Clayton Act outlawed practices that discourage competition.

    c) the Robinson-Patman Act permitted the sale of products at "unreasonably low prices" since consumer surplus would increase.

    d) the Celler-Kefauver Act outlawed asset-purchase merges that would substantially reduce competition.

    e) the Hart-Scott-Rodino Act extended antitrust legislation to proprietorships and partnerships.

25. A "tying contract":

    a) protects a firm against buyer injury that may arise from product defect.

    b) limits the time period over which a buyer is permitted to return a product.

    c) is an agreement between two firms to fix the price at which they sell their output.

    d) requires a consumer who buys one product to buy a second product.

    e) forces buyers of products to use rope instead of twine to tie up merchandise that will be transported on the top of their vehicle.

26. When firms in an industry transfer the decision-making powers of the owners to a small group of individuals who then make decisions for all the participating firms, the firms have created a:

    a) bust.

    b) cartel.

    c) trust.

    d) merger.

    e) block.

27. Which one of the following statements is true?

    a) antitrust policy is designed to prevent corporate mergers between firms if the merger results in the newly formed firm having more than 50% of the market share.

    b) mergers only happen between firms that produce closely substitutable products.

    c) the government opposes all mergers.

    d) the government may permit mergers that reduce competition if the firms can successfully argue that the merger will reduce costs and lead to lower prices, better products, and better service.

    e) all of the above are true.

VI. PRACTICE EXAM: ESSAY QUESTIONS

1. Consider a small city's dry-cleaning market, which is monopolistically competitive. Currently, the typical dry-cleaner is charging $5 an item. The average cost of dry-cleaning is $2. The typical dry-cleaner cleans 1,000 items per week. (Each customer drops off approximately 4 items). Suppose, a new dry-cleaner was to enter the market. Explain what would happen to the price, average cost, output, and profit of a typical dry-cleaner.

2. Discuss the costs and benefits to consumers of having a dry-cleaning market that is monopolistically competitive.

3. Explain why the duopolist's dilemma often leads to price-fixing schemes. Be sure to discuss a number of different price-fixing schemes and what may cause them to break down. Also discuss the enforcement mechanisms that the duopolists might undertake to ensure that a price-fixing scheme does not break down.

4. Suppose you ran the only bakery in town and were currently very profitable. What things might you consider if you wanted to ensure that you continued to enjoy the same success in the future?

5. Explain the circumstances under which a merger would be likely to be granted and under which it would not.

6. Explain why predatory pricing is not a viable long-term strategy.

VII. ANSWER KEY: MULTIPLE CHOICE QUESTIONS

1. Correct answer: d.

Discussion: Statements a and b are correct, so statement d is correct. Entry into a market is motivated by profit potential, which lures entrepreneurs into opening up new firms. Absent the possibility of economic profit, there would be little motivation for an entrepreneur to start up a new business. Entry into a market is also, and in general, only possible when there are smaller economies of scale in production. In other words, entry into a market can occur when the fixed costs of starting up a business are small. Chapter 10 discusses the reasons for why industries with large fixed costs (and thus, large economies of scale) are typically characterized by only one firm serving the market.

Statement c is not correct. Price is greater than marginal revenue for any type of firm that faces a downward sloping demand curve (instead of a horizontal one). This is not a condition for entry to occur but rather a characteristic related to demand. Since statement c is not correct, statement e is not either.

2. Correct answer: c.

Discussion: As entry by another firm into a market previously served by a single firm, the output produced by the original firm, which was in part based on demand condition, will now be "shared" with the other firm (or firms). That is, there will be a loss of consumers for the original firm because there is more competition.

Statement a is not correct because the demand curve facing the original firm will shift left because the firm will lose customers. This is represented by a leftward shift in demand or a decrease in demand. Statement b is not correct because the market price will decline. Entry promotes competition, which in turn reduces the price at which output is sold. Statement d is not correct because average costs of production rise with entry. This is because each firm produces a smaller amount of output than would a single firm serving the market. The lower output levels correspond to higher average costs of production since at lower output levels, economies of scale are less able to be exploited.

3. Correct answer: b.

Discussion: Profit for the firm is based on the demand curve labeled D_2, which represents demand after entry has occurred (it has shifted left). Since demand shifts left, the marginal revenue curve shifts left and so the marginal revenue curve labeled MR_2 must be used to figure out the profit-maximizing output level and price charged by the firm. MR_2 and the marginal cost curve intersect at the output level of 250 units. At that output level, the price charged by the firm, which is read off of the demand curve at the output level of 250 units is $15. At that output level, average cost of production is $7. Thus, the profit of the firm, which is the difference between revenue and total costs is $1,250 ($15 X 250 units - $7 X 250 units).

4. Correct answer: e.

Discussion: Statement e is not true because in a monopolistically competitive market structure, products are close substitutes with each other (e.g. toothbrushes). Goods that are close substitutes have elasticities that are characterized as "price elastic." From Chapter 5, "elastic" means an elasticity of demand greater than 1.

5. Correct answer: a.

Discussion: A monopolistically competitive market structure is characterized by product differentiation, real or perceived. A homogeneous product is virtually identical (apples, sugar, wheat, etc) and is characteristic of a perfectly competitive market structure.

Other characteristics of a monopolistically competitive market structure are many firms in the industry (in contrast to monopoly), elastic demand, and no artificial barriers to entry.

6. Correct answer: c.

Discussion: Economies of scale typically characterize monopolies, particularly natural monopolies. Statements a, b, d, and e are all factors that can cause similar products to be differentiated from one another.

7. Correct answer: b.

Discussion: One of the characteristics of perfectly competitive and monopolistically competitive market structure is that there is ease of entry. With ease of entry comes more competition, which in turn, will thrive until the industry is no longer able to provide a profit for another potential new entrant. Thus, entry stops when economic profits of the industry become zero.

Statement a is not correct. Entry into a monopolistically competitive market structure occurs because there is demand. Statement c is not correct because statement a is. Moreover, if entry stopped when marginal revenue was equal to zero, entering firms would be producing at output levels where marginal revenue would clearly be less than (positive, non-zero) marginal costs. Statement d is not correct; firms maximize profits by producing output where marginal revenue equals marginal cost. Entry is not based on this condition. Statement e is not correct because remember that in a monopolistically competitive industry, firms do not produce at minimum average cost. They all produce at output levels where average cost is higher than minimum. Furthermore, market entry is not dictated by a firm producing at minimum average cost.

8. Correct answer: e.

Discussion: In the long run, competition in the monopolistically competitive market structure leads to entry up until the point at which it is no longer desirable. This occurs where zero economic profits are being earned by the firms in the industry. Monopolistically competitive firms do not produce at minimum average cost because they serve a small portion of the market and because their profit-maximizing strategy is to set marginal revenue = marginal cost. As just mentioned, the profit-maximizing strategy of any firm is to set marginal revenue = marginal cost. Thus, statements a, c, and d are true of a monopolistically competitive market structure.

Statement b describes a version of the profit-maximizing rule that a perfectly competitive firm could use.

9. Correct answer: a.

Discussion: Competition in a monopolistically competitive market structure is what leads to a lower price for the firms' output. This acts to reduce firms' profits. Also, the average cost of production typically rises for monopolistically competitive firms. This too acts to reduce firms' profits. Thus, statement a is the only correct option.

10. Correct answer: c.

Discussion: Statement c is the best example because there are many Italian restaurants each with their own characteristics that differentiate them from each other. Furthermore, entry into the restaurant business is very open.

A sugar farmer is an example of a perfectly competitive firm. Railway transportation is an example of a natural monopoly. A drug company is an example of a patent-generated monopoly. Food service at a national park is an example of a license-generated monopoly.

11. Correct answer: d.

Discussion: Firms in a monopolistically competitive market structure produce at an average cost that is higher than in a perfectly competitive market structure and higher than in a monopoly.

Statements a, b, and c are all examples of benefits from a monopolistically competitive market structure.

12. Correct answer: a.

Discussion: Aircraft and parts is an example of an oligopolistic market structure. Video rental stores and clothing stores are examples of a monopolistically competitive market structure. Apple growers are an example of a perfectly competitive market structure and sewerage and water treatment is an example of a natural monopoly.

13. Correct answer: b.

Discussion: In an oligopolistic market structure, firms have some control over price and act strategically in setting price. That means that each firm considers the reaction of the other firms to the price that it may choose to sell its output. Firms are price-takers in a perfectly competitive market structure.

Statements a, c, d, and e are all true of an oligopolistic market structure.

14. Correct answer: d.

Discussion: A cartel is a group of firms that get together to agree to fix the price at which they sell their output. The purpose of the agreement is to ensure higher profits for all firms than if they acted independently.

Statements a, b, c, and e are all incorrect. Statement b is the definition of a price leader.

15. Correct answer: e.

Discussion: Free trade is a policy that does not prohibit foreign firms from selling in the domestic market. As such, free trade policy promotes competition and works to achieve some of the same objectives as anti-trust policy.

Statement a is not correct. Price-fixing agreements are illegal in the U.S. Statement b is not correct. A four-firm concentration ratio is the percentage of industry output that the biggest four firms in the industry produce. Statement c is not correct. The kinked demand curve is flatter (more elastic) above the kink than below. This is because when a firm raises its price (above the kink point), it will lose a lot of customers. This is just a way of saying quantity demanded is very responsive to price above the kink. Statement d is not correct because a grim-trigger strategy is not designed to lead to losses for firms but rather zero economic profits.

16. Correct answer: d.

Discussion: The duopolist's dilemma means that the two firms end up both picking the low price even though it is not the price at which each firm's profits would be maximized. The reasoning is as follows. Firm A knows that if it picks the high price, Firm B will pick the low price since that way, Firm B will get bigger profits. Thus, Firm A does not have the incentive to pick the high price. For the same reasoning, Firm B knows that if it picks the high price, Firm A will pick the low price since that way, Firm A will get bigger profits. Thus, Firm B will not choose the high price. So, if both firms have to pick the price at which they will sell output without knowledge of what price the other has selected, they will both end up picking the low price.

17. Correct answer: e.

Discussion: A guaranteed price matching strategy never actually has to be enacted by the firm that sets the policy. This is because both firms will end up selling at the high price. Thus, consumers may think that they are being protected when, in fact, the protection is just an "empty promise." The reason the policy leads to a high price by both firms is that once the competitor sees the other firm selling at the high price (albeit with the price matching policy), the other firm is now able to select the price that will guarantee it the biggest profit. That price is the higher price and so both firms end up being able to sell at the higher price.

18. Correct answer: d.

Discussion: Statement d is not correct. The book does not discuss any scenario in which firms are able to impose and effectively collect penalties from the cheater.

Statement a is the definition of a duopoly price retaliation strategy. Statement b is the definition of the grim-trigger retaliation strategy. Statement c is the definition of a tit-for-tat pricing strategy. Statement e cannot be correct because statement d is not correct.

19. Correct answer: b.

Discussion: A duopoly-price strategy leads to smaller profits than would arise under a price-fixing agreement. Predatory pricing, on the other hand, leads to negative economic profits.

Statements a, c, and d are all true.

20. Correct answer: e.

Discussion: A limit-pricing scheme is a strategy of a firm to pick a price for its output below the monopoly price in an effort to deter entry.

Statements a, b, c, and d are all true. You may wish to look at the answer to essay #2 for a detailed discussion related to statement a. Contestable markets are market structures that may be populated by only one or a few firms yet the behavior of the firms is more like the industry is populated by many firms. The threat of entry is what characterizes a contestable market. Government licensing schemes can limit entry and give rise to oligopolies just as can economies of scale in production and the need for a major advertising campaign. Price fixing schemes are illegal under anti-trust laws.

21. Correct answer: e.

Discussion. Statements a-d are all true.

22. Correct answer: a.

Discussion: Antitrust policies have been motivated by a desire to maintain competition in the marketplace and with competition comes lower prices and better quality products.

Statement b is not correct because the purpose of antitrust policies is to ensure competition. Competition, of course, may result in lower prices but that is not the objective of antitrust policies. Statement c is not correct. In fact, as you learned in Chapter 13, price discrimination is not necessarily illegal. It becomes illegal under antitrust legislation if it harms competition. Statement d is not correct. Firms, in their efforts to maximize profits, will obey the dictum of producing an output level where marginal revenue equals marginal cost. Statement e is not correct. Antitrust policies do not have anything to do with banks and trust companies, per se.

23. Correct answer: c.

Discussion: The first piece of antitrust legislation passed was the Sherman Act of 1890. It has subsequently been used to break up the Standard Oil Trust of John Rockefeller in 1911, the American Tobacco Company in 1911, and AT&T in 1982.

Statement a is about the Celler-Kefauver Act. The Celler-Kefauver Act of 1950 outlawed all asset-purchase mergers that would substantially reduce competition. Statement b is about the Hart-Scott-Rodino Act of 1980, which extended antitrust legislation to proprietorships and partnerships. None of the other statements are correct.

24. Correct answer: c.

Discussion: The Robinson-Patman Act prohibited selling products at "unreasonably low prices" with the intent of reducing competition. Unreasonably low prices would naturally increase consumer surplus, albeit temporarily, but the Robinson-Patman Act was legislated with concern about the effects it would have on competition, not on consumer surplus.

All of the other statements are true of antitrust legislation.

25. Correct answer: d.

Discussion: A tying contract requires a consumer who buys one product to buy another.

None of the other statements are correct.

26. Correct answer: c.

Discussion: A trust is an arrangement under which owners of several companies transfer their decision-making powers to a small group of trustees, who then make decisions for all the participating firms. In effect, a trust allows for collusion on price and many other facets of decision-making. In effect, a trust acts (illegally) as a monopoly.

Statement b is not correct. In a cartel, participating firms do not relinquish their decision-making powers to a supra-firm organization. Rather, the participating firms effectively remain separate entities and they jointly agree to set prices. None of the other statements are correct.

27. Correct answer: d.

Discussion: Some cases in which a merger will reduce competition are being argued as permissible mergers if the effect of the merger is similar to what would result if there was competition. That is, if two merging companies can argue that their merger will lead to lower prices, better products, and better services (the outcome expected under competition), then the merger may be granted.

Statement a is not correct. There is not a quantifiable figure (like 50% of market share) used in ruling on whether mergers should be permitted or not. Rulings based on antitrust legislation are determined by how the case impacts competition. Statement b is not correct. Mergers can happen not only between closely substitutable products (Office Depot and Staples), but between products that are not substitutes at all. For example, a merger may arise between an auto manufacturer and an auto parts manufacturer. Statement c is not correct. The government does not oppose all mergers. It opposes only those mergers that will reduce competition.

VIII. ANSWER KEY: ESSAY QUESTIONS

1. In a monopolistically competitive market, there is ease of entry. The ease of entry, however, means that there will be a lot of competition for customers amongst the firms. Thus, firms that are currently making positive economic profit face the threat of entry by entrepreneurs who believe that they, too, could make a profit in the industry. In fact, entry in a monopolistically competitive market structure typically occurs up until the point at which firms are making zero economic profit. At this point, there is no incentive for more entry into the market.

    In the case of the dry-cleaning business of the small city, the typical dry-cleaner is making $2,000 in profit per week based on the approximately 250 customers served (1,000 items per week/4 items dropped off per customer). If a new dry-cleaner enters the market, there will be some competition from him. This means several things. First, the existing dry-cleaners may have to lower the price of their service in order to hold on to their customer base. Since the new dry-cleaner will likely take away customers from the existing dry-cleaners, their demand curves (and marginal revenue curves) will shift to the left. However, the lower price charged by the dry-cleaners will mean that they may not lose as many customers as anticipated. Second, because the existing dry-cleaners will be serving fewer customers (less output), the average cost of serving each customer will rise. (Remember that average costs decline as output increases and vice-versa, i.e. average costs increase as output declines). Third, since the dry-cleaners will be charging a lower price for their service and incurring a higher average cost of production, the dry-cleaners' profits will be reduced. In the end, entry into the small city's dry-cleaning business will stop when economic profits are driven to zero.

2. There are costs and benefits to the dry-cleaning business operating under a monopolistically competitive market structure. With ease of entry, there will be a lot of dry-cleaners serving the market each with their own level of customer service, location, etc. Thus, in a monopolistically competitive market structure, customers get the benefits of being able to select from a variety of slightly differentiated products and services. Also, customers will likely see that the travel time to the dry-cleaner they patronize will decrease since more dry-cleaners in the city means more locations being serviced. The customers also benefit in that competition typically leads to a lower price for the product or service being purchased. The cost to society of a monopolistically competitive market is that the average cost of production is higher. From an efficiency standpoint, this is a cost to society since it would be better off if the dry-cleaners could produce where average cost is minimized and correspondingly, the price consumers pay would be the lowest possible. Of course, competition leads to price being reduced to some degree.

3. The duopolist's dilemma is that each firm, fearful that its profits will be undercut by its competitor, ends up charging a price lower than they would otherwise want to. Thus, each firm makes a smaller profit than they could if they each charged a higher price. Given this dilemma, there is an incentive for the duopolists to get together and agree to a higher price at which they will both sell their output. That way, they can both be guaranteed profits that are more attractive than when they don't agree to fix the price. While such explicit price-fixing schemes are illegal in the U.S, some firms still engage in price-fixing schemes because the fines and legal fees they might have to pay if they are found guilty are less than the profits they anticipate earning over the time the price-fixing scheme is in operation.

    There are a number of different types of price-fixing schemes. Firms can form a cartel and agree to all sell at a fixed price or agree that some firms can sell at price X while others sell at price Y. A price-matching scheme is another pricing strategy. It is not explicitly illegal. In this strategy, a firm announces (through the media) that it will match the prices of its competitor. It is important that the firm be credible in their policy. Since the competitor believes that any low price they try to sell at will be matched, and thus that their profits will be competed for, they will choose to sell at the same high price, too. Thus, the firm announcing the price-matching policy is able to continue selling at the high price. In this way, both firms enjoy higher profits than if there was no matching policy.

Price-fixing agreements, whether explicit or implicit, carry a temptation to cheat. The temptation exists because once the price is fixed, the cheaters know that if they sell at below the fixed price, they will get a larger share of the market and thereby reap increased profits. However, cheaters should think about the long term consequences of cheating since the other firms that are selling at the fixed price might punish the cheaters (and unfortunately, themselves as well) by all selling at a lower price, perhaps the one at which the cheaters were selling ("the duopoly price") or even one low enough that all firms earn zero economic profit (the grim trigger strategy). The threat of retaliation, which arises in a repeated game sequence, may curtail, to some degree, the temptation to cheat.

4. If I ran the only bakery in town and it was very profitable, I would be worried that other entrepreneurs, seeing how profitable I was, would be motivated to open up other bakeries in town. Thus, I would be, in the terms of the textbook, an "insecure monopolist." My insecurity would be that the future success (read profitability) of my bakery may be threatened by the entry of other bakeries into the town. So, what to do? I would consider lowering the price I charge for the array of baked goods I provide to my customers. Of course, I would realize that the lower price might lead to lower economic profits (if my revenue didn't increase and my costs remained the same or even if, at the lower price my revenue increased, but my costs increased by more). The lower price and presumably lower economic profits would make it less attractive for other firms to enter the business and thus I may be able to secure my monopoly status and the long-term prospect of at least positive economic profits.

On the other hand, if I do nothing to deter entry and it occurs, I will likely see my profits reduced. However, if they do not fall by as much as my "low price deterrence strategy," then it would make sense for me to do nothing.

5. A merger may be granted assuming that it does not reduce or threaten competition and thereby lead to higher prices. Typically, mergers that do not reduce competition are mergers between companies that do not sell the same product or product lines. Additionally, under the newer (1997) guidelines, a merger may be granted if the merging firms can establish that the merger will lead to lower average costs of production and lower prices or better products or better services. Better products or better services effectively act as a price reduction.

Mergers are typically blocked in cases where competition in the industry will be harmed. Harm to competition also carries with it the expectation that prices will be higher. A merger between Office Depot and Staples was denied because evidence was presented that higher prices would result. Evidence that competition may be harmed has recently come from price data collected from scanners. In the case of Office Depot and Staples, the price data showed that in cities where Office Depot and Staples were both located, prices charged by Staples was lower than in cities where only Staples was located.

6. Predatory pricing is the practice by a firm of lowering the price of its output, unreasonably, i.e. possibly below the average cost of production, for the purpose of driving out rival firms. The firm that is the price predator expects that by dramatically reducing its prices, it will cause the rival firms to lose their customers, or to lose at least enough of them that the rival firms will be forced to shut down their operation. The price predator knows that this pricing strategy will entail a potentially considerable cost when the lower price is announced; the firm may actually operate at a loss temporarily. But the firm weighs this cost against the expected benefit of monopoly power and profits after the rival firms are eliminated. It is a gamble for the predator firm since it does not know for how long the pricing strategy must be held in place in order to obliterate the rival firms. However, even if successful at achieving monopoly status, the predator firm may again have to invoke predatory pricing to maintain its status. This is because once the predator firm secures monopoly status and begins to earn monopoly profits, entrepreneurs will recognize that they too could participate in the profits by opening up a similar business. With entry, the profits of the predator firm will decrease. With enough entry, economic profits may reach zero. Thus, a predatory pricing strategy may ultimately require a perpetual strategy of cutting price unreasonably if the predator firm hopes to continue to earn monopoly profits. (Of course, further predatory pricing will entail further potential temporary losses to the firm).

Take It to the Net

We invite you to visit the O'Sullivan/Sheffrin page on the Prentice Hall Web site at:

http://www.prenhall.com/osullivan/

for this chapter's World Wide Web exercise.

CHAPTER 8
PUBLIC GOODS, SPILLOVERS,
AND IMPERFECT INFORMATION

I. OVERVIEW

In this chapter, you will learn about public goods -- goods that benefit society but are so expensive to pay for that no individual can pay for it by him or herself. You will learn what distinguishes public goods from private goods and learn of the special challenges that public goods create in a market economy. You will revisit the spillover principle that was learned earlier in Chapter 1.

You will learn about the economic consequences and policy surrounding environmental problems. You will learn how a public policy such as a tax on polluters both leads to firms taking steps to cut the pollution that they create when they produce output and because the tax also reduces the amount of output that polluters produce. You will also learn that the government can use regulation to reduce the amount of pollution that producers may be generating. You will learn about the traditional form of pollution regulation, which is command and control based, and the modern form of pollution regulation, which is market-based. You will learn which policy is most efficient from an economic standpoint. You will learn about global warming, ozone depletion, acid rain, and urban smog and how public policy has been devised to reduce these problems.

You will also learn about the effect of imperfect information on buyers and sellers and the price at which they strike deals. You will learn that markets with imperfect information are typically "mixed markets" meaning that the quality of a goods sold in a particular market is not uniform and that it is difficult for buyers to know whether the quality of the good that they are purchasing is of high or low quality. That is, there is a chance that a buyer will purchase a high-quality good and a chance that a buyer will end up purchasing a low quality version of the same good. You will learn that imperfect information arises when one side of the market (either buyers or sellers) has more information about the good in question than the other side of the market. You will learn that this situation is referred to as an information asymmetry and that it arises most commonly in the market for used goods and insurance. You will learn about the adverse selection problem. You will also learn what a thin market is and why they occur. You will use probabilities to compute expected amounts that uninformed buyers may be willing to pay. You will learn about some methods used to overcome the asymmetric information problem. You will also learn about applications of asymmetric information to the market for used cars, baseball pitchers, auto insurance, malpractice insurance, and health insurance. You will learn about moral hazard and why it is that insurance can actually encourage risky behavior.

II. CHECKLIST

By the end of this chapter, you should be able to:

√   Define a public good and the characteristics of a public good.
√   Compare and contrast public and private goods.

√   List some real world examples of public goods.

√   Explain what spillover benefits (external benefits) are and give some examples.

√   Explain how a subsidy by a government might lead to a more efficient outcome in the case of spillover benefits.

√   Explain the free rider problem and why voluntary contributions will generally not lead to the provision of a public good.

√   Discuss some ways in which organizations can increase the voluntary contributions that they receive.

√   Explain the two ways in which a pollution tax reduces the level of pollution.

√   Explain the effects of a tax on pollution using demand and supply.

√   Use the marginal principle to determine how much abatement a firm would undertake in response to a pollution tax.

√   Discuss how command and control regulations work to reduce pollution.

√   Compare the efficiency of command and control regulations to a tax.

√   Explain the effects of pollution regulation using demand and supply.

√   Explain some of the economic effects of global warming on agriculture.

√   Discuss the economic effects of a carbon tax on reducing global warming.

√   Discuss the economic effects of a ban on CFCs aimed at reducing ozone depletion.

√   Discuss the type of regulation currently used to control urban smog and suggest some alternative policies.

√   Define asymmetric information.

√   Explain the effects of asymmetric information on the price, quality, and volume of a good sold in a market.

√   Apply the asymmetric information problem to a market for used goods or insurance.

√   Explain why asymmetric information typically raises the cost of insurance and lowers the price of used goods.

√   Explain why the actually probability of a buyer purchasing a lemon (low quality good) in a used market is greater than the probability that may be casually assumed.

√   Define the adverse selection problem and explain what gives rise to it.

√   Define a thin market and explain what gives rise to it.

√   Define moral hazard and discuss instances in which moral hazard might arise.

III. KEY TERMS

Public good: a good that is available for everyone to consume, regardless of who pays and who doesn't.

Private good: a good that is consumed by the single person or household who pays for it.

Free-rider problem: each person will try to get the benefit of a public good without paying for it, trying to get a free ride at the expense of others.

Pollution tax: a tax or charge equal to the spillover cost per unit of waste.

Command and control policy: a pollution-control policy under which the government commands each firm to produce no more than a certain volume of pollution and controls the firm's production process by forcing the firm to use a particular pollution-control technology.

Carbon tax: a tax based on a fuel's carbon content.

Adverse-selection problem: the uninformed side of the market must choose from an undesirable or adverse selection of goods.

Asymmetric information: one side of the market — either buyers or sellers — has better information about the good than the other.

Thin market: a market in which some high-quality goods are sold, but fewer than would be sold in a market with perfect information.

Moral hazard problem: occurs because insurance encourages risky behavior.

IV. PERFORMANCE ENHANCING TIPS (PETS)

PET #1

The market demand and supply curves of goods with spillover benefits or spillover costs do not depict the efficient equilibrium outcome.

This means that in the presence of spillover benefits or costs, the equilibrium price and quantity represented by the intersection of market demand and supply curves is not "efficient." This means that the price and quantity outcome does not take into account those consumers (or producers) that receive benefits or incur costs but are not directly using the good. Your book gives a good example using education as the good.

PET #2

A subsidy is a transfer of money from the government to private citizens; a tax is a transfer of money from private citizens to the government.

Since a subsidy is the reverse of a tax, it is sometimes referred to as a "negative tax." It should be pointed out, however, that the ability of the government to extend subsidies to certain private citizens or groups of private citizens comes from the taxes that private citizens (households and businesses) pay to the government. Thus, your tax dollars are used to pay for government subsidies. Thus, indirectly, your tax dollars are transferred to other citizens in society.

PET #3

A spillover cost of production (such as pollution) is a cost that producers do not explicitly pay for unless they are forced to by the government.

Consider a firm that produces chemicals. A by-product of the production process is that some emissions are released into the air. The emissions create pollution, which creates health hazards for which people ultimately pay. The chemical producer generates a spillover cost by polluting the air and creating costs for other members of society. Because air is free, the chemical producer does not have to explicitly pay for the "use of the air." A tax on the chemical producer, in effect, forces it to pay for the cost of the air (and indirectly, assuming the tax revenues are used to help clean up the air) for the health costs that spillover to society.

PET #4

"Abatement" is the term used for "pollution clean-up."

When a firm undertakes an abatement project, it is cleaning up (or at least, reducing) the amount of pollution that it creates.

You should also know that the marginal cost of pollution clean-up increases. That is, the cost of reducing pollution by one unit, and then by one more, and then by one more, increases. For example, Table 1 of Chapter 16 of your textbook shows that as waste per ton of output is reduced from 5 gallons of waste per ton to 0 gallons of waste per ton, the production cost of one ton of output increases. This means, in effect, that the cost of doing more and more clean-up for the same one ton of output increases. Using the numbers from Table 1, the clean up costs increase from $60 to $116. The marginal cost of eliminating a gallon of waste from 5 gallons to 4 gallons is $1 ($61-$60) and the marginal cost of eliminating a gallon of waste from 4 gallons to 3 gallons is $3 ($64-$61), and so on. Thus, the marginal cost increases.

PET #5

A tax imposed on polluters raises their cost of production and hence the price at which they sell their output. This is represented by a leftward shift in supply. The equilibrium quantity of output the producer sells will decline. The tax thus works to reduce the amount of pollution by (1) reducing the amount of production the firm undertakes (and consequently the pollution that results); and (2) by motivating the firm to devise abatement methods so as to avoid having to pay the tax. Thus, new and improved methods of abatement may emerge.

PET #6

The expected (or average) amount that a buyer is willing to pay for a good of unknown quality is computed using the probabilities associated with whether the good is high or low quality (we'll assume only two categories of qualities) and what the corresponding prices would be for a good of a certain quality.

Let's suppose that you are considering buying a used computer. Further, you are aware that more lemon computers are likely to be sold in the used market than not. Suppose the probability of getting a faulty computer is 75% and thus the probability of buying a good computer is 25%. If the going price for a good, used computer were $1,000 and the going price for a faulty, used computer were $200, what is the expected price at which used computers will sell in the mixed market of good and faulty computers?

To answer the question, use the following formula:

(probability of high-quality good/100) X price of high-quality good + (probability of low-quality good/100) X price of low quality good.

Thus, your answer to the question should be:

(25/100) X ($1,000) + (75/100) X $200) = 0.25 X $1,000 + 0.75 X 200 = 250 + 150 = $400.

PET #7

The probability of a low (or high) quality good in the market can be determined by dividing the observations of a low (or high) quality good by the total number of goods (i.e. sum of low plus high quality goods).

Suppose you have done some research on the market for used evening gowns and determined that in your town, 30 used evening gowns are typically for sale each month. Further, you've determined that typically, 20 of the used evening gowns are very high quality and that 10 of the evening gowns are low quality. What is the probability in any given month that you or somebody that you may give advice to will buy a low quality evening gown?

The probability of purchasing a low quality evening gown is (10/30) X 100 = 33.3%

Thus, the probability of buying a high quality evening gown must be 66.7% (100% - 33.3%).

V. PRACTICE EXAM: MULTIPLE CHOICE QUESTIONS

1. Which one of the following describes a public good?
   a) it is rival in consumption and excludable.
   b) it is non-rival in consumption and excludable.
   c) it is rival in consumption and non-excludable.
   d) it is non-rival in consumption and non-excludable.
   e) none of the above.

2. Which pair of the following is an example of a private good and a public good?
   a) preservation of endangered species/space exploration.
   b) public housing/free concert in a city park.
   c) highways/ice cream.
   d) newspapers/golf courses.
   e) law enforcement/national defense.

3. Which one of the following statements is NOT true?
   a) the government spends money only on public goods, not private goods.
   b) public and private goods can both generate spillover benefits.
   c) the interaction of market demand and supply will not necessarily lead to an efficient outcome if a good generates spillover benefits or costs.
   d) education is likely to generate a workplace spillover.
   e) a government subsidy for a good with a spillover (external) benefit can lead to a more efficient outcome.

4. Which one of the following statements is NOT true of a subsidy?
   a) subsidies are often given in the case of private goods that carry spillover (external) benefits.
   b) subsidies internalize a spillover (external) benefit.
   c) subsidies are ultimately paid for by taxpayers.
   d) a subsidy for education might come in the form of federal grants for financial aid.
   e) all of the above are true of subsidies.

5. Which one of the following is NOT an example of a private good with a spillover benefit?
   a) education.
   b) on-the-job training.
   c) the space program.
   d) preventative health care.
   e) research at private universities.

6. Which one of the following is NOT true of voluntary contributions as a way of funding public goods and goods with spillover benefits?

    a) some citizens will not contribute at all.

    b) some citizens will contribute an amount that is small relative to the benefits they receive from the good.

    c) voluntary contributions work better than taxes at ensuring that a project is funded.

    d) voluntary contributions may increase through programs like "matching contributions" and giving coffee mugs, etc. to contributors.

    e) public radio and television have been very successful at overcoming the free rider problem.

7. In economics, pollutions:

    a) is a spillover (external) cost.

    b) is a private good.

    c) generates diminishing returns.

    d) is really a cost of production.

    e) (a) and (d).

8. Which one of the following is an effect of a pollution tax on paper production?

    a) the price of paper will decline.

    b) paper producers will have an incentive to abate.

    c) the quantity of paper produced will rise.

    d) the marginal cost of paper production will decline.

    e) none of the above.

9. Use the table below to decide how many gallons of water per ton of output produced a firm will decide to emit.

Waste per ton	Clean-up Cost per ton	Tax Cost per ton
20 gallons	$100	$60
19 gallons	$102	$57
18	$106	$54
17	$112	$51
16	$120	$48

    a) 20 gallons.

    b) 19 gallons.

    c) 18 gallons.

    d) 17 gallons.

    e) 16 gallons.

10. Which one of the following is true of traditional pollution regulation (command and control policy)?
    a) the policy imposes that a single abatement technology (method of clean-up) be used.
    b) it creates an incentive to pollute.
    c) it encourages innovation in new and less costly methods of abatement.
    d) it is less costly than imposing a tax on polluters.
    e) all of the above are true.

11. Which one of the following is true of a comparison between a pollution tax and traditional pollution regulation?
    a) regulation raises the price of the output of the polluter more than would a pollution tax.
    b) firms produce and sell less output under regulation than a tax.
    c) pollution is reduced by less with a regulation than with a tax.
    d) regulation does not produce any tax revenue that can be used to fund other clean-up projects.
    e) all of the above.

12. Which one of the following is NOT true of global warming?
    a) it is due to an accumulation of carbon dioxide in the atmosphere.
    b) there is uncertainty about how much the earth's temperature will actually rise.
    c) total rainfall is expected to decrease.
    d) a carbon tax (a tax on the burning of fossil fuels like oil, coal, and gasoline) is one solution aimed at reducing the pace of global warming.
    e) sea levels are expected to increase.

13. A mixed market is one in which:
    a) consumers can be buyers and sellers and producers can be sellers and buyers.
    b) there are different qualities of a good being sold in the market and there is imperfect information about the quality of each good.
    c) a seller of a good requires that the purchase of one good be tied to the purchase of another.
    d) demand is positively sloped and supply is negatively sloped.
    e) none of the above.

14. In a market for used goods,
    a) the seller has more information than the buyer about the quality of the good.
    b) the buyer has more information than the seller about the quality of the good.
    c) there are no high-quality used goods for sale.
    d) low quality used goods will be under-priced.
    e) the quality of used goods sold in the market will typically rise over time.

15. Which one of the following is an example of asymmetric information?
    a) a grocery store selling cookies that are stale.
    b) a builder building a house with 2" instead of 4" studs.
    c) a company hiring an employee that has an addiction to sleeping pills.
    d) a seller at a flea market selling stolen goods.
    e) all of the above.

16. Which one of the following is true of a used market, e.g. used market for cars?
    a) a consumer typically overestimates the probability of getting a lemon (low quality car).
    b) the more pessimistic buyers become that their chance of buying a high quality car is high, the lower will the price of all (low and high quality) used cars become.
    c) there is an adverse information problem.
    d) the willingness to pay and the willingness to accept are equal.
    e) (b) and (d).

17. The adverse selection problem is that:
    a) the informed side of the market pays more for a good than the less informed side of the market.
    b) a seller does not inform a buyer of all of the add-on fees that will be incurred upon the purchase of a good.
    c) product differentiation makes it difficult to decide which product to buy.
    d) the uninformed side of the market must choose from an undesirable selection of goods.
    e) all of the above.

18. Which one of the following is an equilibrium?
    a) buyers assume a 40% chance of getting a lemon and 8 lemons and 2 plums are supplied.
    b) buyers assume a 60% chance of getting a lemon and 6 lemons and 4 plums are supplied.
    c) buyers assume a 40% chance of getting a lemon and 4 lemons and 4 plums are supplied.
    d) buyers assume an 80% chance of getting a lemon and 2 lemons and 8 plums are supplied.
    e) buyers assume a 75% chance of getting a lemon and 7 lemons and 3 plums are supplied.

19. Which one of the following is NOT true of a thin market?
    a) it may be caused by asymmetric information.
    b) there are relatively few high-quality goods sold.
    c) in a thin market, there may be some sellers of high-quality goods because of extenuating circumstances (moving out of the country; increased family size, etc.)
    d) the price of a high quality good will be higher than if the market was thick.
    e) all of the above.

20. A mixed market is:
    a) dominated by low-quality goods.
    b) one in which there is asymmetric information.
    c) one where buyers encounter an adverse selection problem.
    d) typical of used goods and insurance.
    e) all of the above.

21. Use the following information to complete the sentence below:

    Average cost of settling a lawsuit of a careful plastic surgeon = $6,000.
    Average cost of settling a lawsuit of a reckless plastic surgeon = $36,000.
    Probability that a careful doctor will want insurance = 25%
    Probability that a reckless doctor will want insurance = 75%

    Assuming insurance companies cannot distinguish between careful and reckless plastic surgeons, an insurance company will charge $____ for malpractice insurance and a careful plastic surgeon would be incline to _____ insurance.
    a) $28,500; not buy.
    b) $21,000; not buy.
    c) $36,000; not buy.
    d) $21,000; buy.
    e) $42,000; not buy.

22. Which one of the following is an example where the problem of moral hazard would be likely to occur?
    a) insurance against theft.
    b) high and low quality used computers being sold by the same store.
    c) commercial dating services.
    d) a real estate company providing homeowner's warranties on appliances and plumbing for each "used" house it sells.
    e) the national blood supply.

VI. PRACTICE EXAM: ESSAY QUESTIONS

1. Suppose that you are the head of a government agency that oversees re-training programs for the unemployed. Discuss whether the service that your agency delivers is a public or private good. Will the private market of demand and supply lead to an efficient outcome? Why or why not? Discuss how your agency is funded. How well do you think a voluntary contribution scheme work in funding your program?

2.   Explain how a tax on polluters works to help reduce the amount of pollution.

3.   Suppose you are a college admissions director and every year you receive 5,000 applications for admission to your school while your school only has 1,000 slots open. Your school is prestigious and has a reputation for producing some of the best and brightest college graduates on the national market. What problems might you encounter as the admission director? How might you handle them?

4.   Explain the effects of asymmetric information on the price, quality, and volume of used computers sold in a market.

VII. ANSWER KEY: MULTIPLE CHOICE

1.   Correct answer: d.

Discussion: A public good is both non-rival and non-excludable in consumption. Non-rival means that one person's consumption of the good does not rival another person's ability to consume/use the good. That is, more than one person can consume/use the good at the same time. Non-excludable means that people who do not pay for the good cannot be excluded from using and receiving the benefits of the good. Thus, even if one person were to pay for the good, others could use it without having to pay for it.

Statement a describes a private good. A private good can only be consumed and thus enjoyed by the consumer. That is, it is rival in consumption. A private good can also only be consumed/used by the person paying for it. That is, a private good is excludable. Reading a book, attending a movie, going to a private school, buying a house, and eating an ice cream cone are some examples.

As an aside, you should remember that a private good can have spillover benefits as can a public good.

2.   Correct answer: b.

Discussion: Public housing is both rival and excludable in consumption even though it is a government-provided good. A free concert in a city park is non-rival and non-excludable. More than one person can enjoy it and people can enjoy it regardless of whether or not they pay for it. Of course, citizens who live around the park who may not prefer the noise of the concert will experience a spillover (external) cost.

Statement a is an example of two public goods. Statement c is an example of a public good/private good (instead of vice-versa). Statement d is an example of two private goods. Statement e is an example of two public goods.

3. Correct answer: a.

Discussion: Statement a is not true because a government spends money on public goods like highways, law enforcement, and space exploration as well as on education (a private good with spillover benefits), and housing and food (a private good).

Statement b is true because a public good like the space exploration program can generate spillover benefits -- high-tech companies may learn new and improved ways to do things from the space exploration program. Private goods like education, health care, and even deodorant create spillover benefits. Statement c is true because when a private good has spillovers, not all of the benefits and costs of the good are revealed in the demand and supply curves. That is, not all of the consumers or even producers are represented in the demand and supply curves. Statement d is true -- education generates not only workplace but civic spillovers. Statement e is true because the government, by subsidizing particular goods, is attempting to achieve a more desirable (truthful) market outcome.

4. Correct answer: e.

Discussion: All of the above are true of a subsidy. While statement a is true, it does not mean that the government provides subsidies to any and every private good that carry a spillover benefit. Statement b means that a subsidy forces an external benefit to be reflected in the market demand curve. Statement d suggests that there are many ways in which the government can give money back to citizens for the purchase of a private good. Statement c is also true, as discussed in PET #2.

5. Correct answer: c.

Discussion: Statement c is an example of a public good, not a private good, which has spillover benefits. All of the other examples are examples of private goods with spillover benefits.

6. Correct answer: c.

Discussion: Statement c is not true; taxes work better at ensuring that a project is funded than voluntary contributions. In effect, a tax ensures that everybody pays for the project, not just those willing to contribute.

Statements a and b reflect a common problem with voluntary contributions. Statement d suggests that there are ways (that are costly to somebody, however) to increase voluntary contributions to a specific project. Statement e is true; in fact, public radio and television have used some of the tactics listed in statement d as a way of increasing voluntary contributions.

7. Correct answer: e.

Discussion: Pollution is a spillover cost of production because it imposes costs on other segments of society that bear the cost of pollution such as health costs, inability to use a river to fish or a lake to swim, etc. Pollution should also rightly be considered a cost of production because a firm that pollutes a river or the air is using the river or the air in the production process. Thus, it should be treated as a cost just like the use of labor and raw materials is considered a cost of production.

Statement b is not correct because pollution is a public good (that is, in fact, bad). Statement c is not correct because the reduction of pollution entails increasing marginal costs.

8. Correct answer: b.

Discussion: A tax forces the polluting firm to bear some of the cost of polluting in production. Since the tax imposes a cost on the firm, the firm has an incentive to avoid it by finding methods of abatement.

Statement a is not correct because the price of paper will rise. Statement c is not correct because the quantity of paper produced will decline. Statement d is not correct because the marginal cost of abatement will increase. Statement e cannot be correct because statement b is true.

9. Correct answer: b.

Discussion: The marginal cost of reducing pollution from 20 gallons to 19 gallons per ton is $2 whereas if the polluter did not clean up, the tax cost would be $3. (The government forces the polluter to pay $3 more dollars to pollute 20 gallons instead of 19 gallons). Thus, the marginal cost of abatement is less than the tax cost so the firm should abate.

The marginal cost of reducing pollution from 19 gallons to 18 gallons per ton is $4 whereas if the polluter did not clean up that one more gallon of waste, the tax cost would be $3. Since the tax cost of polluting by one more gallon is less than the cost of cleaning up, the polluter will not clean up and instead pay the tax cost. The same reasoning applies to the 17th and 16th gallons.

10. Correct answer: a.

Discussion: A command and control pollution policy imposed by regulators forces all firms in the same industry to use the same method of abatement.

Statement b is not true; regulation does not create the incentive to pollute but rather forces the polluter not to pollute. Statement c is not true because the policy discourages innovation in pollution abatement by dictating that all firms use the same method of clean-up. Statement d is not true because command and control regulation is more costly to polluters than a tax. Statement e is not true because statement a is true.

11. Correct answer: e.

Discussion: A pollution tax is more efficient than traditional pollution regulation. All of the statements above are reasons why it is more efficient.

12. Correct answer: c.

Discussion: Global warming is expected to increase, not decrease, the amount of rainfall. All of the other statements are true.

13. Correct answer: b.

Discussion: In a mixed market, there are different qualities of a good being sold and unfortunately the buyer or seller of the good may not know for sure (has imperfect information) what the quality of the good is. The market for used goods is typically a mixed market as is the market for insurance.

All of the other statements are bogus.

14. Correct answer: a.

Discussion: A used market is a market for which there is asymmetric information — in this case, the information is asymmetric because the seller knows more about the true quality of the good than does the buyer.

Based on the above, statement b is not true. Statement c is generally not true (only in extreme cases would no high quality used goods be for sale) because a used market is also one that is "mixed" in that high and low quality versions of the same good will be offered for sale. Statement d is not true because the price of low quality used goods is based on the price at which a high and low quality version of the good would be priced. This leads to a higher price for a low quality good than reflects its true value. Statement e is not true because there is a tendency for the quality of goods sold in a used market to decrease over time.

15. Correct answer: e.

Discussion: While asymmetric information typically arises in a market for used goods, it can occur elsewhere. All of the above examples are cases in which one party (the buyer or the seller) has more information about the product than the other party.

16. Correct answer: b.

Discussion: When buyers become more pessimistic that their chance of buying a high quality car is high, they will attach a lower probability to the price they would be willing to pay for a high quality car and thus a higher probability to the price they would be willing to pay for a low quality car. This necessarily lowers the price that a buyer would be willing to pay for a car about which they have no information as to its quality.

You may wish to review PET #1 and attach different probabilities to that associated with buying a good computer and a faulty one and then see what happens to the expected price of the computer.

Statement a is not true; consumers typically underestimate the probability of purchasing a lemon. Statement c is not correct because the term is "adverse selection" not "adverse information." Statement d is not true because there are typically differences in the willingness to pay and accept (which is why buyers and sellers bargain with each other). Statement e is not true because statement d is not true.

17. Correct answer: d.

Discussion: The adverse selection problem arises in a mixed market because the buyer does not know the quality of every good being sold in a particular market. That is, the uninformed side of the market must choose which good to buy knowing that some of the selection is of poor quality but not knowing which of the goods are poor quality.

18. Correct answer: b.

Discussion: An equilibrium will be reached in the market when the assumed (or perceived) chance of purchasing a lemon is equal to the actual chance. In statement b, the actual chance is $(6/10) \times 100 = 60\%$. (See PET #2 for review).

Statement a is not correct because the actual chance is 80%. Statement c is not true because the actual chance is 50%. Statement d is not true because the actual chance of getting a lemon is 20%. Statement e is not true because the actual chance of getting a lemon is 70%.

19. Correct answer: d.

Discussion: A thin market is a market in which there are relatively few high quality goods but an abundance of low quality goods being offered for sale. This drives down, not up, the price of the good in a thin market. If the market were thicker, the price of the good would be higher than in a thin market. Thus, in a thin market, where both qualities of good are being sold at the same price, it will generally be the case that low quality goods are overpriced (relative to their true value) and high quality goods under-priced (relative to their true value).

A thin market, in part, exists because of asymmetric information. Asymmetric information leads to a lower price for the high quality good and thus induces many of the sellers of the high quality good not to sell.

However, there will be some high quality goods being sold perhaps because sellers find themselves in extenuating circumstances where they are forced to sell their good.

20. Correct answer: e.

Discussion: Your book stresses that all of the above are true of a mixed market and hopefully so too will your instructor because then you'll be prepared for a question like this!

21. Correct answer: c.

Discussion: In this example, insurance companies face an adverse selection problem about plastic surgeons because they do not have as much information about how careful or reckless a plastic surgeon is while the plastic surgeon knows more about himself or herself than the insurance company. Faced with the adverse selection problem, insurance companies protect themselves against it by charging a price that is equal to the average settlement that the reckless plastic surgeon pays. In this example, that price is $36,000. However, since careful doctors know that they are careful and that their average settlement is $6,000, they find it less costly to settle than to pay for malpractice insurance. Thus, careful doctors will not buy the insurance.

Based on the above reasoning, statements a, b, d, and e are not correct.

22. Correct answer: a.

Discussion: The problem of moral hazard is that the provision of insurance leads to riskier behavior than would otherwise occur without the insurance. When insurance companies provide insurance coverage for valuables that are stolen, people knowing that they will be monetarily reimbursed for the stolen items may not be as vigilant about where they leave their valuables and about who may have access to their valuables. People may not be as vigilant about locking their car doors or doors to their houses or about keeping their valuables hidden. Thus, by having insurance against theft, individuals take riskier behavior with respect to the care of their valuables than they would if they had no insurance at all.

Statements b-e are examples of mixed markets where adverse selection, asymmetric information, and a thin market may prevail.

VIII. ANSWER KEY: ESSAY QUESTIONS

1. The worker re-training program is a private good with spillover benefits. It is a private good because only those enrolled in the re-training program are able to use it. Furthermore, only companies that pay for the program, also supported by subsidies from the government, are able to use it. However, there are spillover benefits to the re-training program. Not only do the unemployed and the companies using the program benefit, but society benefits as well. People who are employed pay taxes and are less likely to get involved in illegal activities. Since the re-training program has spillover benefits, the government may subsidize the worker re-training programs. This gets the private market to take advantage of the external benefits. While my agency is funded through subsidies provided by the government and also through companies paying into the program for its use, the government subsidies ultimately come from tax-paying citizens. A voluntary contribution scheme would probably not lead to the level of support currently provided because of the free-rider problem. What typically happens under a voluntary contribution scheme is that some people who use the program will not contribute anything at all while others will contribute but not in accordance with the actual benefits they receive. Thus, a voluntary contribution scheme would likely lead to an under-funded program which thus may not be able to continue to run. Of course, I might suggest that our agency's fundraising efforts include matching contributions and free gifts. However, somebody will have to pay for these.

2. A tax on polluters implicitly raises their cost of production as they must pay for the tax or adopt methods of abatement to avoid the tax. Abatement, of course, is a cost to the firm. However, since the tax creates the incentive to adopt methods of abatement, pollution will be reduced by the abatement actions of the firms. Secondly, a pollution tax raises the cost of output that the polluter produces. (This is represented by a leftward shift in supply). A higher cost of production is, in part, passed on to consumers through a higher consumer price. The higher price reduces the equilibrium quantity of the output demanded. Firms respond by producing less of the output, which means they, in turn, end up polluting less. It may also happen that firms invent a similar product that has a manufacturing process that does not pollute or pollutes by much less.

3. As the admissions director and having read Chapter 8 of my textbook, I would recognize that I am facing an adverse selection problem that arises because of asymmetric information. There is asymmetric information because the students (the sellers of their talents and aptitude) have more information about themselves (the product they are selling) than I might have about their true abilities. Students vary a good deal in quality and their high school academic record may not always be the best reflection of the quality of a student. That is, some students may have shining academic records but in fact be very poor students. In the language of the used car market, some students are "lemons." In fact, the pool of students applying to the school represents a mixed market — there are high quality and low quality students in the pool together. As the admissions director, I would like to avoid the problem of admitting lemons, particularly because the admittance of such students could ultimately harm the prestigious reputation of the college.

4. So, as admissions director, I may not only use high school transcripts and SAT or ACT scores to determine who should be admitted, but I may also require a written essay, personal interviews, letters of reference, and evidence of extracurricular activity involvement. The additional information may help reduce the probability that I will admit lemons to my college. In a way, you could say that essays, interviews, and the like are the school's form of insurance against admitting a poor student.

5. In a market with asymmetric information, the price of a used good is typically lower than it would otherwise be. The reason is that a used market is a mixed market where high and low quality goods are being sold without obvious information on which of the goods are high quality and which are low quality. In such a market, the seller has more information about the quality of the good being sold than the buyer has. Thus, buyers attach a probability to the possibility that they will end up buying (unbeknownst to them) a low quality good rather than a high quality good. Since buyers are not willing to pay very much for a low quality good, the probability that they will end up buying one is factored into the price that they will offer to pay. This means that high quality used goods will also have to be sold at a lower price. For example, a buyer may be willing to pay $1,000 for a high quality, used computer but only $200 for a low quality used computer. Thus, the price they are willing to offer will range between $200 and $1,000 and will depend on how likely the buyer thinks he may end up getting a low quality computer. That is, the equilibrium price for used computers (regardless of their quality) will range between $200 and $1,000. The higher the probability that buyers attach to getting a low quality computer, the lower will be the equilibrium price at which used computers sell.

6. Since the equilibrium price of used computers (both high and low quality) will be lower than otherwise, the quality of used computers offered for sale will be lower than otherwise, too. This is because sellers with high-quality computers will not, unless extraordinary circumstances dictate, be willing to part with their computers for such a low price. This means that in the used market for computers, there will be a lot more low quality computers for sale than one might expect had they not taken account of how the

price feeds into determining the quality of used computers offered for sale. The market may also end up being a "thin" market in the sense that there will be fewer high quality computers for sale in because the sellers of the high quality computers have elected not to sell at the low price.

Take It to the Net

We invite you to visit the O'Sullivan/Sheffrin page on the Prentice Hall Web site at:

http://www.prenhall.com/osullivan/

for this chapter's World Wide Web exercise.

CHAPTER 9
THE LABOR MARKET

I. OVERVIEW

In this chapter, you will learn about the labor market using demand and supply analysis where the price of labor is the wage rate. You will learn that demand for labor is a derived demand since the demand for labor is derived from the demand for the output that labor produces. You will learn what will cause the wage rate and employment to change. You will learn why the wage rate differs for different occupations and for different groups of people. You will analyze the effects of various public policies aimed at the labor market: a minimum wage law and occupational licensing. You will learn about labor unions. You will learn about the labor market in a setting where the employee has more information than the employer about how productive he or she will be on the job. Finally, you will learn that "efficiency wages" may be paid by an employer to reduce the problems that may arise with the information asymmetry.

II. CHECKLIST

By the end of this chapter, you should be able to:

√ Discuss a firm's short run demand for labor and relate it to diminishing returns.

√ Explain why the demand for labor is negatively sloped.

√ Use the marginal principle to determine whether a firm would benefit by hiring one more worker.

√ Explain why the short run labor demand curve is more steeply sloped than the long run labor demand curve.

√ Explain the income and substitution effects of an increase in the wage rate. Also explain it in terms of a decrease in the wage rate.

√ Explain why the market supply of labor is positively sloped.

√ Explain what will cause the demand for and supply of labor to shift and analyze the effects on the equilibrium wage and employment.

√ List four explanations for why wages differ across different occupations.

√ Explain why women and blacks on average earn less for an hour of work than do white males.

√ Discuss the learning and signaling effect to explain why college graduates typically earn more than high school graduates.

√ Discuss the tradeoffs associated with a minimum wage law.

√ Discuss occupational licensing and its effect on wages and employment.

√ List some examples of craft unions and labor unions.

√ Discuss the history of labor unions in the United States.

√   Discuss three ways in which a labor union attempts to raise the wage of the union members.

√   Discuss whether unions can create more productive workers.

√   Explain efficiency wages and why they may be paid by a firm.

III. KEY TERMS

Marginal product of labor: the change in output per unit change in labor.

Marginal revenue product of labor: the extra revenue generated from one more unit of labor; equal to price of output times the marginal product of labor.

Short-run demand curve for labor: a curve showing the relationship between the wage and the quantity of labor demanded in the short run.

Market supply curve for labor: a curve showing the relationship between the wage and the quantity of labor supplied.

Output effect: the change in the quantity of labor demanded resulting from a change in the quantity of output.

Input substitution effect: the change in the quantity of labor demanded resulting from a change in the relative cost of labor.

Long-run demand curve for labor: a curve showing the relationship between the wage and the quantity of labor demanded in the long run.

Learning effect: the increase in a person's wage resulting from the learning of skills required for certain occupations.

Signaling or screening effect: the increase in a person's wage resulting from the signal of productivity provided by completing college.

Labor union: an organized group of workers, the main objective of which is to improve working conditions, wages, and fringe benefits.

Craft union: a labor organization that includes workers from a particular occupation, for example, plumbers, bakers, or electricians.

Industrial union: a labor organization that includes all types of workers from a single industry, for example, steelworkers or autoworkers.

Marginal labor cost (or marginal factor cost): the increase in total labor cost from hiring one more worker.

IV. PERFORMANCE ENHANCING TIPS (PETS)

PET #1

The wage rate is the price of labor.

Since the wage rate is the price of the commodity, labor, demand and supply analysis can be used to examine what happens to the price of labor (wage rate) when the demand or supply of labor change.

PET #2

Factors other than a change in the wage rate that are relevant to the labor market may cause the demand and supply curves for labor to shift. Changes in the wage rate cause a movement along the demand and supply curves.

For review, you may wish to review PET #1 of Chapter 1 of the Practicum as well as PET #1-5 of Chapter 4 of the Practicum.

PET #3

A higher wage rate will cause some workers to work more (quantity of labor supplied increases) and will cause some workers to work less (quantity of labor supplied decreases).

For workers that work more hours when the wage rate rises, they are behaving according to the law of supply. That is, for these workers, the supply of labor is positively sloped. These workers will reduce the amount of leisure time they take (because the opportunity cost of leisure time has increased since the wage rate has increased) and therefore work more hours. We could say that these workers substitute more work for less leisure time.

For workers that work fewer hours when the wage rate rises, they are not behaving according to the law of supply since they increase the amount of leisure time they take and thus work fewer hours. That is, for these workers, the supply of labor is negatively sloped. A worker may choose to respond this way to a higher wage rate because they recognize that they can now work fewer hours (more leisure time) and still maintain the same income. We could say that these workers substitute more leisure time for less work.

You should be aware this chapter points out some other reasons why the supply curve will be positively sloped.

PET #4

The marginal revenue product of labor is equal to the price at which a firm sells its output multiplied by the marginal product (productivity) of labor.

To see this, note that the price of output (P) is measured as $ per unit of output. The marginal product of labor is measured as the addition to output produced by one more worker (or from one more hour of work). That is, (Δ output/one unit of labor). When price is multiplied by the marginal product of labor, the result is:

$$P \times (\Delta \text{ output/one unit of labor}) = (P \times \Delta \text{ output })/\text{one unit of labor}$$

where (P X Δ output) = Marginal Revenue. Thus, the marginal revenue product of labor is the addition to revenue that one more worker generates for the firm.

PET #5

Factors that cause an increase in the demand for output that labor produces will lead to an increase in the demand for labor and thus an increase in the equilibrium wage.

A firm's demand for labor is a derived demand for labor. It is derived from the demand for the output that labor helps to produce. An increase in the demand for output leads to an increase in the price of output. The increase in the price of output means that each worker's work effort (productivity) will add more to the revenue of the firm than before the price increase. That is, the marginal revenue product of labor increases. Using the marginal principle, the marginal benefit to the firm of additional workers has increased. If the wage rate (marginal cost of an additional worker) is unchanged, the firm will find it profit-maximizing to hire more workers.

PET #6

A minimum wage policy is like a minimum price (or price floor, price support).

Remember from Chapter 4 that a minimum price is a price below which the price may not fall. For a minimum price policy to be effective, it must be set above the equilibrium price. In the case of minimum wage policy, a minimum wage that is set above the equilibrium wage will create a surplus of labor (quantity of labor supplied will exceed quantity of labor demanded). If the minimum wage is set below the equilibrium wage, the policy is ineffective since there is no tendency for the equilibrium wage to fall below the minimum wage. You may want to review PET #9 from Chapter 4 of the Practicum.

PET #7

An efficiency wage is a wage that is paid by a firm that is above the equilibrium wage (or going market-rate) for a particular job or occupation.

An efficiency wage may be paid by a firm in order to attract high quality, productive workers, to reduce the worker's incentive to shirk (i.e. make them work harder), and to reduce absenteeism and turnover. The higher wages paid by the firm may not necessarily mean that the firm's profits will suffer. The workers may be more productive than their counterparts working for other firms in the same industry who are not being paid an efficiency wage. Thus, even though the firm's wage cost may be higher with efficiency wages, the cost of production may not rise because the productivity increase acts to offset the higher labor costs.

V. PRACTICE EXAM: MULTIPLE CHOICE QUESTIONS

1. If an increase in the wage rate causes workers to reduce the amount of hours they work and increase the amount of leisure time they take, then:

    a) the labor supply curve for these workers is positively sloped.

    b) the labor supply curve for these workers is negatively sloped.

    c) these workers are obeying the law of supply.

    d) the demand for these workers is derived.

    e) the marginal product of these workers is negative.

2. Which one of the following would be considered a possible response to a higher wage rate for computer technicians in Palo Alto?

    a) a decrease in the amount of hours worked.

    b) an increase in the amount of hours worked.

    c) an increase in the number of individuals who pick computer technician over other occupations.

    d) migration to Palo Alto.

    e) all of the above.

3. Which one of the following is an explanation for why the long run demand curve for labor is negatively sloped?

    a) an increase in the wage rate raises the price at which output is sold and thus increases the profits of firms.

    b) a decrease in the wage rate causes fewer people to be willing to work.

    c) a decrease in the wage rate lowers the cost of labor and causes firms to use more labor instead of other more expensive inputs.

    d) an increase in the wage rate reduces the productivity of workers.

    e) all of the above.

4. The substitution effect of a decrease in the price of labor (wage rate):
   a) would lead to a decrease in the amount of hours worked and a decrease in leisure time.
   b) would lead to a decrease in the amount of hours worked and an increase in leisure time.
   c) would lead to an increase in the amount of hours worked and a decrease in leisure time.
   d) would lead to an increase in the amount of hours worked and an increase in leisure time.
   e) would have no effect on the amount of hours worked.

5. According to the income effect, a decrease in the price of labor (wage rate):
   a) leads to a decrease in the amount of labor supplied.
   b) leads to a decrease in the consumption of goods.
   c) leads to an increase in the demand for leisure time.
   d) leads to a decrease in the demand for labor.
   e) all of the above.

6. In which country would labor be likely to be most expensive?
   a) India.
   b) Haiti.
   c) Mexico.
   d) Italy.
   e) the Philippines.

7. Consider the market for lawyers. Suppose the number of lawyers passing the Bar exam in 1998 is larger than it has ever been in the past. What effect would this have on the market for lawyers?
   a) a decrease in the wage rate (salary) paid to lawyers and an increase in the demand for lawyers.
   b) a decrease in the wage rate (salary) paid to lawyers and an increase in the supply of lawyers.
   c) an increase in the wage rate (salary) paid to lawyers and a decrease in the demand for lawyers.
   d) an increase in the wage rate (salary) paid to lawyers and an increase in the supply of lawyers.
   e) (a) and (b).

8. Which one of the following would increase the demand for labor?
   a) an increase in the price of output that labor produces.
   b) an increase in the productivity of labor.
   c) an increase in the price of capital.
   d) a minimum wage law.
   e) (a), (b), and (c).

9. Which one of the following is a reason for why the relative wage of certain occupations is high?

   a) few people who have the skills necessary to perform the job.

   b) high education and training costs.

   c) undesirable job features.

   d) licensing restrictions.

   e) all of the above.

10. Which one of the following has NOT been suggested as an explanation for the gender and race gap in earnings?

   a) women and blacks have, on average, less education than white males.

   b) women and blacks have, on average, less work experience than white males.

   c) gender/race discrimination.

   d) women and blacks are only a small percentage of the total work force.

   e) all of the above.

11. Which one of the following statements is true?

   a) In 1997, a typical college graduate earned 78% more than the typical high-school graduate.

   b) a college education provides a signal to a potential employer that the job candidate has desirable skills.

   c) the "learning effect" of a college education is that students learn new skills that enable them to work in higher-skill jobs.

   d) over the last twenty years, technological change has created a big increase in the demand for high-skilled workers

   e) all of the above.

12. Suppose the current wage rate in the service industry is $5.00/hour. A minimum wage policy for the service industry that sets the minimum wage at $5.25 will create a _____ of jobs and a minimum wage policy for the service industry that sets the minimum wage at $4.50 will create a _____ of jobs.

   a) loss; gain.

   b) gain; loss.

   c) loss; no effect.

   d) no effect; gain.

   e) loss; loss.

13. Which one of the following statements is true?

    a) a minimum wage policy may lead to a decrease in the price of output that minimum wage workers produce.

    b) an industrial union is made up of workers from a particular occupation.

    c) an example of occupational licensing is a requirement that a worker complete a certain number of hours of education and re-training every three years in order to remain licensed.

    d) a labor union has monopsony power.

    e) none of the above are true.

14. Occupational licensing schemes:

    a) restrict entry into the profession.

    b) increase wages.

    c) increase production costs.

    d) are designed to protect consumers.

    e) all of the above.

15. Which one of the following statements is NOT true?

    a) the Wagner Act guaranteed workers the right to join unions and required each firm to bargain with a union formed by a majority of its workers.

    b) the Taft-Hartley Act gave government employees the power to strike when their health or safety was imperiled.

    c) The Landrum-Griffin Act guaranteed union members the right to fair elections, made it easier to monitor union finances, and made the theft of union funds a federal offense.

    d) Fewer than 20% of all U.S. workers belong to unions.

    e) The number of government workers in unions has more than doubled in the last forty years.

16. Unions attempt to increase the wages of their members by:

    a) negotiating with the firm.

    b) advertisements that encourage people to buy products with the union label.

    c) featherbedding.

    d) striking.

    e) all of the above.

17. Which one of the following statements is true?

    a) a firm that pays efficiency wages may see an increased work effort by its employees as well as a reduction in absenteeism and turnover.

    b) featherbedding may lead to lower costs of production.

    c) a firm knows more about the productivity and skill level of a potential employee than the potential employee knows about his or her own productivity and skill level.

    d) the labor market is a fixed market.

    e) a monopsonist in the labor market uses its power to increase the wage rate.

VI. PRACTICE EXAM: ESSAY QUESTIONS

1. Consider the market for graphic designers in Charlotte. Let the current equilibrium wage be $11/hour. Suppose that the demand for graphic designers in Charlotte increases by 10%. Discuss what will happen to the equilibrium wage in the short and long run. Be sure to explain why the results are different. Assume the elasticity of labor supply in the short run is 0.5 and in the long run is 2.

2. Discuss the purpose of unions and their intended impact on wages and employment. What are some ways in which union membership leads to more productive workers?

VII. ANSWER KEY: MULTIPLE CHOICE QUESTIONS

1. Correct answer: b.

Discussion: The labor supply curve is a graph of the wage rate against the amount of labor (or labor time) supplied. An increase in the wage rate that reduces the amount of labor supplied reflects a negative or inverse relationship between the wage rate and the amount of labor supplied.

Statement a is not correct based on the above reasoning. Statement c is not correct because if the workers were obeying the law of supply, then the labor supply curve would be positively sloped. Statement d is not correct because the relationship between the wage rate and labor supplied tells us nothing about the demand for labor.   Statement e is not correct because the marginal product of labor is a component of the demand for labor, not the supply. Furthermore, if the marginal product of workers was negative, no firm would hire them.

2. Correct answer: e.

Discussion: A higher wage rate may induce some workers to work fewer hours (because they can maintain the same income at a higher wage but working fewer hours) and thus take more leisure time. Some workers may do the opposite -- they may choose to work more hours and thereby increase their earnings substantially. The choice depends on the workers' preferences for leisure time over income (and thus increased consumption and saving). A higher wage rate also has the effect of attracting workers to the profession. Many students choose college majors based on what they expect the wage (salary) to be for that particular job when they graduate. Higher expected wages tend to attract students into those majors. A higher wage rate also causes people to move to those places where they can earn a higher wage.

3. Correct answer: c.

Discussion: A decrease in the wage rate creates a substitution effect -- the firm finds it less costly to use labor to help produce output than to use other relatively more expensive inputs. Thus, the firm will decide to use more labor and fewer of the other inputs, (e.g. conveyor belt) as a less costly, alternative way to produce output.

Statement a is not correct because it is not an explanation for why the demand curve is negatively sloped. It is also not a correct statement because a higher wage (unless it is an efficiency wage that creates offsetting productivity gains) typically reduces a firm's profits. Statement b is not correct because it is a reference to labor supply not labor demand. Statement d is not correct because it is not an explanation for why the demand curve is negatively sloped. Since statements a, b, and d are not correct, statement e cannot be correct.

4. Correct answer: b.

Discussion: The substitution effect says that an increase in the price of labor (the wage rate) will increase the amount of hours worked and at the same time, decrease the amount of leisure time an individual takes would lead to a decrease in the amount of hours worked and an increase in leisure time. This works in reverse as well. When the wage rate declines, the amount of hours worked will also decline and correspondingly the amount of leisure time taken will increase. The reason according to the substitution effect is that when the wage rate is lower, the opportunity cost of not working (taking leisure) declines. Thus, since it is, in effect, less costly to take leisure, more of it will be taken.

5. Correct answer: b.

Discussion: The income effect works the opposite of the substitution effect. A decrease in the wage rate, because it reduces the real income, reduces the demand for goods.

Statement a is not correct because the income effect says that a decrease in the wage rate will cause individuals to work more (in order to maintain their previous income). When an individual works more, he has less time for leisure. Thus statement c is also incorrect since according to the income effect, a decrease in the wage rate will decrease the demand for leisure time. Statement d is not correct. The income effect is a concept related to the supply of labor, not the demand for labor. Statement e is not correct since statement b is the correct answer.

6. Correct answer: d.

Discussion: Labor is likely to be most expensive in countries where the population is relatively small and/or where the skill level of workers is high. Conversely, labor is likely to be less expensive in countries where labor is abundant (big population) and/or the skill level of workers is low. India, Haiti, Mexico, and the

Philippines are all countries with big populations and low skilled-workers. Italy, a Western European country, has relatively more skilled workers and a relatively smaller population.

7. Correct answer: b.

Discussion: The big increase in the number of lawyers passing the Bar exam would be represented by a rightward shift in the supply of lawyers. The shift would have the effect of lowering the equilibrium wage (salary) paid to lawyers. As the wage decreased, the quantity of lawyers demanded (movement along the labor demand curve) would increase.

Statement a is not correct because the demand for lawyers does not increase (i.e. labor demand does not shift to the right); the quantity of lawyers demanded increases (movement along the labor demand curve). Statements c and d are not correct because the wage rate decreases, not increases. Statement e is not correct because statement a is not correct.

8. Correct answer: e.

Discussion: Statement a will cause an increase in the demand for labor. When the price of output that labor produces increases, the marginal revenue each worker generates for the firm increases and thus workers become more valuable to the firm. This would lead to an increase in the demand for labor. Statement b will also cause an increase in the demand for labor. More productive (higher marginal product) workers are more beneficial to a firm (generate more output and thus more revenue). Thus, firms will demand more labor when workers' productivity increases. Statement c will also cause an increase in the demand for labor. When capital becomes more expensive, firms will decide to substitute labor in production for capital (since labor would be relatively less costly). Statement d will cause a decrease in the quantity of labor demanded. That is, a minimum wage policy causes a movement along the demand curve, but not a shift in the demand for labor (decrease in demand).

9. Correct answer: e.

Discussion: Higher wages are paid to workers who have skills that few people have. This is why chemical engineers are paid more than a clerk at a shoe store. Doctors, professors, lawyers, veterinarians, etc. all are professions which entail more than a college education and thus are more costly professions to enter. Jobs with undesirable features (perhaps risky jobs like oil rig drillers) tend to be paid more because there are fewer people willing to work in dangerous situations. Thus, the supply of labor in these professions is typically not as large as in say, retail sales, and the wages are thus correspondingly higher. Licensing restrictions limit the supply of workers in the licensed professions. This too leads to correspondingly higher wages.

10. Correct answer: d.

Discussion: Statement d has not been used as an explanation for the gender and race gap. The gender and race gap in earnings is that women and blacks typically earn less than a white male counterpart that is doing the same job. The difference in earnings has been explained in several ways (that are not necessarily mutually exclusive). The gender gap may be due to the fact that women and blacks typically have less education and less work experience than white males. That is, these groups of workers, on average, are less valuable to a firm than a worker with more education and work experience. Gender and race discrimination have also been suggested as explanations for the earnings gaps between men and women and white males and black males.

11. Correct answer: e.

Discussion: All of the above are true. Statement a provides evidence that workers who have more education are better paid. Statement b is an example of the "screening" or "signaling" effect that graduation from college provides to potential employers. Statement c suggests that a college education produces workers with higher skills and thereby, admission into better paid professions. Statement d suggests that workers in fields like engineering and computer technology have seen (and may continue to see) increases in wages bigger than those in other professions.

12. Correct answer: c.

Discussion: A minimum wage is a floor below which the wage may not drop. A minimum wage law set at $5.25/hour is a policy that will not permit the wage to drop below that rate. Since the current wage is $5.00/hour, the minimum wage policy raises the wage to $5.25/hour. The increase in the wage rate reduces the quantity of labor demanded (movement along the demand curve) and thus causes a loss of jobs. An increase in the wage rate also raises the quantity of labor supplied (movement along the supply curve). A minimum wage of $4.50/hour is not effective because the equilibrium wage is $5.00/hour. Since $5.00/hour is an equilibrium wage, there is no tendency for it to drop below $5.00/hour. Thus, a restriction that the wage not be permitted to fall below $4.50 is meaningless. This means that the policy will not have an effect on the quantity of labor demanded or supplied or on the equilibrium wage of $5.00/hour. Thus, statement c is the only correct answer.

13. Correct answer: c.

Discussion: Occupational licensing requirements typically place restrictions on workers in the profession. Workers typically must fulfill a certain set of conditions in order to become licensed or remain licensed. The conditions may be that the workers meet certain educational requirements or a specified number of hours spent on the job per year.

Statement a is not correct because a minimum wage typically raises the price of output that minimum wage workers produce. This is because a minimum wage typically raises a firm's cost of production (without leading to increased worker productivity), which in turn is passed on to consumers in the form of higher prices. Statement b is not correct because an industrial union is made up of all types of workers from a particular industry. An autoworkers union may include janitors to assembly line operators to auto designers that work in the auto industry. A craft union is made up of workers from a particular occupation such as electricians (regardless of what industry they work in). Statement d is not correct because a labor union is a seller of labor in the labor market. A monopsonist in the labor market is defined as a single buyer of labor (not seller). Since statement c is true, statement e cannot be correct.

14. Correct answer: e.

Discussion: All of the above are true. However, while occupational licensing schemes are designed to protect consumers from incompetent workers, such schemes may not always be effective. To wit, there are surgeons who are licensed to practice who have amputated the wrong leg or removed the wrong kidney from a patient.

15. Correct answer: b.

Discussion: Statement b is not true. The Taft-Hartley Act gave the government the power to break up strikes if they imperiled national health or safety. For example, former president Ronald Reagan fired all striking air traffic controllers and hired non-union air traffic controllers since such a strike imperiled air safety. All of the other statements are true.

16. Correct answer: e.

Labor unions (of which the AFL-CIO is the umbrella organization) attempt to increase the wages of their members as well as to improve working conditions and enhance fringe benefits. Unions do this through (1) negotiation with the firm (which may lead to a strike as part of the negotiation tactic), (2) by creating a demand for the product they produce (remember that the demand for labor is a derived demand; the stronger the demand for output, the higher the wage paid to employees that produce the output), and/or (3) through featherbedding (dictating that a firm must hire so many workers for a particular task). That is, featherbedding is designed to increase the demand for labor and thus the wage. Featherbedding, however, can backfire and actually reduce the wage paid to workers. This can happen if featherbedding leads to higher production costs and thus a higher price for the output the workers produce. If the price of the output rises, the amount sold will decline and this will have a tendency to reduce the demand for labor and thus the wage.

17. Correct answer: a.

Discussion: Efficiency wages may lead workers to work harder (and thus not shirk), but also to reduce the frequency with which they call in sick and their desire to quit the job. When Henry Ford raised the wage he paid his workers from $3/ day to $5/day, he effectively paid them an efficiency wage since the going market rate was $3/day.

Statement b is not true because featherbedding raises costs of production. Statement c is not correct because employees know more about their own productivity and skill level than does a potential employer. Statement d is not correct; a labor market is a mixed market meaning that both high and low-skill workers exist in the market and it can be difficult for a firm to know which type of worker it is hiring. Statement e is not correct because a monopsonist uses its power in the market to reduce the wage rate.

VIII. ANSWER KEY: ESSAY QUESTIONS

1. An increase in the demand for graphic designers would be represented by a rightward shift in the demand for graphic designers. The increased demand for graphic designers would raise the wage above $11/hour. The degree to which the wage rises depends on how elastic the labor supply curve is. In the short run, the supply of labor is less elastic than in the long run. This means that the short run supply of graphic designers will be steeper than the long run supply of graphic designers. In the short run, the influence of migration and choice of graphic designer as an occupation cannot be felt on the labor market. That is, the short run is a time period that is not long enough to allow for individuals to migrate to Charlotte to fill the increased demand for graphic designers or for college students and others to alter their career decisions so that they can be hired as a graphic designer. Thus, the increased demand puts a lot more pressure on the wage to rise (because of the limited response on the supply side). If the short run elasticity of supply is 0.5% and the demand for graphic designers increased by 10%, then the increase in the wage rate would be 20%. The formula to be used is analogous to the elasticity of demand formula that was covered in Chapter 5 of your textbook and is reviewed in Chapter 5 of the Practicum. The formula is:

    $$\text{Elasticity (E)} = \%\Delta Q / \%\Delta P$$

    where in this case, you know that the elasticity of supply is 0.5% and that the $\%\Delta Q$ is 10% since that is how many more graphic designers are demanded. Since we are analyzing the labor market, the $\%\Delta P$ is the $\%\Delta$wage. (The wage rate is the price of labor). Thus, plugging in the numbers and solving for $\%\Delta P$ yields:

    $$\%\Delta P \text{ (i.e. wage)} = \%\Delta Q / E = 10\%/0.5 = 20\%.$$

    Thus, in the short run, the wage rises by 20% which in dollar terms is equal to (0.20 X $11/hour) = $2.20. The new wage, in the short run, is $13.20/hour.

    In the long run, the higher wage and demand for graphic designers causes people to migrate to Charlotte and enter the profession of graphic design. This takes some pressure off of the wage. With a long run elasticity of supply is 2, the equilibrium wage in the long run will change by:

    $$\%\Delta P = 10\%/2 = 5\%$$

    Thus, in the long run, the wage rises by 5% which in dollar terms is equal to (0.05 X $11/hour) = $0.55. The new wage, in the long run, is $11.55/hour.

    In the long run, the wage rises by less than in the short run because the increased demand for graphic designers is matched by a bigger pool of available graphic designers. Existing firms do not have to compete as strongly with each other (by offering better wage rates) in order to attract graphic designers to work for them as they do in the short run when the pool of available graphic designers is limited.

2. Unions (which came into being in the late 1800s) are organized groups of employees that attempt to negotiate with the firm for higher wages, better working conditions, and better benefits. Unions also attempt to maintain employment for the union members. Since a union is an organization within a firm, the union has more power than an individual in negotiating with the management of the firm.

While unions attempt to increase the wages of the union members, they confront a problem. A negotiation for higher wages may raise production costs and thus the price of the output the firm sells. If the higher price reduces the amount of output the firm is able to sell, the firm has an incentive to layoff workers. (Remember that the demand for labor is derived from how much output and at what price the output can be sold). Naturally, unions want to avoid any loss of employment for their union members. This is why some unions try to hold membership down. A smaller membership means that a firm would have to think twice about laying off some of its workers because these employees are vital to the firm's operation. Without them, the firm may not be able to operate at all.

Unions also recognize that there are other ways to increase wages without directly asking for higher wages. Unions may promote products produced under the union label. That is, unions attempt (through advertising) to increase the demand for the product(s) that they produce. Unions may also advocate work rules that establish how many workers must be used to fulfill certain tasks. This is called "featherbedding." For example, unions may dictate that a roadside construction crew consists of 4 workers when perhaps 3 could do the job just as well. Featherbedding thus leads to an artificially increased demand for labor and supposedly would lead to a higher wage -- just what the union is after in the first place. However, featherbedding can backfire. If featherbedding leads to higher production costs and thereby a higher price for the output the workers are producing, the demand for labor could actually decline. This is because a higher price of output will reduce the amount of output sold and thus fewer workers are needed.

In terms of a graph, featherbedding is designed to shift out (to the right) the demand for labor. Thus, the wage will rise and employment will increase. However, as the price of output rises, the demand for labor shifts back in (to the left). If the price increase is big enough, the demand for labor could shift back in by enough that the new wage and employment level are below what the initial wage and employment level were.

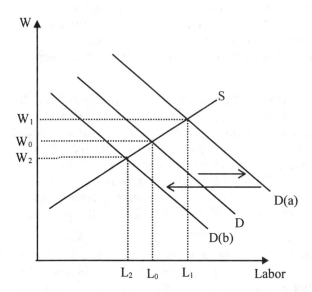

To see this, look at the graph above. The curves labeled S and D are the initial supply and demand curves prior to featherbedding. The hoped for impact of featherbedding is to increase the demand for labor to D(a). However, as the price of output rises (because of production cost increases associated with the featherbedding), the demand curve may shift back to D or even worse D(b). At D(b), the new equilibrium wage and employment level is below what the starting wage and employment level were.

One of the assumptions so far has been that the higher wage that union members are paid is not offset by an increase in union member productivity. That is, the higher wage (without any corresponding rise in worker productivity) is what leads to higher production costs and a higher price for the output, which, unfortunately for the union, reduces the demand for labor. However, this turn of events can be avoided if the higher wage leads to more productive workers. That is, if the higher wage is offset by employees becoming more productive, the firm's production costs may not increase and thus the price at which output is sold need not necessarily increase with the higher wage rate. There are two ways in which union members may have an incentive to be more productive. First, since the union promotes communication between the management of the firm and the workers, workers may be more satisfied on the job because any problems they have may be dealt with more swiftly by management. Furthermore, the more satisfied workers are, the less likely they are to quit. Thus, turnover rates of union members may be lower. This translates to more experienced workers (the longer one stays on the job the more experienced he becomes). More experienced workers are assumed to be more productive. Second, the higher wage may be viewed as an "efficiency" wage in the sense that the higher wage motivates workers to work hard (so as to keep their well-paying jobs).

Take It to the Net

CHAPTER 10
MEASURING A NATION'S PRODUCTION AND INCOME

I. OVERVIEW

In this chapter, you will learn about Gross Domestic Product (GDP) -- a measure of a nation's total production. You will also learn about national income -- a measure of a nation's total income. You will see, through the circular flow diagram, that a nation's production and its income are related. You will learn about the way GDP is measured and the basic categories that the government defines in calculating GDP. You will learn about the way national income is measured and what constitutes it. You will learn about the difference between nominal and real GDP by revisiting the reality principle. Along the way, you will also learn about the GDP deflator, which is one price index that tracks inflation. Finally, you will consider whether GDP is a good measure of a nation's welfare. And, you will learn about some problems with obtaining an accurate measure of a nation's production.

II. CHECKLIST

By the end of this chapter, you should be able to:

√ Explain the study of macroeconomics.

√ Define a recession.

√ Define gross domestic product (GDP).

√ Explain why intermediate goods are not included in GDP.

√ Give two reasons why nominal GDP can change.

√ Describe the four main categories of purchasers of GDP.

√ Discuss the subcategories of consumption expenditures, private investment expenditures, government expenditures, and net exports.

√ Define depreciation.

√ Discuss the distinction between "investment" to economists and "investment" in common parlance.

√ Define transfer payments and explain why they are not considered a government purchase of GDP.

√ Explain why imports are subtracted from purchases of GDP and exports are added to purchases of GDP.

√ Define a trade deficit and explain how it relates to foreigners' purchases of U.S. assets.

√ Explain the relationship between GDP and GNP.

√ Define value added.

√ Describe the five main categories of national income.

√ Define personal income and personal disposable income.

√ Define and be able to calculate the GDP deflator.

√ Explain the difference between real and nominal GDP and which measure is used for assessing economic growth.

√ Explain the limitations of GDP (what it does not measure) and explain whether or not these limitations lead to an over or underestimate of GDP.

III. KEY TERMS

Macroeconomics: the branch of economics that looks at the economy as a whole.

Gross Domestic Product (GDP): the total market value of all the final goods and services produced within an economy in a given year.

Intermediate goods: goods used in the production process that are not final goods or services.

Real GDP: a measure of GDP that controls for changes in prices.

Nominal GDP: the value of GDP in current dollars.

Economic growth: sustained increases in the real production of an economy over a period of time.

Capital: the buildings, machines, and equipment used in production.

Consumption expenditures: purchases of newly produced goods and services by households.

Non-durable goods: goods that last for short periods of time, such as food.

Durable goods: goods that last for a long period of time, such as household appliances.

Services: reflect work done in which individuals play a prominent role in delivery and range from haircutting to health care.

Private investment expenditures: purchases of newly produced goods and services by firms.

Depreciation: the wear and tear of capital as it is used in production.

Gross investment: actual investment purchases.

Net investment: gross investment minus depreciation.

Government purchases: purchases of final goods and services by all levels of government.

Net exports: exports minus imports.

Trade surplus: another name for net exports or exports minus imports.

Trade deficit: negative net exports or imports minus exports.

Transfer payments: payments to individuals from governments that do not correspond to the production of goods and services.

Gross National Product (GNP): GDP plus net income earned abroad.

Net National Product: GNP less depreciation.

Indirect taxes: sales and excise taxes.

National Income: Net National Product less indirect taxes.

Value-added: the sum of all the income (wages, interest, profits, rent) generated by an organization.

Personal income: income (including transfer payments) that is received by households.

Personal disposable income: personal income after taxes.

Chain index: a method for calculating changes in prices that uses base years from neighboring years.

IV. PERFORMANCE ENHANCING TIPS (PETS)

PET #1

Nominal GDP may increase because of an increase in the price level and/or because of an increase in output (production). Real GDP may increase because of an increase in output (production).

Nominal GDP is the "market value" or "current-dollar" (today's prices) measure of the amount of output an economy in total produced over a given time period (usually a year). If prices rise, without any increase in the amount of output produced, nominal GDP will increase. Such an increase, however, should in no way be construed as economic growth since output did not grow at all.

To make an analogy, suppose you are the financial analyst for a particular firm and you observe that its revenue has increased. The firm's revenue may have increased either because (1) the price at which the firm sells its output has increased; (2) the firm sold more output (while there was no increase in price); or (3) some combination of the two.

The same is true of nominal GDP. However, economic analysts and policymakers are interested in what has happened to output exclusively. This is because an increase in output typically means that more people were employed and/or that labor was more productive and this is good news for the economy. Nominal GDP unfortunately isn't an accurate picture of what has happened to output because a change in nominal GDP is influenced by what has happened to prices as well as production. Real GDP, which takes out the effects of price changes on nominal GDP, gives a more accurate picture of what has happened to production.

PET #2

Economic growth is measured by the percentage change in real GDP, not by the percentage change in nominal GDP.

Suppose you calculate the growth rate of real GDP to be 3.2% and the growth rate of nominal GDP to be 6%. Which measure is appropriate to evaluate economic growth and what can you infer about inflation?

The appropriate measure of economic growth is the rate of change in real GDP. In this case, we would say that the economy grew by 3.2%. Since nominal GDP increased by 6%, we could infer that the inflation rate was roughly 2.8% (= 6% - 3.2%). We should not say that the economy grew by 6%.

PET #3

The expenditure approach to measuring U.S. GDP is to sum up the purchases, whether purchases of U.S. or foreign-produced goods and services, by U.S. consumers (or "households"), businesses and the government, add expenditures by foreign residents on goods and services produced in the U.S (exports of the U.S.) and subtract expenditures by U.S. consumers, businesses, and the government on foreign-produced goods and services (imports of the U.S.).

Your professor may write it as:

GDP = C + I + G + EX - IM

where:

C = consumption expenditures by households on goods and services whether produced domestically or abroad.

I = gross investment expenditures by firms. This is primarily spending on plant and equipment, whether produced domestically or abroad.

G = government expenditures on goods and services, whether produced domestically or abroad.

EX = exports.

IM = imports.

PET #4

An increase in businesses' inventories reflects production that took place in the current year and should be added to GDP, even though the output was not purchased. A decrease in businesses' inventories reflects purchases of output that was produced in a prior year and should be subtracted from GDP.

PET #5

Net investment that is positive is the addition to a nation's stock of capital above and beyond its current level. Net investment that is zero means that a nation's stock of capital is neither increasing nor decreasing beyond its current level. Net investment that is negative means that a nation is not investing enough to replace capital that is being worn out.

To illustrate the difference between gross investment and net investment, consider the stock of shoes that you currently have. Suppose you have 10 pairs of shoes. Over the course of the year, 3 of the pairs wear out (depreciate) and are no longer any good. If you buy 7 more pairs of shoes that year, your gross investment in shoes is 7 pairs. However, because you are replacing 3 pairs that have worn out, your net investment in shoes is 4 pairs. That is, at the end of the year, you will now have 14 pairs of shoes. You have, on net, added 4 (7-3) pairs to the stock of 10 pairs of shoes that you started out with.

Suppose instead that you bought 3 pairs of shoes that year. While three pairs would be your gross investment, your net investment would be zero. You have only replaced what you have worn out. Thus, you are no better off at the end of the year since your stock of shoes remains at 10 pairs.

Now, suppose that you bought 1 pair of shoes that year. While three pairs would be your gross investment, your net investment would be -2 (1-3). You have not invested enough to replace the 3 pairs of shoes worn out. Thus, your stock of shoes will decline from 10 pairs to 8 pairs.

The same is true for a country. A country whose net investment is zero will not be adding to its capital stock; a country that is not replacing its worn out capital will see its capital stock shrink. As you will see in later chapters, this can have implications for the rate of growth an economy will be able to achieve.

PET #6

Government purchases of GDP is government spending on goods and services for which there was productive effort. Thus, government spending on transfer payments (e.g. social security, unemployment compensation) and interest on the national debt are not part of the government purchases included in GDP.

While your textbook makes this PET quite clear, it is worth repeating.

PET #7

A country that runs a trade deficit (the value of imports is greater than the value of exports) is on net borrowing from foreigners. A country that runs a trade surplus (the value of exports is greater than the value of imports) is on net lending to foreigners.

For example, suppose the U.S. has a trade deficit of $100 billion. This means that the U.S. is not earning enough foreign currency on its exports to cover payments in foreign currency on its imports. Where can the U.S. get the extra $100 billion in foreign currency to cover the trade deficit? The U.S. must borrow the funds from foreigners (i.e. foreigners lend foreign currency to the U.S). Since residents of the U.S. can also lend to foreigners, we say that the trade deficit implies that the U.S. is borrowing $100 billion more from foreigners than it is lending to them. In other words, on net the U.S. is borrowing from foreigners.

Another way of saying that the U.S. is on net borrowing from foreigners is to say that foreigners are on net lending to the U.S. They are lending to the U.S. by taking their savings and using them to buy U.S. assets (e.g. U.S. stocks and bonds). As an analogy, if you buy a bond from a company, you are in effect, lending your savings to the company and the company is borrowing from you.

The reverse holds true for a country with a trade surplus.

V.   PRACTICE EXAM: MULTIPLE CHOICE QUESTIONS

1. Which one of the following would NOT be considered a macroeconomic issue?

   a) inflation.

   b) economic growth.

   c) international trade.

   d) national unemployment.

   e) consumer behavior.

2. The output of an economy is called:

   a) market goods.

   b) gross domestic product.

   c) national volume.

   d) the net balance.

   e) national product.

3. GDP is the total market value of:

   a) all final goods and services sold in an economy in a given year.

   b) all goods and services purchased by households in a given year.

   c) all final goods and services produced within an economy since 1900.

   d) all goods and services produced within the borders of a country in a given year.

   e) intermediate and final goods produced in a given year.

4. Which one of the following would NOT be included in current GDP?

   a) the purchase of a new jet ski.

   b) services rendered by a financial planner.

   c) a trip to Hilton Head.

   d) the purchase of a two-year old used set of Ping golf clubs.

   e) the purchase of flour by a househusband or housewife.

5. The most common measure of economic growth is:

   a) changes in real GDP because only changes in output are measured.

   b) changes in nominal GDP because it considers changes in both output and prices.

   c) changes in the consumer price index because it measures changes in the income of a typical family of four.

   d) changes in the chain-type price index because it measures the ability of the economy to respond to higher costs of production.

   e) changes in labor productivity since it measures whether workers' standard of living is changing.

6. Which one of the following defines a "recession"?

   a) a one-month decline in real GDP.

   b) a protracted period of low economic growth.

   c) a decline in real GDP that lasts for six consecutive months or longer.

   d) a growth rate of real GDP that is negative.

   e) the movement of real GDP from trough to peak.

7. Which one of the following would NOT be considered a component of GDP?

   a) spending by a household on a used television set.

   b) spending by the government on social security benefits.

   c) a decline in the level of businesses' inventories over last year.

   d) spending by a firm on a foreign-made piece of equipment.

   e) none of the above.

8. Which one of the following sectors purchases the largest share of GDP?

   a) consumers.

   b) firms.

   c) the government.

   d) foreigners.

   e) proprietors.

9. Which one of the following statements is true?

   a) durable goods are those that last for a short period of time.

   b) an example of a non-durable good is a dishwasher.

   c) services are the fastest growing component of consumption spending.

   d) net investment = gross investment + depreciation.

   e) an example of investment in economics would be the purchase of a stock.

10. Which one of the following would give a correct measure of GDP?

    Let C = consumption expenditures, I = gross investment expenditures, G = government expenditures, EX = exports, and IM = imports.

    a) GDP = C + I + G + EX + IM.

    b) GDP = C + I + G + EX - IM.

    c) GDP = C + I + G.

    d) GDP = C + I + G - EX - IM.

    e) GDP = C + I - G + EX + IM.

11. If the U.S. runs a trade surplus,

    a) U.S. exports are greater than U.S. imports.

    b) U.S. imports are greater than U.S. exports.

    c) the U.S. is a net lender to foreign countries.

    d) U.S. sales of assets to foreigners are greater than U.S. purchases of assets from foreigners.

    e) (a) and (c).

12. Which one of the following is NOT included in national income?

    a) wages.

    b) savings by households.

    c) corporate profits.

    d) net interest earnings.

    e) rental income.

13. Which one of the following statements is true?

    a) GDP calculations include the value of services performed by a homemaker such as cleaning or cooking.

    b) under the table transactions lead to an overestimate of GDP.

    c) personal income is the sum of all payments made to households minus taxes they paid to the government.

    d) manufactured goods are the fasted growing component of consumption expenditures.

    e) the GDP deflator is calculated as (nominal GDP divided by real GDP) x 100.

VI.   PRACTICE EXAM: ESSAY QUESTIONS

1. Suppose you are an economic advisor to a tiny island country that produces only volleyballs. As part of your job, you must help the president of the island prepare the "State of the Island" address. In the first quarter of 2001, you find that island produced a market value (or current dollar value) of $1,000,000 volleyballs. In the second quarter of 2001, the island produced a market value of $1,200,000 of volleyballs. Furthermore, your statistics tell you that annual inflation (based on the GDP deflator) for the tiny island country from the first quarter to the second quarter of 2001 was 80%. What would you tell your president to report in her "State of the Island" address?

2. Discuss the four components of spending on GDP and explain why intermediate goods purchased by businesses are not included in GDP.

VII. ANSWER KEY: MULTIPLE CHOICE QUESTIONS

1. Correct answer: e.

Discussion: Consumer behavior is an issue studied in microeconomics. Statements a-d are all macroeconomic issues.

2. Correct answer: b.

Discussion: No discussion necessary.

3. Correct answer: d.

Discussion: GDP is the total market value of all final goods and services produced within the borders of a country in a given year. The terms that are bolded in the sentence are important to the definition.

Statement a is not correct because GDP is a measure of what is produced, not what is sold, in a given year. There may be goods sold in a given year that were produced in a prior year. These goods would be "used goods" and should not be part of current year GDP. Statement b is not correct because GDP is the purchase of final (for end use) goods and services. Households and businesses purchase goods and services for end use. For example, a business may purchase a computer for its use. Statement c is not correct because GDP is the value of what is produced in a particular (or given) year. It is not the sum of the value of production since the turn of the century. Statement e is not correct because GDP does not include the market value of intermediate goods (such as plastics used in auto production or wood used in furniture).

4. Correct answer: d.

Discussion: GDP is a measure of the value of goods and services produced in a given year. Since the golf clubs are used, they were produced two years ago and hence should not be included in current GDP.

Statements a, b, c, and e are all examples of either goods or services purchased for "end use." In other words, they are "final" goods or services.

5. Correct answer: a.

Discussion: Economic growth is measured as the percentage change in real GDP, typically reported on an annualized basis. Real GDP takes out the effects of price changes on nominal GDP. (See PET #1 of this chapter for review).

Statement b is not correct because nominal GDP is influenced by not only changes in output (production) but changes in prices as well. Changes in prices do not reflect economic growth and so should not be considered. This last sentence also means that statements c and d are not correct. Statement e is not correct although labor productivity and economic growth are related.

6. Correct answer: c.

Discussion: A recession is a decline in real GDP that lasts for six months or longer. This also means that economic growth would be negative for two quarters.

Statement a is not correct because decline in real GDP must last at least six months, not just one month. Statement b is not correct. Low (but positive) economic growth does not define a recession. Statement d is not correct because it needs a qualifier on how many quarters there was negative growth. For example, a one-quarter negative growth rate would not constitute a recession. Statement e is not correct because a movement from trough to peak would define an economic expansion.

7. Correct answer: e.

Discussion: Only spending for goods and services produced domestically, this year, is a component of GDP. Spending on a used television set constitutes spending this year on a prior year's production. Spending by the government on social security benefits is spending on a good or service for which there is no underlying productive effort and thus does not constitute spending on this year's GDP. A decline in businesses' inventories over last year means that businesses sold goods this year that were produced in a prior year. (Likewise, an addition to businesses' inventories means that there were goods produced this year that did not get sold this year -- an addition to inventories that is included in GDP). Spending by a firm (or individual) on a foreign-made good or service (imports) constitutes spending on good or service not produced in the domestic (home) country. Thus, such spending does not reflect spending on domestically-produced GDP.

8. Correct answer: a.

Discussion: Consumers are, by far, the largest spending sector in the U.S. economy. The government is a larger spending sector than are firms.

9. Correct answer: c.

Discussion: Services are the fastest growing component of consumption spending. This is partly driven by demographic changes.

Statement a is not correct; durable goods are goods that last a long time. Statement b is not correct. In fact, a dishwasher is an example of a durable good. Most households will keep a new dishwasher at least three years. Statement d is not correct. Net investment = gross investment minus depreciation. Statement e is not correct. In economics, investment is defined as the purchase of plant, machinery, and equipment. Investment in economics, is not "financial investment."

10. Correct answer: b.

Discussion: Remember that GDP is the total dollar value of the goods and services an economy produces in a given year. That production is purchased by consumers, businesses, the government and foreigners. Thus, it must be a truism that the total dollar value of production equals the total dollar value of spending on that production. However, since consumers, businesses, and the government can also purchase foreign-made goods and services (termed "imports"), we must subtract these out of C, I and G in order to have a measure of spending by consumers, businesses, and the government on only domestically-produced goods and services (which constitute GDP). We add spending by foreigners on domestically-produced goods and services (termed "exports") to spending by the other sectors of the economy to arrive at the total amount of spending for the goods and services our economy has produced in a given year.

11. Correct answer: e.

Discussion: A trade surplus is defined as an excess of exports over imports. Thus, statement a is correct and means that the U.S. is selling more goods and services to foreigners than it is in total purchasing from foreign countries. Alternatively, this means that foreigners are purchasing more goods and services from the U.S. than they are selling to us. This means that through trade, foreigners are not earning enough dollars on their sales of goods and services to the U.S. to pay for their purchases of goods and services from the U.S. The way in which foreign countries can finance their trade deficits is for them to borrow dollars from the U.S. In other words, the U.S. (the trade surplus country in this example) is on net lending dollars to foreign countries. Thus, statements a and c are correct.

Statement b is not correct; it would imply a trade deficit. Statement d is not correct. Statement d is a way of saying that the U.S. would be on net borrowing from foreign countries (i.e. issuing bonds, etc. -- assets -- that foreigners are in turn, buying). If foreigners were buying U.S. assets, they would be in effect lending to the U.S. (This would imply that the U.S. had a trade deficit).

You may wish to review PET #7 of this chapter.

12. Correct answer: b.

Discussion: National income is the sum of wages and benefits, corporate profits, proprietors' income, interest earnings, and rental income. Saving does not make up national income. It, however, comes from national income. That is, a country can save from its national income.

13. Correct answer: e.

Discussion: Statement e is correct. For example, if nominal GDP in the year 2000 was $8 trillion dollars and real GDP in the same year was $7.5 trillion dollars, the GDP deflator would be $[8/7.5] \times 100 = 106.7$. This means that, compared to the base year (where the GDP deflator is 100), prices of goods and services included in GDP increased on average by about 6.7%.

Statement a is not correct. GDP calculations do not consider the value of services provided by a homemaker. If the value of services (such as laundry service, cleaning service, chauffeur, etc.) provided by homemakers were considered, the GDP figures would be higher. In fact, it is estimated that a homemaker's services should be valued at roughly $40,000. Statement b is not correct because under the table transactions are unrecorded. They escape government calculations and hence government statistics. It is believed that if the value of these transactions were recorded they would add an additional 7% to GDP (since they do constitute production of a good or service). Statement c is not correct; personal disposable income is personal income minus taxes paid. Personal income is all payments earned by households prior to paying taxes. Statement d is not correct because services, not manufactured goods, are the fastest growing component of consumption expenditures.

VIII. ANSWER KEY: ESSAY QUESTIONS

1. First of all, the figures on the market value of output are in current dollars and thus are measures of the island's nominal GDP. The growth rate in nominal GDP between the first and second quarter is [($200,000)/$1,000,000] X 100 = 20%. The 20% figure, if annualized as is common for reporting of GDP growth rates, would be 20% X 4 = 80%. So, on an annualized basis, nominal GDP has increased by 80%. However, nominal GDP can increase because (1) output (production of volleyballs) has increased; (2) the price of volleyballs has increased; or (3) some combination of the two. Since inflation (increase in prices) does not constitute economic growth, the growth rate in nominal GDP should not be used to assess whether or not the economy has grown. The effects of higher prices on the nominal GDP growth rate must be taken out. Since you also know that inflation, on an annualized basis for your country was 80% between the first and second quarter of 2001, you can infer what has happened to the growth rate of output (real GDP). The growth rate of real GDP can be roughly measured as the difference between the growth rate of nominal GDP and the GDP deflator inflation rate. Thus, you would report that the growth rate in real GDP for the island was 0%. So, you would tell the president to sadly report that the economy did not grow. Moreover, the economy suffered double-digit inflation on the order of 80% on an annualized basis (or 20% = (80%/4) on a quarterly basis).

2. The four components of spending on GDP (I will consider U.S. GDP) are:

   (1) Consumption expenditures. This is spending by U.S. households on final goods and services, whether the goods and services are produced in the U.S. or abroad. That is, some consumption expenditures by U.S. households are for foreign-produced goods and services. For example, suppose that consumption expenditures in the U.S. totaled $5 trillion; further if $1 trillion of the spending was on foreign-produced goods and services, then we could say that households purchased $4 trillion worth of U.S. produced goods and services.

   (2) Investment expenditures. Investment expenditures have several components. The main component of investment spending is spending by businesses on plant and equipment. Businesses, of course, can purchase U.S.-produced equipment or foreign-made equipment. A second component of investment expenditures is residential housing. Purchases of new housing are considered investment expenditures even though households, not businesses, are typically the buyers. A third component of investment expenditures is "inventory investment." When businesses decide to add to their inventories from last year, they are investing in their inventory. Businesses may choose to build up their inventories in anticipation of a strong sales year.

(3) Government expenditures. This is spending by the government on goods and services for which there was productive effort. The government buys legal services from lawyers, paper from paper manufacturers, computers from computer manufacturers, guns from gun manufacturers, and so on. The government, too, can buy from U.S. manufacturers or from foreign manufacturers.

(4) Net Exports. This is spending by foreigners on U.S. made goods and services minus spending by U.S. entities on foreign-made goods and services. Since items (1), (2), and (3) above contain spending by households, businesses, and the government on foreign-made goods and services, these must be subtracted out to arrive at an estimate of how much spending was undertaken by U.S. households, businesses, and the government on only U.S. produced goods and services (i.e. U.S. GDP). However, since foreigners can purchase U.S. output just as U.S. residents purchase U.S. output, we must also include export spending in constructing a measure of GDP.

In sum, U.S. GDP is equal to consumption expenditures plus investment expenditures plus government expenditures plus exports minus imports.

The purchase of intermediate goods by businesses is not a component of GDP. To do so would lead to double-counting (which would lead to an overestimate of GDP). Here's why. Suppose you buy a computer system and pay $2,000 for it. The $2,000 price tag reflects the value of all of the production that went into producing the computer and making it available to a retail store where it can be sold to you. Thus, the $2,000 price tag is a measure of all of the production that has taken place. This number is used in computing GDP.

Suppose that of the $2,000 price tag on the computer system, $1,300 was due to the components used in the computer system. (We'll assume the components were produced in the U.S). If we included the $1,300 in addition to the $2,000 in computing U.S. GDP, we would be double-counting the value of production that has actually taken place. The $2,000 already reflects $1,300 worth of production.

Take It to the Net

We invite you to visit the O'Sullivan/Sheffrin page on the Prentice Hall Web site at:

http://www.prenhall.com/osullivan/

for this chapter's World Wide Web exercise.

CHAPTER 11
UNEMPLOYMENT AND INFLATION

I. OVERVIEW

In this chapter, you will learn about unemployment and inflation. You will learn about different types of unemployment and the problems they present for the economy. You will learn about the problems that inflation creates for a society. You will learn how the unemployment rate and the inflation rate are measured. You will see that these statistics may not always portray the most accurate picture of the state of the economy. You will learn that limitations to these statistics are caused by the difficulties in accurately measuring prices around the country and who exactly is unemployed. You will learn how the government compiles information on the unemployed. You will learn about "discouraged workers" and the "underemployed." You will learn how the government compiles information on the consumer price index (CPI) and how this measure of the price level differs from the chain-type price index. Finally, you will learn why the percentage change in the CPI may overstate inflation.

II. CHECKLIST

By the end of this chapter, you should be able to:

√ Define the unemployed.

√ Define the labor force.

√ Distinguish the unemployed from individuals who are not in the labor force.

√ Define the labor force participation rate and distinguish it from the unemployment rate.

√ Explain how the unemployment rate is calculated.

√ Explain who would be considered unemployed.

√ Define a discouraged worker and address whether or not a discouraged worker is considered unemployed.

√ Define an underemployed worker and address whether or not an underemployed worker is considered unemployed.

√ Describe the different types of unemployment (cyclical, frictional, structural) and their causes.

√ Define the natural rate of unemployment and "full employment."

√ Discuss the Consumer Price Index (CPI).

√ Discuss the types of goods included in the CPI.

√ Compare the CPI to the chain-price index for GDP.

√ Define inflation and explain how it hurts society.

√ Explain why and by how much it is believed that the percentage change in the CPI overstates inflation.

√ Explain some consequences of overstating the rate of inflation.

√   Define deflation and the problems caused by it.

III. KEY TERMS

Unemployed: individuals who are looking for work but do not have jobs.

Employed: individuals who currently have jobs.

Labor force: the employed plus the unemployed.

Unemployment rate: the fraction of the labor force that is unemployed.

Discouraged workers: workers who left the labor force because they could not find jobs.

Underemployed: workers who hold a part-time job but prefer to work full time or hold jobs that are far below their own capabilities.

Labor force participation rate: the fraction of the population over sixteen years of age that is in the labor force.

Cyclical unemployment: the component of unemployment that accompanies fluctuations in real GDP.

Frictional unemployment: the part of unemployment associated with the normal workings of the economy such as searching for jobs.

Structural unemployment: the part of unemployment that results from the mismatch of skills and jobs.

Natural rate of unemployment: the level of unemployment at which there is no cyclical unemployment.

Full Employment: the level of employment that occurs when the unemployment rate is at the natural rate.

Consumer Price Index (CPI): a price index that measures the cost of a fixed basket of goods chosen to represent the consumption pattern of individuals.

Inflation rate: the rate of change of the price level in the economy.

Cost of living adjustments: automatic increases in wages or other payments that are tied to a price index.

IV. PERFORMANCE ENHANCING TIPS (PETS)

PET #1

To be considered unemployed, an individual must be 16 years or older, have actively sought paid employment in the last four weeks, and must not be employed in a part-time job.

The government's definition about who is considered unemployed is very specific. Several pre-conditions must be satisfied before the government identifies an individual as unemployed. First, the individual must be 16 years or older. Second, the individual must have actively sought paid employment in the last four weeks. That is, if an individual does nothing but read the newspaper want ads in search of a job; the government would not consider this person unemployed. The individual would be classified as "not part of the labor force." In other words, the individual may not have a job but they're actions signal that don't really care to work either. An individual must also have sought paid employment. For example, an individual that does not have a job and applies for a position as a volunteer at a hospital would not be considered unemployed (nor as part of the labor force). Finally, an individual must have looked for a job in the last four weeks. That is, if it's been two months since an individual has actively searched for a job, that individual would not be classified as "unemployed" by the government. The government would classify that individual as not part of the labor force. Finally, if an individual has a part-time job, even if it is a job the individual doesn't want to be doing or is planning on leaving, the government would, in this case, classify the individual as "employed."

PET #2

To be considered part of the labor force, an individual must either have a paying job (full-time or part-time) or have actively sought paid employment in the last four weeks.

This PET tells you that the labor force consists of those individuals with jobs (the employed) and those individuals who do not have a job but who would like to work if they could (the "unemployed").

PET #3

Discouraged workers are not considered as unemployed because they are not actively seeking paid employment. Hence, they are also not considered part of the labor force. Underemployed workers hold jobs and are thus considered employed and therefore part of the labor force but not part of the unemployed.

V. PRACTICE EXAM: MULTIPLE CHOICE QUESTIONS

1. The labor force is defined as:
    a) all persons age 16 and over who are currently employed in a paying job.
    b) all persons age 16 and over who are either working for pay or have actively sought paid employment in the last four weeks.
    c) all persons willing and able to work for pay.
    d) all persons of voting age who are working for pay.
    e) the population minus those in the armed services.

2. Which one of the following statements is true?
    a) the government counts anybody who does not have a job as "unemployed."
    b) the unemployment rate is calculated as the number of unemployed individuals/labor force.
    c) the labor force is equal to a country's population.
    d) during the Great Depression, the unemployment rate reached a high of 10%.
    e) all of the above are true.

3. The government considers a discouraged worker as:
    a) someone who does not have a job but is actively seeking paid employment.
    b) someone who is working at a job that is below his or her skill level.
    c) not part of the labor force.
    d) someone who has a part-time job but seeks full-time employment.
    e) someone who has a job but is discouraged about getting a pay raise.

4. Frictional unemployment occurs when:
    a) a worker can't find a job because he/she lacks the skills necessary to be employed.
    b) a corporation transfers a worker to another city.
    c) a worker quits one job in order to search for another.
    d) a worker is laid off due to a downturn in the business cycle.
    e) (c) and (d).

5. Which one of the following is an example of a structurally unemployed individual?
    a) J. Martin, who lacks the skills necessary to be employed.
    b) Lee, who lost his job as an art director because of a recession.
    c) Jan, who has a Ph.D. in economics but is a bus driver.
    d) Helena, who has just graduated from college and is searching for a job as an architect.
    e) none of the above.

6. Which one of the following may be a reason why the unemployment rate doesn't reflect the true unemployment picture?
    a) the unemployment rate counts underemployed individuals as employed.
    b) the unemployment rate is based on a telephone survey where individuals may not give truthful answers.
    c) the unemployment rate does not count discouraged workers.
    d) the unemployment rate counts part-time workers as employed.
    e) all of the above.

7. Economists say that the economy is at "full employment" when:
    a) the structural unemployment rate is zero.
    b) the total unemployment rate is zero.
    c) the frictional unemployment rate is zero.
    d) the natural unemployment rate is zero.
    e) none of the above.

8. Which one of the following statements is true?

    a) people with part-time jobs are counted as "unemployed."

    b) an underemployed individual is someone who is temporarily without a job.

    c) the labor force participation rate is the percentage of the labor force that is employed.

    d) all individuals over 16 years of age that do not have a job are considered unemployed.

    e) married men and women tend to have the lowest unemployment rates.

9. Which one of the following statements is NOT correct?

    a) the natural rate of unemployment is estimated to be 4 - 5.5% in the U.S.

    b) the term "full employment" means that 100% of the labor force is employed.

    c) an inflation rate of 5% may arise even if some prices are falling.

    d) inflation is the percentage change in the price level.

    e) deflation occurs when the price level declines.

10. The consumer price index is:

    a) an index of the prices of a basket of goods and services purchased by a typical household.

    b) the broadest price index.

    c) an index of the prices of goods and services typically produced in an economy.

    d) an index of retail prices.

    e) a leading indicator of the producer price index.

11. Which price index is the most widely used by the government and the private sector?

    a) producer price index.

    b) consumer price index.

    c) the GDP deflator.

    d) the chain-type price index.

    e) the core index.

12. Which one of the following statements is true of the Consumer Price Index?

    a) it does not take account of the price of imported goods and services.

    b) the goods and services used to construct the index do not change from month to month.

    c) it does not take into account the price of used goods.

    d) it understates the true rate of inflation.

    e) all of the above are true.

13. Suppose that in 1994 the CPI was 150 and that in 1995 the CPI was 165. The inflation rate between 1994-95 would be:

   a) 15%.

   b) 10%.

   c) 65%.

   d) 5%

   e) not enough information to answer question.

VI. PRACTICE EXAM: ESSAY QUESTIONS

1. Describe the different types of unemployment and discuss which type may be most problematic for a country.

2. Explain why the CPI overstates the true rate of inflation. What impact does this have for cost-of-living adjustments and social security payments?

VII. ANSWER KEY: MULTIPLE CHOICE

1. Correct answer: b.

Discussion: The labor force consists of the employed plus the unemployed. Thus, it is these individuals that are age 16 and over who currently have a job (the "employed") plus those individuals age 16 and over who do not have a job and have actively looked for or are looking for a job (the "unemployed").

Statement a is a definition of for individuals or are employed. Statement c is not a definition of the labor force since the labor force also counts individuals that are working. Statement d is not correct. Statement e is a definition of the civilian population.

2. Correct answer: b.

Discussion: Statement b is true. The unemployment rate is percentage (or fraction) of the labor force that is currently without a job and actively seeking employment.

Statement a is not true. The government only counts individuals who do not have a job but who are actively seeking a job as "unemployed." Individuals without a job and not seeking employment are counted as "not in the labor force." Statement c is not correct. A nation's labor force is not equal to its population. If it was, infants would be considered unemployed! Statement d is not correct. Unbelievable as it may seem, the unemployment rate was 25% meaning that one-fourth of the nation's labor force was unemployed during the Great Depression. That statistic is very high by historical standards and fortunately, the U.S. has not experienced unemployment like that since the Great Depression. It should be mentioned that by 1940 (11 years after the Great Depression commenced), the unemployment rate was 17%, which is still rather high by post-World War II standards. Statement e is not correct since only statement b is correct.

3. Correct answer: c.

Discussion: Discouraged workers are individuals that have stopped searching for employment (because they are so discouraged about their prospects of actually finding work). Since these workers are not actively seeking employment, they are not considered unemployed and thus are not part of the labor force, either.

Statement a is not correct based on the discussion above. Statement b defines an individual who is "underemployed." Statement d does not define a discouraged worker. In fact, someone who has a part-time job is considered employed and part of the labor force. Statement e is included for a laugh:).

4. Correct answer: c.

Discussion: Individuals are considered to be "frictionally unemployed" under a few circumstances. One of those circumstances arises when an individual quits one job to search for another. Your textbook mentions several other instances which give rise to frictional unemployment.

Statement a is an example of structural unemployment. Statement b is not a statement about unemployment. Statement d is an example of cyclical unemployment. Statement e is not correct because statements c and d are not examples of frictional unemployment.

5. Correct answer: a.

Discussion: Statement a is an example of a structurally unemployed individual. A structurally unemployed individual is someone who lacks the skills necessary to be employed.

Statement b is an example of a cyclically unemployed individual. Statement c is an example of an individual who has a job, albeit a job for which her skills are above the level used on the job. Thus, the individual is underemployed. Statement d is an example of a frictionally unemployed individual. A frictionally unemployed individual is someone who has either newly entered the labor market in search of a job, re-entered the labor market after an absence (perhaps to raise a child) in search of a job, or left their job in search of another job. Thus, Helena would be considered a new entrant into the labor market. She is frictionally unemployed because she has yet to find a job. Statement e is not correct because statement a is the answer.

6. Correct answer: e.

Discussion: There are many reasons why the unemployment rate may not necessarily reflect the true unemployment picture. Statements a-d are all reasons why the unemployment rate may be a potentially misleading indicator of the extent to which a nation's labor resources are being used.

7. Correct answer: e.

Discussion: An economy is said to be at "full-employment" even in the presence of a non-zero unemployment rate. This is because there will naturally be in any healthy, functioning economy some individuals who are newly entering the labor market, re-entering the labor market, or searching for another job (either because of frictional or structural unemployment). That is, there will naturally always be some unemployment." For the U.S., the estimate of the natural unemployment rate is 4-5.5%. Thus, full-employment is said to be achieved when the national unemployment rate is in the range of 4-5.5%.

8. Correct answer: e.

Discussion: Whereas married men and women tend to have the lowest unemployment rates, teenagers tend to have the highest unemployment rates. Thus, statement e is correct.

Statement a is not correct because even people with part-time jobs are counted as employed since they do have a job. Statement b is not true; an underemployed individual is someone who has a job but is working at a job below his/her skill level. Statement c is not correct; the labor force participation rate is calculated as the labor force (sum of employed plus unemployed individuals) divided by the population age sixteen and over. Statement d is not correct because only individuals over 16 years of age that have actively sought paid employment in the last four weeks are considered unemployed. Thus, an individual who is 16 years or older, but is not looking for a job, is not counted as unemployed.

9. Correct answer: b.

Discussion: The term full-employment allows for there to be frictional and structural unemployment. Some unemployment is always to be expected in the natural functioning of an economy. Thus, 100% of the labor force will not typically be employed. This is a way of saying that there will always be some "natural unemployment" in an economy.

Statement a is correct since the current estimate of the natural unemployment rate for the U.S. is 4 - 5.5%. Statement c is a correct statement because inflation measures what happens to the average level of prices. Since the price level is an average of prices of all different types of goods and services, it may turn out that some prices have actually fallen while other have risen in such a way that, on average, the price level may rise by 5%. Statement d is correct since inflation is measured as the percentage change in the price level. Statement e is correct since a decline in the price level is referred to as "deflation" (that is, negative inflation).

10. Correct answer: a.

Discussion: The consumer price index (CPI) is an index of the prices of a basket of goods and services purchased by a typical consumer. The goods and services in the basket do not change in calculating the CPI and for this reason, the basket of goods and services used in the calculation is said to be "fixed."

Statement b is not correct. The broadest price index is the chain price index for GDP. It is the broadest price index since it covers the prices of a broader range of goods and services than the CPI does. Statement c is a statement about the chain price index for GDP. Statement d is a made-up answer. Statement e is not correct. The producer price index (which your book does not mention) is viewed as a leading indicator (an "omen") of changes in the CPI.

11. Correct answer: b.

Discussion: The Consumer Price Index (CPI) is the price index that is most widely used by the government. The government uses the CPI to make cost-of-living adjustments to social security benefits it pays out to retirees. Such cost-of-living adjustments are given so as to keep the "real" or "purchasing power" value of the benefits the same from year to year. The private sector also uses the CPI to make cost-of-living adjustments to wages, particularly to union wages.

The producer price index (not discussed in your textbook) is a price index of goods and services used by producers. It is sometimes referred to as the "wholesale price index." The GDP deflator and the chain-type price index are price indices that are constructed from the prices of the goods and services in GDP. The core index is (not discussed in your textbook) a price index that subtracts food and energy prices out of the CPI. Food and energy prices tend to be the most volatile (fluctuating) prices in the index.

12. Correct answer: b.

Discussion: The Consumer Price Index is based on a basket of goods and services that a typical household buys. The goods and services included in the basket do not change from month-to-month when the government collects the price data. Thus, the CPI is based on a fixed basket of goods and services.

Statement a is not correct because the CPI can include the price of imported goods and services. The chain-type price index and GDP deflator do not include the price of imported goods and services. Statement c is not correct because the CPI may include the price of used goods. Statement d is not correct; it is currently estimated that the percentage change in the CPI overstates the true rate of inflation by 0.5% - 1.5%. Thus, if the government reports a rate of inflation of 4%, the true rate of inflation is likely to be 2.5 - 3.5%.

13. Correct answer: b.

Discussion: The inflation rate is calculated as the percentage change in the CPI. The percentage change in the CPI is calculated as $[(165-150)/150] \times 100 = 10\%$. Thus, statement b is correct. None of the other statements is correct.

VIII. ANSWER KEY: ESSAY QUESTIONS

1. The three types of unemployment are cyclical, frictional, and structural. The sum of the three is the unemployment rate. The sum of the frictional and structural unemployment rates is called the "natural rate of unemployment." Cyclical unemployment is caused by the ups and downs of the economy.

Sometimes the economy booms and sometimes it goes into a recession. People who lose their jobs because the economy goes into a recession are categorized as cyclically unemployed. It is presumed that once the economy comes out of the recession, these people will be re-employed. Cyclical unemployment is of a fairly short-term nature, particularly in comparison to structural unemployment. Frictional unemployment occurs as people re-enter the labor force or enter the labor force for the first time (say upon graduation from high school or college). These people may be unemployed for a time as they search for a job to which their skills are matched. Frictional unemployment also arises because people leave their jobs in search of another job -- perhaps a better paying one or one that is more satisfying. Frictional unemployment is also of a fairly short-term nature, particularly in comparison to structural unemployment. New entrants, re-entrants, and job switchers are part of a natural functioning economy. There will always be, at any point in time, these types of people looking for jobs. In other words, we should not expect that the frictional unemployment rate could be pushed to 0%. The third type of unemployment is structural unemployment. Structural unemployment occurs because of a mismatch between the skills a worker possesses and the skills necessary to obtain a job. Structural unemployment is of a longer-term nature. The structurally unemployed tend to have a more difficult time finding work and may even require re-training or new skills in order to find work. Structural unemployment is also a natural part of the economy in the sense that the structure of the economy changes over time and so, too, the demand for different types of workers. For example, the U.S. economy has become a more high-tech economy and the service industry has grown as an employer relative to the manufacturing industry. This structural change in the economy leads to unemployment in pockets of industry across the nations that are outmoded.

2. The CPI overstates the true rate of inflation because the basket of goods and services that are priced from month-to-month do not change. Implicitly, this means that consumers do not change their consumption spending patterns, either. However, consumers are able to alter and do alter their spending patterns in response to price changes. For example, suppose the price of a name-brand medicine goes up and that this brand is one of the goods in the basket used to construct the CPI. Consumers may switch to a generic brand of the medicine, thus avoiding the higher price for the name brand. However, the CPI will not register this switch to a lower price brand because it is constructed based on a fixed basket of goods and services. In fact, the CPI will increase because the price of the name-brand medicine that is included in the CPI has increased, even though consumers have been able to avoid the price increase. Thus, percentage changes in the CPI may overstate the actual rate of inflation to consumers.

The CPI may also overstate the rate of inflation because any increases in the prices of goods and services in the CPI are all considered to be inflationary. However, some prices increase because the good or service being purchased has improved. For example, suppose the new safety features of automobiles cause automobile prices to rise. An automobile today is now a different product from what it was in the past. It is a safer vehicle. The higher price tag should thus not be considered as inflationary because consumers are paying a higher price but getting more for their money.

For both of these reasons, it is estimated that percentage changes in the CPI overstate the true rate of inflation by 0.5% - 1.5%.

Cost-of-living adjustments and social security benefits are tied to the rate of change in the CPI. This means that they will be adjusted upward by the percentage increase in the CPI. For example, if the CPI inflation rate for 1996 was 2%, then social security benefits will automatically increase by 2%. This means that if a retiree was receiving a $1,000 per month social security payment, the payment would increase by 2% to $1,020. The same would be true for any worker or individual who has a payment tied to the CPI.

If the CPI currently overstates the true rate of inflation, then, in effect too much in social security benefits are being paid out. In the example above, if the true rate of inflation is actually 1%, then the retiree's benefit would only rise to $1,010 and the government would save $10 per month. While this may seem like a small saving for the government, multiply it by 12 months and the number of people receiving social security benefits. As you can imagine, the savings to the government (and ultimately the taxpayers) could end up being quite large.

However, retirees may argue that the CPI rate of inflation isn't relevant to compute their purchasing power. That is, the basket of goods and services used to construct the CPI is not the basket that they typically purchase. Since retirees are older, they may argue that they spend more of their income on medical services than that reflected in the CPI. Since medical fees are increasing at a much faster pace than, say entertainment or transportation prices, retirees may feel that the government should continue to make cost-of-living adjustments based on a number that overstates the true rate of inflation.

Take It to the Net

We invite you to visit the O'Sullivan/Sheffrin page on the Prentice Hall Web site at:

http://www.prenhall.com/osullivan/

for this chapter's World Wide Web exercise.

CHAPTER 12
WHY DO ECONOMIES GROW?

I. OVERVIEW

In this chapter, you will learn how capital deepening and technological progress can affect a country's ability to grow. You will learn how saving and investment play a role in capital deepening as well as what determines technological progress. You will also learn how international trade and public policy ultimately affect economic growth through their effects on saving and investment. You will learn how research and development and investment in education may affect the growth rate a country is able to achieve. You will also see how population growth affects economic growth and real wages. You will use a production function to illustrate how capital deepening and technological progress alter the level of output a country is able to produce. You will be re-introduced to the difference between gross investment and net investment and will see why it is important in understanding the basis for economic growth. You will learn about growth accounting, which is an attempt to estimate the contributions of capital deepening, labor growth, and technological progress to economic growth. You will learn about productivity and how capital deepening and technological progress affect productivity and real wages. You will learn about the sources of technological progress and how policy can be directed at enhancing technological progress. You will also learn about real GDP per capita as a basis for comparing living standards across countries.

II. CHECKLIST

By the end of this chapter, you should be able to:

√ Define economic growth.

√ Explain how a growth rate is calculated.

√ Use the Rule of 70 to analyze how long it will take a country to double its standard of living if it grows at X% per year.

√ Use the Rule of 70 to analyze what growth rate it would have to achieve in order for its standard of living to double in X years.

√ Discuss how a country's standard of living can be measured and some problems with making direct comparisons to another country's standard of living.

√ Define capital deepening and illustrate its effects on real wages, the production function, and the level of output.

√ Explain how saving and investment are related.

√ Explain the distinction between gross and net investment. Explain which type of investment is important to economic growth.

√ Explain the effect of population growth on output per worker and discuss ways in which policy can be used to mitigate the effect.

√ Explain how government spending and a trade deficit can be used to enhance capital deepening.

√ Define technological progress.

√ Discuss growth accounting.

√ Define labor productivity.

√ Discuss what has happened to U.S. labor productivity since the 1970s and offer possible explanations.

√ Discuss some causes of technological progress.

√ Define creative destruction.

√ Give some examples of government policy that would raise the rate of technological progress.

√ Define human capital.

√ Discuss the importance to education and health and fitness on productivity and growth.

√ Discuss the merits of a public policy aimed at educating a society versus improving the sanitation system of a country.

III. KEY TERMS

Capital deepening: increases in the stock of capital per worker.

Technological progress: an increase in output without any increases in inputs.

Real GDP per capita: inflation-adjusted gross domestic product per person. It is the usual measure of living standards across time and between countries.

Exchange Rate: the rate at which one currency trades for another.

Convergence: the process by which poorer countries "catch up" with richer countries in terms of real GDP per capita.

Growth rate: the percentage change in a variable.

Rule of 70: if an economy grows at x percent per year, output will double in 70/x years.

Saving: total output minus consumption.

Growth Accounting: a method to determine the contribution to economic growth from increased capital, labor, and technological progress.

Labor productivity: output per hour of work.

Creative destruction: the process by which competition for monopoly profits leads to technological progress.

Human capital: investments in education and skills.

New growth theory: modern theories of growth that try to explain the origins of technological progress.

IV. PERFORMANCE ENHANCING TIPS (PETS)

PET #1

Real GDP per capita is a country's real GDP level divided by its population. It is not an appropriate measure of what a typical individual's before or after-tax real income is.

Real GDP per capita is not a useful measure of average income for a working individual or household. The reason is that the calculation for real GDP per capita assumes that the dollar figure for real GDP is a measure of the income that accrues to every individual in the population, whatever their age, and whether they are working or not. Also, real GDP, while an approximate measure of national income, is not a good measure of personal income (i.e. before-tax household income) or of disposable income (i.e. after-tax household income) -- income that accrues to working individuals. In fact, real GDP exceeds aggregate real personal and aggregate real disposable income by a substantial amount. Thus, when this chapter reports that real GDP per capita in the U.S. was $29,010 in 1997, it does not imply that on average, every working individual earns $29,010. It also does not imply that on average, a family of four's before or after-tax real income is $116,040 ($29,010 X 4).

PET #2

GDP per capita (per person) is not necessarily the best measure of the standard of living of a country's residents.

GDP per capita is often used as a measure of comparing the standards of living across countries; high GDP per capita countries are presumed to have higher standards of living than low GDP per capita countries. However, the use of GDP per capita to compare living standards does not take into account quality of life issues like crime, pollution, traffic congestion, access to health care, status of the educational system, etc. Thus, the country with the highest GDP per capita may not necessarily offer the highest "quality of life."

PET #3

(The growth factor minus 1) X 100 equals the growth rate.

Suppose that you are told that real GDP in 2000 is $150 billion and real GDP in 2001 is $165 billion. The growth factor is $165/$150 = 1.10. The growth rate is thus (1.10 - 1) X 100 = 10%.

Alternatively, as your book points out, the growth factor is 1 plus (the growth rate/100). That is, if the growth rate is 10%, the growth factor is 1 + 10/100 = 1.10.

PET #4

The Rule of 70 can be used to determine either the time periods it will take for a variable to double or the growth rate necessary for a variable to double in X time periods.

For example, suppose you are told that the U.S. growth rate is 3% per year and that the Japanese growth rate is 5% per year. Which country's real GDP will double more quickly? Using the rule of 70, it will take the U.S. approximately 23 years (70/3) to double its real GDP whereas Japan's real GDP will double in 14 years (70/5). For another example, suppose you are told that Canada has undertaken an ambitious economic plan. One goal is for real GDP to double in 10 years. What growth rate must Canada sustain each year for 10 years in order to achieve the goal? Using the rule of 70, the answer would be 7% per year (70/10 years).

One word of caution: if the growth rate is stated on a monthly or quarterly basis, the time period to double should be stated in monthly or quarterly terms (instead of yearly) as well. For example, suppose the government reported that they expected real GDP to grow at 2% each quarter. Using the rule of 70, at that growth rate, it would take 70/2 = 35 quarters for real GDP to double. Thirty-five quarters is 8.75 years.

PET #5

The pool of savings available to fund investment in Country A can come from the savings of country A's residents or from the savings of foreign countries' residents who lend their savings to country A.

Suppose that U.S. residents in total save $500 billion a year, $450 billion of which is placed in the U.S. and the remaining $50 billion is lent to other countries. Further, suppose that foreigners save $1 trillion a year, $100 billion of which is lent to the U.S. On net, the U.S. pool of private saving will be $450 billion + $100 billion = $550 billion. This pool of saving will be available to fund private and/or government investment projects.

PET #6

Net investment is the change in a country's capital stock after taking account of depreciation. Thus:

> *net investment = gross investment - depreciation.*

You can also re-arrange the equation above as:

> *gross investment = net investment + depreciation.*
> *depreciation = gross investment - net investment.*

PET #7

Net investment that is positive is the addition to a nation's stock of capital above and beyond its current level. Net investment that is zero means that a nation's stock of capital is neither increasing nor decreasing beyond its current level. Net investment that is negative means that a nation is not investing enough to replace capital that is being worn out.

PET #5 of the chapter on Measuring a Nation's Production and Income covered this principle and used an illustration that is worth repeating here. To illustrate the difference between gross investment and net investment, consider the stock of shoes that you currently have. Suppose you have 10 pairs of shoes. Over the course of the year, 3 of the pairs wear out (depreciate) and are no longer any good. If you buy 7 more pairs of shoes that year, your gross investment in shoes is 7 pairs. However, because you are replacing 3 pairs that have worn out, your net investment in shoes is 4 pairs. That is, at the end of the year, you will now have 14 pairs of shoes. You have, on net, added 4 (7-3) pairs to the stock of 10 pairs of shoes that you started out with.

Suppose instead that you bought 3 pairs of shoes that year. While three pairs would be your gross investment, your net investment would be zero. You have only replaced what you have worn out. Thus, you are no better off at the end of the year since your stock of shoes remains at 10 pairs.

Now, suppose that you bought 1 pair of shoes that year. While three pairs would be your gross investment, your net investment would be -2 (1-3). You have not invested enough to replace the 3 pairs of shoes worn out. Thus, your stock of shoes will decline from 10 pairs to 8 pairs.

The same is true for a country. A country whose net investment is zero will not be adding to its capital stock and so will not experience the benefits of capital deepening; a country that is not replacing its worn out capital will see its capital stock shrink and will not experience the benefits of capital deepening.

PET #8

In order for a country to grow through capital deepening, its saving must be greater than the depreciation of the capital stock.

This PET is just an application of PETS #6 and #7. That is, a country must save enough to ensure that its level of net investment is positive (greater than zero).

V. PRACTICE EXAM: MULTIPLE CHOICE QUESTIONS

1. Which one of the following statements is NOT true of real GDP per capita?

    a) if a country's real GDP per capita grows at 2% per year, it will take 35 years for real GDP per capita to double.

    b) it is difficult to compare real GDP per capita across countries because of differences in consumption patterns.

    c) it is difficult to compare real GDP per capita across countries because of differences in currencies.

    d) if U.S. real GDP per capita is $25,000, German real GDP per capita is 60,000 marks and the exchange rate is 2 marks per U.S. dollar, then we can be sure that Germany has a higher real GDP per capita than the U.S.

    e) all of the above are true.

2. Which one of the following statements is NOT true?

    a) there has been a convergence of real GDP per capita among the developed (industrialized) countries.

    b) there is strong evidence that less developed countries grow at faster rates than developed countries.

    c) real GDP per capita may decline if the growth rate in real GDP is less than the population growth rate.

    d) the average growth rate in real GDP per capita between 1960-97 for Japan was about 5% per year.

    e) the level of real GDP per capita amongst countries will eventually converge if the low real GDP per capita countries grow at rates faster than the high real GDP per capita countries.

3. Which one of the following is the correct growth factor assuming real GDP in 1998 is $5,000 trillion and real GDP in 1999 is $6,000 trillion?

    a) 0.56

    b) 1.20

    c) 0.65

    d) 1.83

    e) 1.44

4. Suppose the economy was expected to grow at 4% a year for the next five years. If GDP this year is $100 billion, what will it be at the end of five years?

    a) $120 billion.

    b) $121.67 billion.

    c) $104 billion.

    d) $537.82 billion.

    e) $305.18 billion.

5. Suppose that you would like to see your salary double in ten years. What must the growth rate of your salary be each year in order for you to achieve your goal?

    a) 7%.

    b) 1.7%.

    c) 1.4%.

    d) 10%.

    e) 14%.

6. Suppose that a country's real GDP was growing at a rate of 5% per year. How many years would it take for the country's real GDP to double?

    a) 10 years.

    b) 20 years.

    c) 14 years.

    d) 40 years.

    e) cannot be determined without more information.

7. Labor productivity depends on the amount of _____ an economy has.

    a) machines.

    b) buildings (or factories).

    c) equipment.

    d) technology.

    e) all of the above.

8. In an economy with no government or foreign sector:

    a) saving must equal gross investment.

    b) saving must equal net investment.

    c) saving must equal depreciation.

    d) saving will be less than investment.

    e) saving will be greater than investment.

9. A change in a country's capital stock is equal to:

    a) the level of gross investment.

    b) the level of net investment.

    c) the rate of depreciation of a country's capital stock.

    d) the level of saving.

    e) (a) and (d).

10. Which one of the following statements is true of capital deepening?

    a) for a fixed amount of capital, increases in a country's work force will lead to increases in the amount of output per worker.

    b) a government that uses its tax revenues to fund the construction of new highways and bridges is not engaging in capital deepening because the government creates a budget deficit.

    c) trade deficits always hurt the ability of a country to deepen its capital stock.

    d) capital deepening will stop when depreciation is zero.

    e) capital deepening is a source of economic growth.

11. Which one of the following would NOT be an example of technological progress?

    a) discovery of a new tax loophole which enables companies to reduce the amount of taxes they pay to the government.

    b) the invention of the computer.

    c) the invention of a conveyor belt.

    d) the discovery of converting steam to energy.

    e) the invention of the washing machine.

12. Which Nobel-prize winning economist developed a method for measuring technological progress?

    a) Franco Modigliani.

    b) Milton Friedman.

    c) Robert Solow.

    d) Sir Charles Godfrey.

    e) Gerard Debreu.

13. Which one of the following statements is true of growth accounting?

    a) technological progress has accounted for roughly 1% of the growth rate in U.S. output.

    b) growth accounting determines how much of a country's growth in output is due to growth in worker productivity and to growth in prices (inflation).

    c) a country whose main source of growth in output is through technological progress will typically be able to enjoy a higher level of consumption than a country whose main source of growth is through increases in the capital stock.

    d) the slowdown in U.S. labor productivity has been explained by a reduced rate of capital deepening.

    e) the effect of advances in information technology on labor productivity is easily measured.

14. Which one of the following has NOT been considered a potential source of technological progress?

    a) research and development in fundamental sciences.

    b) monopolies that spur innovation.

    c) inventions designed to reduce costs.

    d) the scale of the market.

    e) all of the above have been considered potential sources of technological progress.

15. Which one of the following statements is NOT true?

    a) technological progress enables a country to produce more output with the same amount of labor and capital.

    b) education can promote technological progress.

    c) creative destruction is the process of replacing plant and equipment before it has fully depreciated.

    d) patents may promote technological progress.

    e) the protection of intellectual property rights may promote technological progress.

16. Suppose country A's real GDP per capita is $10,000 and country B's real GDP per capita is $20,000. If country A's real GDP per capita is growing at 7% per year while country B's real GDP per capita is growing at 3.5% per year, after how many years will country A's real GDP per capita exceed country B's real GDP per capita?

    a) 10 years.

    b) 60 years.

    c) 80 years.

    d) 7 years.

    e) 20 years.

17. Which one of the following would be an example of an investment in human capital?

    a) purchase of an automated assembly line.

    b) sending a crew of factory workers to a year-long training program.

    c) buying stock in a biotechnology firm.

    d) installing a new sewer system in the rural part of a country.

    e) (b) and (d).

VI.   PRACTICE EXAM: ESSAY QUESTIONS

1. Explain why the citizens of a country that experiences economic growth through only technological progress may enjoy a better standard of living than a country that experiences economic growth only through an increase in the capital stock.

2. Discuss the different sources of technological progress.

VII. ANSWER KEY: MULTIPLE CHOICE QUESTIONS

1. Correct answer: d.

Discussion: Statement d is not true. It is not appropriate to compare real GDP per capita across countries by using the going exchange rate to convert the real GDP per capita of one country to another country's currency. Thus, even though using the exchange rate, Germany's real GDP per capita would equal $30,000 (60,000 marks / 2 marks per dollar) and thus exceed U.S. real GDP per capita, it is not correct to infer that Germany's real GDP per capita and thus the standard of living is better than in the U.S.

Differences in consumption patterns and the prices of goods across countries must be evaluated in arriving at a correct comparison of real GDP per capita. Thus, statements b and c are true. Statement a is an application of the rule of 70. With a growth rate of 2% per year, it will take 35 years (70/2) for a country's real GDP per capita to double.

2. Correct answer: b.

Discussion: Statement b is not true. Economists have found only weak evidence that less developed countries have grown at a rate faster than developed countries.

Statement a is true for developed countries. Statement c is necessarily true. Since real GDP per capita is equal to a country's real GDP divided by its population, then an increase in the population growth rate that exceeds the growth rate in real GDP will necessarily lead to a decline in real GDP per capita. Statement d is true. Statement e is true. (For a numerical example of the principle, see the answer to question 15).

3. Correct answer: b.

The growth factor is calculated by dividing the most recent number by the more distant number. Thus, the growth factor is $6,000/$5,000 = 1.20. The growth factor implies a 20% growth rate of real GDP between 1998 and 1999.

4. Correct answer: b.

Discussion. The formula to use is GDP in year n = current GDP X $(1 + \text{growth rate})^n$. Thus, GDP after five years will be $100 billion X $(1.04)^5$ = $100 billion X 1.2167 = $121.67 billion. Based on this, none of the other statements are correct.

If you used $100 billion X (1.40), you would incorrectly get $537.82 billion.

5. Correct answer: a.

Discussion: You must use the Rule of 70 to arrive at the answer. The Rule of 70 is: Number of years to Double = 70/growth rate. Since you know the number of years to double is ten years, you have 10 = 70/growth rate. Thus, the growth rate must be 7% in order for your goal to be achieved.

6. Correct answer: c.

Discussion: The Rule of 70 can be used to answer this question, as it was used to answer question 5. Using the Rule of 70 (see PET #4), the years it would take real GDP to double is calculated by dividing 70 by 5. Since 70/5 is equal to 14, it will take real GDP fourteen years to double.

7. Correct answer: e.

Discussion: The productivity of labor (how much output each worker is able to produce over a given time period) is affected by the amount (including quality and age) of machines that the workers use; by the building or factory (including quality and age) that workers work in; by the equipment they have to work with (tools, computers, fax machines, etc); and by the state of technology.

8. Correct answer: a.

Discussion: A country's saving (in the absence of a government or foreign sector) is used by (lent to) businesses that in turn purchase plant and equipment, i.e. invest or add to the capital stock. The investment by businesses may be undertaken to replace worn out capital (depreciation) or to purchase new capital. Gross investment is the sum of these two activities and saving provides the funds necessary for both.

Statements d and e cannot be true of an economy that does not have a government or a foreign sector. It is necessarily true that saving must equal (gross) investment.

9. Correct answer: b.

Discussion: A country's capital stock will change when its net investment changes. If net investment is positive, a country's capital stock will increase. This is because the country will not only be replacing worn out capital, it will be adding more new plant and equipment to its capital stock. If net investment is negative, a country's capital stock will decrease. This is because the country will not even be totally replacing its worn out capital. Remember that net investment is gross investment minus depreciation. You may wish to review PET #7 of this chapter for more detail.

10. Correct answer: e.

Discussion: Capital deepening is an increase in the amount of capital available per worker. Since capital deepening enables workers to produce more output per day, capital deepening leads to economic growth (increases in output).

Statement a is not true. For a fixed amount of capital, increases in a country's work force will lead to a decline in capital per worker (i.e. total capital/number of workers), not an increase. Statement b is not true. When a government spends your tax dollars on such things as highway and bridge construction (or research and development, or education for that matter), it is adding to the stock of capital (physical or human) and thereby engaging in capital deepening. Statement c is not true. A country that runs a trade deficit may incur the trade deficit because it is importing a lot of plant and equipment (capital). Thus, a trade deficit is not necessarily a bad thing for a country since it can promote capital deepening. This, of course, assumes that the country is deficit spending on capital goods not on consumption goods. Statement d is not true. Capital deepening will stop when net investment is zero (i.e. when gross investment equals depreciation).

11. Correct answer: a.

Discussion: Technological progress is defined as progress that enables a country to produce more output with the same amount of capital and labor. The discovery of a new tax loophole does not add to the amount of output a country can produce with the same amount of capital and labor. It simply keeps dollars in the hands of businesses and out of the hands of the government.

12. Correct answer: c.

13. Correct answer: c.

Discussion: Your book discusses a comparison of the growth rates achieved by Hong Kong and Singapore. The discussion points out that technological progress enables the citizens of a country to consume more than a country that grows through increases in the capital stock. This is because increases in the capital stock are funded from saving. That is, in order to increase the capital stock, a country must save more. This means that a country must consume less. Thus, a country that experiences growth because of increases in the capital stock is probably a country where the level of consumption is not very high. In contrast, if growth occurs through technological progress (which presumably is not being funded from saving), then a country does not have to reduce its consumption level in order for growth to occur.

Statement a is not true. Technological progress has accounted for roughly 35% of the growth rate in U.S. output. That is, with a U.S. growth rate in output of 3% a year, 1% of that 3% is attributed to technological progress, i.e. $1/3 = 33\%$ of the growth rate is attributed to technological progress. Statement b is not true. Growth accounting determines how much of a country's growth in output is due to growth in the capital stock, the labor force, and technological progress. Statement d is not true. The slowdown in U.S. labor productivity has not been explained by a reduction in the capital stock. A number of explanations (discussed in your text) have been offered but none seem to do a good job of explaining why U.S. labor productivity has declined since the 1970s. Statement e is not true. The effects of advances in information technology on labor productivity have been very difficult to quantify. This, in part, is due to the fact that the information technology advances primarily affected the service sector where output per worker is much harder to quantify than, say, for the manufacturing sector.

14. Correct answer: e.

Discussion: Research and development, either private or government-funded leads to technological advances not only within the industry conducting the research and development but for other related industries. Monopolies, particularly those granted through patents, can spur innovation. Monopoly status confers the possibility of long-term profits to a firm, which in turn spurs a firm to innovate. Secondly, as other firms try to break the monopoly status by producing a similar product (a process called "creative destruction"), other innovations are generated. Inventions that are designed to reduce costs are another source of technological progress. Here again, the profit-maximizing motive of the firm can promote innovation. A firm that reduces its costs through innovation will see bigger profits. The scale of the market also spurs innovation. The possibility that a product, once developed, will be mass marketed (e.g. disposable diapers) also creates an incentive to innovate. That is, if firms see a huge profit potential in an innovative product, they will produce it.

15. Correct answer: c.

Discussion: Creative destruction is a process whereby firms compete with an innovating monopolist by introducing a new, better, version of the product, which generates more innovation.

Statement a is true and means that technological progress can increase the productivity of labor, as well as capital. Statement b is true. Your book discusses a case in which education (investment in human capital) is thought to be the key to technological progress. A more educated society is a more intelligent society and a more intelligent society is more likely to innovate than one that is not as well educated. Statement d is true. Successful patents guarantee an innovator profits for a long period of time. The incentive to reap profits thus leads to innovation and technological progress. Statement e is true. If property rights are not protected, neither are profits from innovations. Thus, without property rights, there is a reduced incentive to innovate and technological progress is likely to be shunted.

16. Correct answer: e.

Discussion: Country A's real GDP per capita will double to $20,000 in 10 years (70/7). In another 10 years, it will double from $20,000 to $40,000. Country B's real GDP per capita will double in 20 years (70/3.5). Thus, country B's real GDP per capita will be $40,000 in 20 years. After the 20th year, assuming country A will continue to grow at 7% a year while country B grows at 3.5% a year, it must be true that country A's real GDP per capita will surpass country B's real GDP per capita after the 20th year.

17. Correct answer: e.

Discussion: Statements (b) and (d) are both examples of investments in human capital. Investments in human capital come in two forms: investments in the education of a workforce and investments in the health and fitness of a workforce. Mandatory attendance to a four-year college would be one example of an investment in the education of a country's workforce. For some countries, mandatory attendance through grade eight is an investment in a country's workforce. Investment in food supplies to a country's population (it's hard to be productive when you're chronically hungry) as well as in its sewer and water infrastructure is another.

Statement a is an example of investment in a country's capital stock. Statement c is an example of "financial investment".

VIII. ANSWER KEY: ESSAY QUESTIONS

1. Technological progress enables a country to produce more output with the same amount of capital and labor as before. Because more output can be produced without any increase in the capital stock, a country's citizens do not have to reduce their consumption spending (i.e. increase the level of their saving today) in order to fund additions to the capital stock. Thus, citizens can consume a higher share (percentage) of output than citizens of a country that grows through additions to its capital stock. In this way, we might say that the citizens are able to enjoy a better standard of living. When a country experiences economic growth through additions to its capital stock, its citizens are in effect sacrificing current consumption (i.e. they are saving more today) so that businesses can purchase new plant and equipment with the saving. The purchases of new plant and equipment benefit society as a whole in the future by enabling the country to grow at a faster rate than it would have if it's citizens had not been willing to reduce consumption spending today. However, there is a cost to the citizens in that their standard of living may not be as enjoyable because of reduced consumption. So, technological progress permits economic growth without the sacrifice of reduced consumption in the present whereas economic growth through additions to the capital stock comes at a cost.

    This, of course, assumes that technological progress is not funded through saving. Some types of technological progress (innovations) may arise without any necessary increase in saving required. If they did, then what is true of economic growth through additions to the capital stock would be true of economic growth through technological progress.

    A good example of the sacrifices that a country's citizens must make in terms of reduced consumption spending is present-day Russia. The country is trying to rebuild itself and requires a lot of new, updated plant and equipment. The funds to pay for the new plant and equipment must come from somewhere. They must come from the saving of Russian citizens who lend their saving to businesses (i.e. business borrow from the citizens). Another way to look at the problem is to apply the principle of crowding out. If a country can only produce $X of output, it must be divided up between consumers and businesses (assuming no government). Thus, if a country wants to add to its capital stock, businesses must be able to increase their spending on plant and equipment which means consumers must reduce their spending on consumption goods since the country as a whole can only produce a limited amount of output.

2. Technological progress has many sources. Technological progress can occur through the research and development efforts of the government or the privately sector. Sometimes research and development has spillover benefits for other industries, which can, in turn, promote further technological progress. Technological progress also arises through the creative, educated, and talented minds of a nation's workforce. Thus, education (particularly in engineering and the sciences) can promote technological progress. The granting of patents to firms that innovate (which gives the firm a monopoly status) also promotes technological progress. A firm's desire to innovate is affected by the potential profit reward. A firm that is awarded a patent has more assurance that the profits it will earn on its innovation will not, at least for a time, be reduced by other firms competing with it. A legal framework for the protection of intellectual property rights also promotes technological progress through assuring innovative firms that profits they make from new ideas will be justly protected. This also helps to ensure that innovative firms will have a continued desire to innovate. Without such protection, firms may decide that the payoff from innovating is not enough and so technological progress is held back. Technological progress can also be influenced by the market potential. A bigger market presents a bigger potential profit opportunity. This is why free trade, which is a way of broadening a firm's market potential, may also encourage technological progress. Just think of the profit opportunities if U.S. firms were able to

freely export to China, the world's biggest market and almost 30 times the size of the U.S. market! Now, there's an incentive to come up with new and improved products! Technological progress also occurs through a firm's desire to reduce its costs (and thereby increase its profits).

A careful look at the list above suggests that innovation and therefore technological progress is fundamentally prompted by two things: an educated society and a profit motive.

Take It to the Net

We invite you to visit the O'Sullivan/Sheffrin page on the Prentice Hall Web site at:

http://www.prenhall.com/osullivan/

for this chapter's World Wide Web exercise.

CHAPTER 13
AGGREGATE DEMAND AND AGGREGATE SUPPLY

I.   OVERVIEW

In this chapter, you will learn about the historical behavior of real GDP in the United States. You will learn about U.S. experiences with recessions and the Great Depression. You will learn about some explanations for recessions as well as for periods of economic expansion. The model you will use to understand the behavior of real GDP (and other economic variables) over time is the model of aggregate demand and aggregate supply. You will use this model to study the short and long run effects of changes in aggregate demand and aggregate supply on output and the price level. You will learn what causes aggregate demand and aggregate supply to shift and what determines the slope of each curve. You will learn about "shocks" that can move an economy in one direction or another and the short and long run effects of such shocks. You will also learn how changes in government spending and the money supply can affect the behavior of real GDP in one direction or another, at least in the short run. You will learn about these policies' effects in the long run. You will learn why, in a market-based economy, the price system may not act to coordinate economic activities. You will see that some government spending policies can lead to "crowding out" and/or "crowding in." That is, you will see how changes in government spending can lead to changes in consumption, investment and net exports. You will see that such government spending policies come at an opportunity cost when the economy is operating at its full-employment level.

II.   CHECKLIST

By the end of this chapter, you should be able to:

√   Explain the key problem of the Great Depression.

√   Define a depression.

√   Define a recession and identify the peak and trough of economic fluctuations.

√   Discuss the historical behavior of real GDP for the United States.

√   Discuss the behavior of unemployment, investment spending, and consumption during recessions and address whether they are procyclical or countercyclical.

√   Define and explain Okun's Law.

√   Discuss what happens to unemployment and inflation when the economy grows faster than the trend rate of growth of real GDP.

√   Discuss Romer's explanation for why it may appear that economic fluctuations have become more stable since World War II.

√   Explain the difference between auction prices and custom prices and the implications for bringing about market equilibrium.

√   Explain why wages and prices may be sticky.

√ Give some examples of economic shocks and discuss their impact on output and the price level.

√ Describe the "short run" and the "long run" in macroeconomics.

√ Explain why the aggregate demand curve is negatively sloped.

√ List factors that would cause the aggregate demand curve to shift and in which direction.

√ List factors that would cause the Keynesian (short run) aggregate supply curve to shift and in which direction.

√ List factors that would cause the Classical (long run) aggregate supply curve to shift and in which direction.

√ Explain why the aggregate supply curve is drawn very flat for the short run and vertically for the long run.

√ Compare and contrast the effects of shifts in aggregate demand on output and the price level in the short run and the long run.

√ Describe the effects of shifts in Keynesian (short run) aggregate supply on output and the price level.

√ Define crowding out and crowding in.

√ Explain what causes crowding out and crowding in and which sectors of the economy may be crowded out or in as a result of an increase in government spending.

III. KEY TERMS

Economic fluctuations: movements of GDP above or below normal trends.

Business cycles: another name for economic fluctuations.

Peak: the time at which a recession begins.

Trough: the time at which output stops falling in a recession.

Recession: six consecutive months of negative economic growth.

Depression: the common name for a severe recession.

Keynesian economics: a school of economic thought that provides insights into the economy when it operates away from full employment.

Okun's Law: a relationship between changes in real GDP and the unemployment rate.

procyclical: moving in the same direction as real GDP.

countercyclical: moving in the opposite direction as real GDP.

Short-run in macroeconomics: the period of time that prices are fixed.

Aggregate demand: the relationship between the level of prices and the quantity of real GDP demanded.

Wealth effect: the increase in spending that occurs because the real value of money increases when the price level falls.

Aggregate Supply: the relationship between the level of prices and the quantity of output supplied.

Classical Aggregate Supply: a vertical aggregate supply curve. It reflects the idea that in the long run, output is determined solely by the factors of production.

Keynesian aggregate supply curve: a relatively flat aggregate supply curve. It reflects the idea that prices are sticky in the short run and firms adjust production to meet demand.

Supply shocks: external events that shift the aggregate supply curve.

Classical economics: the study of the economy as it operates at full employment.

Crowding out: reductions in consumption, investment, or net exports caused by an increase in government purchases.

Full employment output or potential output: the level of output that results when the labor market is in equilibrium.

Real business cycle theory: an economic theory that emphasizes how shocks to technology can cause fluctuations in economic activity.

IV. PERFORMANCE ENHANCING TIPS (PETS)

PET #1

Changes in output in the Keynesian economic model (short run model) are associated with changes in employment.

For example, if an economy produces more output (i.e. real GDP increases), employment is expected to have increased. If an economy produces less output (i.e. real GDP decreases), employment is expected to have decreased.

PET #2

Economic fluctuations are defined as changes in the level of output (real GDP) over time.

Economic fluctuations are also referred to as "the business cycle."

PET #3

Shifts in aggregate demand are caused by factors that lead to changes in spending other than changes in the price level.

This is just an application of PETS #1 and #6 from Chapter 4 of the Practicum which you may want to review. Since aggregate demand is composed of spending by households (consumers), businesses (firms), the government, and the foreign sector, any change in these spending components not caused by a change in the price level will be represented by a shift in aggregate demand. These spending components may change for a variety of reasons (change in taxes, interest rates, money supply, exchange rate, etc).

For example, suppose the interest rate increases. A rise in the interest rate makes it more costly for households and businesses to borrow money to fund their purchases. Thus, a rise in the interest rate may reduce consumption and business spending. This would be represented by a leftward shift in the aggregate demand curve.

PET #4

Shifts in the Keynesian (short run) aggregate supply curve are caused by factors that lead to changes in the cost of inputs used to produce output.

Labor and oil are key inputs used in the production of just about everything. Changes in the cost of labor (wages) as well as changes in the price of oil are represented by shifting the Keynesian aggregate supply curve. Increases in input costs (wages or price of oil) are represented by a leftward shift in the Keynesian aggregate supply curve. Decreases in input costs are represented by rightward shifts in the Keynesian aggregate supply curve.

PET #5

Shifts in the Classical (long run) aggregate supply curve are caused by factors that lead to changes in an economy's capacity to produce output.

An economy's capacity to produce depends on a number of factors: the size and productivity of its labor force, the age and amount of the capital stock, and the state of technology. Changes in these factors will be represented by a shift in the aggregate supply curve. Your book, in this chapter, does not consider the effect of technology on the aggregate supply curve.

For example, suppose the government increases spending on highways and telephone lines. An improvement in the capital stock means that an economy will be able to produce more output with its given set of resources than before. The improvement to the nation's capital stock would then be represented by a rightward shift in the aggregate supply curve.

PET #6

Crowding out occurs at the full-employment level of output because any increase in government purchases of output necessarily requires a reduction in purchases by some other sector(s) of the economy (consumers, businesses, foreign).

First of all, you may wish to replace the term "crowding out" with "reduction in" if it makes it easier for you to understand what crowding out is about. That is, when government spending increases, spending by other sectors of the economy will be reduced.

Let's look at some examples of crowding out. Suppose country A is operating at the full-employment level of output and at this level is producing $2 trillion worth of goods and services. Further, suppose that consumers purchase total $1.2 trillion; businesses purchases total $0.4 trillion, and government purchases total $0.6 trillion. Thus, total purchases equal $2.2 trillion, which is more than the $2 trillion produced by country A. Thus, it must be that the foreign sector, i.e. exports minus imports, purchases total -$0.2. That is, $0.2 trillion of the $2.2 trillion purchased by consumers, businesses, and the government of Country A is satisfied through foreign supply.

Now, suppose the government increases its spending from $0.6 trillion to $1.0 trillion. With the economy operating at full-employment, only $2 trillion worth of output can be produced by Country A even though total spending by Country A's consumers, businesses, and government now totals $2.6 trillion. Something has to give -- consumer, business, and foreign sector spending will have to be re-arranged to accommodate the increase in government spending.

Let's look at one example of crowding out. Suppose country A's consumers and businesses do not change their spending behavior (so they continue to purchase 1.2 + 0.4 = $1.6 trillion) while government spending has increased to $1 trillion. Thus, country A's consumers, businesses, and government in total purchase $2.6 trillion worth of output. The $2.6 trillion worth of purchases by consumers, businesses, and the government must be satisfied through $2 trillion worth of production by country A supplemented with $0.6 trillion worth of (net) production from abroad. That is, country A must import $0.6 trillion more than it will export. Thus, country A's trade balance declines to -$0.6 trillion. That is, the trade deficit gets worse. In this sense, we would say that net exports are crowded out (reduced) by $0.4 billion because the trade balance worsens from -$0.2 trillion to -$0.6 trillion.

Let's look at another example of crowding out. Suppose that consumers and businesses both cut back their purchases by $0.2 trillion but that the trade deficit remains at -$0.2 trillion. Here, we would say that consumption and investment spending are crowded out (reduced) by a total of $0.4 billion (0.2 + 0.2). The crowding out of spending by the private sector accommodates the increased government spending. Thus, purchases by country A's consumers, businesses, and government would total $2.2 trillion (1.0 + 0.2 + 1.0). Since the country can only produce $2 trillion worth of output, the foreign sector brings in an additional $0.2 trillion (i.e. country A imports $0.2 trillion more than it exports) to satisfy the purchases of country A's residents.

V. PRACTICE EXAM: MULTIPLE CHOICE QUESTIONS

1. According to Keynes, the main cause of the Great Depression in the U.S. was:
   a) insufficient demand for goods and services.
   b) excess capacity in production.
   c) the stock market crash.
   d) unemployment.
   e) low real wages.

2. Which one of the following statements is true?
   a) Keynesian economic thought deals with the behavior of the economy in the long run.
   b) in the short run, the aggregate supply curve is relatively flat.
   c) a recession is defined as a two-year or longer decline in real GDP.
   d) after an economic peak, an economy enters a recovery period.
   e) unemployment is considered to be a procyclical variable.

3. Assume the potential growth rate in real GDP is 4% and the current unemployment rate is 6%. Based on this, Okun's Law explains that:

    a) a 2% point increase in the growth of real GDP will raise the unemployment rate by 12%.

    b) a 2% point decline in the growth of real GDP will raise the unemployment rate 1% points.

    c) a 2% point decrease in the growth of real GDP will raise the unemployment rate to 14%.

    d) a 2% point decline in the growth of real GDP will increase the unemployment rate to 7%.

    e) (b) and (d).

4. Which one of the following variables is "countercyclical" with real GDP?

    a) consumption spending.

    b) investment spending.

    c) the unemployment rate.

    d) prices of stocks.

    e) all of the above are countercyclical.

5. If the economy grows at a rate above its trend rate of growth in real GDP:

    a) the unemployment rate will rise.

    b) the inflation rate will be likely to increase.

    c) the price of oil will decline.

    d) wage rates will decline.

    e) a depression will occur.

6. Christina Romer's explanation for why movements in real GDP (economic fluctuations) appear more stable after World War II than before is that:

    a) government spending and taxation were stabilized after World War II.

    b) the money supply was stabilized after World War II.

    c) there have been no more World wars.

    d) the data used to measure movements in real GDP was incomplete prior to World War II and thus led to over-exaggerations in how much real GDP actually fluctuated.

    e) inflation has been on average very low since World War II.

7. In which market would the price be least likely to be "sticky"?

    a) wages of union teachers.

    b) steel rods.

    c) fresh fruit.

    d) trucks.

    e) wages of government workers.

8. A consequence of sticky prices in the aircraft industry would be:
   a) a shortage or surplus of airplanes.
   b) a shortage or surplus of labor in the aircraft industry.
   c) a shortage or surplus of aircraft parts.
   d) a vertical production function.
   e) (a), (b), and (c).

9. Which one of the following is a reason for why the aggregate demand curve is negatively sloped?
   a) a decrease in the price level raises the purchasing power of money and wealth.
   b) a decrease in the price level raises interest rates, which reduces spending.
   c) an increase in the price level raises exports.
   d) an increase in the price level reduces the amount of output produced.
   e) a decrease in income causes people to save more.

10. Which one of the following would shift the aggregate demand curve to the left (decrease aggregate demand)?
    a) an increase in the money supply.
    b) an increase in government spending.
    c) an increase in exports.
    d) an increase in taxes.
    e) a decline in the capital stock.

11. In the short run, an increase in aggregate demand will increase _____ and in the long run will increase _____.
    a) the price level and output/the price level.
    b) the price level and output/output.
    c) output/the price level.
    d) the price level/the price level.
    e) output/the price level and output.

12. Which one of the following statements is true?
    a) In the Keynesian model, the level of output is determined by demand.
    b) In the Classical model, the level of output is determined by demand.
    c) In the Classical model, the aggregate supply curve is horizontal.
    d) where aggregate demand and aggregate supply intersect is the full-employment level of output.
    e) (b) and (c).

13. In the short run, a drop in oil prices will lead to:

    a) a lower price level with no change in output.

    b) a lower price level and a higher output level.

    c) a lower price level and a lower output level.

    d) a higher price level and a higher output level.

    e) a higher price level and a lower output level.

14. Assuming a country is operating at the full-employment level of output, a government that increases its share of purchases of its country's GDP:

    a) incurs an opportunity cost.

    b) may find that its exports decline and its imports increase.

    c) may find that investment spending declines.

    d) may find that consumer spending declines.

    e) all of the above.

15. Suppose you are given the following information on GDP and shares (percentages) of GDP purchased by consumers, businesses, the government, and the foreign sector:

    GDP = $3 trillion.

    Share of consumption expenditures = 50%

    Share of investment expenditures = 15%

    Share of government expenditures = 15%

    Share of net exports = 20%.

    Based on these numbers, which one of the following statements is true?

    a) an example of crowding out would be if the share of consumption expenditures increased to 60% and the share of investment expenditures decreased to 5%.

    b) an example of crowding out would be if the share of consumption expenditures increased to 75% and the share of net exports declined to -5%.

    c) an example of crowding out would be if the share of government expenditures increased to 25% and consumption expenditures fell by 7% and investment expenditures fell by 3%.

    d) an example of crowding out would be if all of the shares fell by, say, 5%.

    e) if the share of government expenditures increased to 30% and investment expenditures increased to 20% but consumption expenditures decreased to 30%, we would conclude that the private sector, on net, had been crowded in.

VI. PRACTICE EXAM: ESSAY QUESTIONS

1. Explain the short and long run effects of an increase in the money supply on the price level and output. Assume the economy is initially operating at the potential level of real GDP. Be sure to address why the results are different.

2. Explain the short run effects of an increase in the price of oil on the price level and output. Assume the economy is initially operating at the potential level of real GDP.

VII. ANSWER KEY: MULTIPLE CHOICE QUESTIONS

1. Correct answer: a.

Discussion: Keynes thought that the Great Depression was caused by too little spending taking place in the U.S. economy. This insufficient demand for goods and services led to a reduced demand for workers, which consequently led to a very high unemployment rate.

Statements b, c, and e may be consequences (not causes) of the Great Depression. While the stock market crash may have been partly responsible for the Great Depression, it is not the reason that Keynes stressed.

2. Correct answer: b.

Discussion: In the short run, a time period over which prices may not be able to adjust to equilibrate demand and supply, prices (and wages) are "sticky." This price stickiness is represented by a relatively flat aggregate supply curve. In the long run, with full adjustment of prices and wages, the aggregate supply curve is drawn as vertical.

Statement a is not correct; Keynesian economic thought deals with the behavior of the economy in the short run. Statement c is not correct; a recession is defined as a two consecutive quarter (six months) or longer decline in real GDP. Statement d is not correct. An economic recovery starts as an economy moves out of a trough (low point), not a peak. Statement e is not correct. Unemployment is countercyclical, not procyclical. That is, as real GDP rises, the unemployment rate declines and as real GDP declines, the unemployment rate rises.

3. Correct answer: e.

Discussion: Statements b and d are both correct. Okun's Law relates movements above the potential level of real GDP to declines in the unemployment rate. Okun's Law states that for every 1% point that real GDP grows faster than the normal rate of increase in potential output, the unemployment rate falls by 0.5 percentage points. Thus, with real GDP growing 2% points below the normal rate, the unemployment rate will increase by 2% points multiplied by 0.5. Thus, the unemployment rate will increase by 1% point and it will thus rise from 6% to 7%.

Based on the discussion, statements a and c cannot be correct.

4.   Correct answer: c.

Discussion: The unemployment rate is "countercyclical." That means that changes in the unemployment rate move in the opposite (counter) direction of changes in real GDP. So, increases in real GDP correspond to declines in the unemployment rate and vice-versa.

Statements a, b, and d are examples of "procyclical" variables. That is, increased consumption spending, investment spending, and the prices of stocks will be associated with increases in real GDP and vice-versa.

5.   Correct answer: b.

Discussion: When the economy grows above its "trend" or "potential" rate of growth, inflation is likely to occur. This is because, an economy growing above its potential rate is likely doing so because of increases in aggregate demand. The increases in aggregate demand strain the production capacity of the economy and ultimately, the production capacity may no longer be able to satisfy the increases in aggregate demand -- labor and other goods and services may be in "short supply" relative to the demand for them. Consequently, prices of goods and services, including wages may begin to rise resulting in inflation.

Statement a is not correct. As Okun's Law points out, increases in output above the potential level, correspond to reductions in the unemployment rate, not increases in it. There is no economic rationale for statements c and e. Statement d is not correct since wages would be likely to increase, not decrease, at least in the long run.

6.   Correct answer: d.

Discussion: Christina Romer's explanations for the stability of real GDP since World War II than before it was based on a non-economic argument. That is, the "observed" moderation in fluctuations (movements) in real GDP starting in the mid-1940s had more to do with the quality of the data and the techniques used to study the behavior of real GDP than with economic policy. Her conclusion was quite controversial since many economists believed that the stability in real GDP achieved subsequent to World War II had to do with sound fiscal and monetary policies that were put into practice.

7.   Correct answer: c.

Discussion: When prices are "sticky," it means that prices don't move up or down immediately in response to changes in demand or supply. Such price stickiness may be due to contracts that have been set that fix the price at which a good or service sells for a period of time. Thus, wages of union and government workers (and most workers in general) are considered sticky. The price for durable goods like steel rods, trucks, etc. are also typically set by a contract. Even prices on pre-printed brochures and menus may be sticky since businesses may not be able to quickly change the price for their output when there is a shift in demand or supply. Fresh fruit, however, is a good that is much less likely to be sticky.

8. Correct answer: a.

Discussion: The consequence of sticky prices is that when demand and/or supply shift, the price does not immediately change. Consequently, an excess demand or supply can be created. Examples of completely sticky prices are price ceilings and price floors discussed in Chapter 4. You may wish to review PETS #8 and #9 of Chapter 4 of the practicum. If a shortage or surplus of airplanes emerges, then the amount of labor and aircraft parts used in producing airplanes will also be affected. If wages in the aircraft industry and prices in the aircraft parts industry are not sticky, then a shortage or surplus may not arise. A production function shows the relationship between output and labor for a given capital stock and state of technology. It has nothing to do with sticky prices.

9. Correct answer: a.

Discussion: When the price level drops, the average level of prices of goods and services declines. This means goods and services are less costly to consumers. This, in turn, means that the purchasing power of consumers' money and wealth (how many goods and services they can buy) will have increased. Since the real value of consumers' money and wealth has increased, they will be inclined to buy more when the price level drops. This is a way of saying that aggregate demand is negatively sloped. As the price level drops, the amount of total output desired to be purchased will increase.

Statement b is incorrect because a decline in the price level lowers interest rates, not raises them. Statement c is incorrect because an increase in the price level implies that exports are becoming more expensive to foreign residents. Thus, an increase in the price level would reduce exports, not raise them. Statement d is incorrect; the relationship between the price level and the amount of output produced is an aggregate supply concept, not an aggregate demand concept. Statement e is incorrect; aggregate demand shows the relationship between the price level and the amount of output in total demanded by an economy. It does not show the relationship between income and saving.

10. Correct answer: d.

Discussion: A leftward shift in the aggregate demand curve means that aggregate demand for goods and services has declined. An increase in taxes would reduce the amount of spending in the economy and thus translate to a decrease in aggregate demand for goods and services.

Statements (a), (b), and (c) are all events that would raise the amount of spending in an economy and thus would be represented with a rightward shift in the aggregate demand curve. Statement e is an aggregate supply concept. A decline in the capital stock (a factor of production) would be represented by an upward shift in the short run aggregate supply curve and a leftward shift in the long run aggregate supply curve.

11. Correct answer: a.

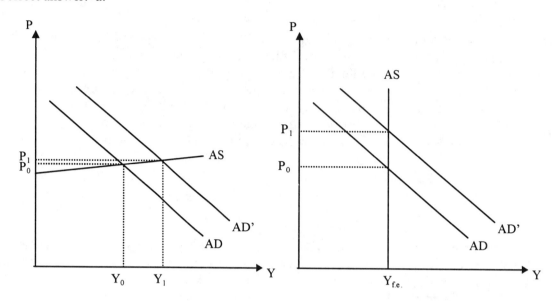

Discussion: To see this, look at the graphs above. Your text represents the short run with a relatively flat aggregate supply curve and the long run with a vertical aggregate supply curve. Compare what happens to the price level and output (real GDP) in the short and long run when aggregate demand increases.

As you can see, in the short run, output increases with a modest increase in the price level. In the long run, the economy is assumed to be producing at full-capacity (full-employment, or potential). This means that physically, the economy does not have the resources to produce any more. Thus, when aggregate demand increases, businesses cannot respond by, in the aggregate, producing any more output. However, with buyers wanting to purchase more output, they will compete with each other for the limited output by offering to pay a higher price for it (much like at an auction). Ultimately, the price level rises. It rises by enough to keep aggregate demand equal to the amount the economy is able to produce. Thus, the price level rises in the long run with no change in the level of output produced.

Given the discussion above, statements b, c, d, and e cannot be correct.

12. Correct answer: a.

Discussion: The Keynesian model is a "demand-driven" model meaning that the level of output an economy produces is determined by the demand for the goods and services it produces. Low demand will mean a low output level.

Statement b is not true; in the Classical model, the level of output is determined by the factors of production an economy has. Statement c is not true; in the Classical model, aggregate supply is represented as a vertical line. Statement d is not true; the intersection of aggregate demand and supply produce an "equilibrium" output level but the equilibrium output level may not be the full-employment output level. For example, the full-employment output level may be $1.5 trillion worth of goods and services whereas the intersection of aggregate demand and supply produce an output level of $1 trillion.

13. Correct answer: b.

Discussion: A drop in oil prices is an example of a supply shock. Oil is a key input into production and when its price changes, it affects the aggregate supply curve. In effect, the lower price of oil makes production less costly. This would be represented by a downward shift in the short run aggregate supply curve (i.e. the same amount of output can be produced as before, but now at a lower price level). As the short run aggregate supply curve shifts down along the aggregate demand curve, you will see that the equilibrium price level will drop and the equilibrium output level will rise. Output rises because the lower price level creates a real wealth, interest rate, and trade effect which all lead to increased spending. Since the cause of the increased spending is a drop in the price level (which is graphed on the axis), the increased spending is represented by a movement along the aggregate demand curve (not a rightward shift in it). With increased spending, businesses respond by producing more, which is why output rises.

Given the discussion above, none of the other statements are correct.

14. Correct answer: e.

Discussion: An increase in government spending incurs an opportunity cost because it crowds out spending by other sectors of the economy. Thus, an increase in government spending may incur an opportunity cost (giving up something) of decreased spending by consumers. That is, the economy, as a whole must give up some spending by consumers. The increased government spending also leads to crowding out of net exports (i.e. exports will decline but imports will rise) and investment spending. This is not to say that some groups of consumers or businesses will not be crowded in. For example, your book mentions that an increase in government spending on highways may crowd in (increase) some types of investment spending.

15. Correct answer: c.

Discussion: Crowding out is caused by an increase in government expenditures. Crowding out means that an increase in government spending causes a reduction in spending by consumers and/or businesses and/or through net exports. Thus, statements a and b cannot be correct because there is no basis for crowding out. Government spending has not changed. Statement d cannot be correct because government expenditures along with consumption and investment expenditures decline. Statement e is not correct because the share of government expenditures increased by 10% but investment expenditures increased by 5% while consumption expenditures declined by 20% so that in total, private sector spending was crowded out (reduced) by -15% = (+5% - 20%), not crowded in, on net. Statement d is the only statement that reflects crowding out. In this case, while government expenditures rise by 10%, consumption expenditures are reduced by 7% and investment expenditures by 3% for a total of a 10% reduction in private sector spending. That is, private sector spending is crowded out by the increase in government spending.

VIII. ANSWER KEY: ESSAY QUESTIONS

1. In the short run, prices are sticky and output is demand determined. Thus, the increase in the money supply, which raises spending by households and businesses, leads to an increase in aggregate demand. As aggregate demand shifts out to the right, with prices sticky, there is hardly any change in the price level. This is represented by the aggregate demand curve shifting rightward along a relatively flat aggregate supply curve as below which moves the economy from point A to point B:

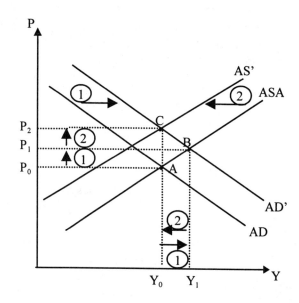

However, in the short run, businesses respond to the increased demand by producing more output and so the level of output produced rises. It rises from Y_0 to Y_1. The price level rises modestly from P_0 to P_1.

However, the economy cannot continue to operate for a sustained period of time above its full-employment or potential level of output. The increase in aggregate demand cannot be satisfied for a long period of time given the production capability of the economy, which is at Y_0. This is because the full-employment level of output is determined by supply conditions -- labor, capital, and technology and these have not changed. So, in the long run, given the increases in demand for goods and services as well as for labor, prices and wages will begin to rise. The rise in wages and other input prices is represented by a leftward shift in the aggregate supply curve as marked in the graph above. Thus, eventually, the economy returns to the potential level of output, Y_0, but with a higher price level, P_2. (movement from B to C).

2. An increase in the price of oil is represented by a leftward shift in the Keynesian (short run) aggregate supply curve. Oil is a key input into production and an increase in its price raises the price of nearly all goods and services. The oil price increase is represented by a leftward shift in the Keynesian aggregate supply curve illustrating that at all output levels, the price level would now be higher than before the oil price increase. See the graph below.

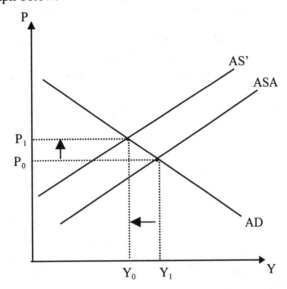

As the aggregate supply curve shifts leftward along the aggregate demand curve, the effect is to raise the price level, as you might have expected. At the same time, there is a corresponding decline in the level of output the economy is capable of producing. Thus, the oil price increase creates two problems in the economy: a higher price level (inflation) and a reduction in real GDP (more unemployment). This was the experience of the U.S. economy in 1973 and again in 1979.

Take It to the Net

We invite you to visit the O'Sullivan/Sheffrin page on the Prentice Hall Web site at:

http://www.prenhall.com/osullivan/

for this chapter's World Wide Web exercise.

CHAPTER 14
KEYNESIAN ECONOMICS AND FISCAL POLICY

I. OVERVIEW

In this chapter, you will learn about a short run model of the economy referred to as a Keynesian economic model. You will learn that the model emphasizes how changes in spending, particularly government spending, can influence the level of output in the short run. You should remember that the model is simple in the sense that it holds a number of factors like prices, interest rates, exchange rates, and wages constant in order to highlight the affect of spending on output. You will see how spending by households, businesses, the government and the foreign sector determines how much is in total produced in an economy. You will be introduced to multiplier analysis and see how some initial change in spending can lead to a multiple change in the level of output. You will learn about fiscal policy, which is the use of government spending and changes in taxes to influence the level of output produced by an economy. You will learn a little of the history of Keynesian economic policy in the U.S. You will learn about the automatic stabilizers and properties of a tax and transfer payments system.

II. CHECKLIST

By the end of this chapter, you should be able to:

√   Discuss the key features of a Keynesian economic model.

√   Discuss Keynesian economic policy.

√   Explain autonomous spending.

√   Use the Keynesian cross diagram to show how changes in spending create changes in output.

√   Discuss macroequilibrium and situations of disequilibrium using the Keynesian cross diagram.

√   Discuss the role of inventories in situations of disequilibrium.

√   Explain the consumption function and the equation for the consumption function.

√   Define the marginal propensity to consume, save, and import.

√   Define the multiplier.

√   Describe how the multiplier works in an economy.

√   Compare the effects on output of an increase (or decrease) in government spending of $X to a cut in taxes of $X.

√   Define the government spending multiplier, the tax multiplier, and the balanced budget multiplier.

√   Give a brief history of the application of Keynesian economic ideas to the U.S. economy.

√   Define automatic stabilizers and explain what they do.

III. KEY TERMS

Equilibrium output: the level of GDP where the demand for output equals the amount that is produced.

Consumption function: the relationship between the level of income and consumption spending.

Autonomous consumption: the part of consumption that does not depend on income.

Marginal propensity to consume (MPC): the fraction of additional income that is spent.

Marginal propensity to save: fraction of additional income that is saved.

Multiplier: the ratio of changes in output to changes in spending. It measures the degree to which changes in spending are "multiplied" into changes in output.

Keynesian fiscal policy: the use of taxes and government spending to affect the level of GDP in the short run.

Disposable personal income: the income that ultimately flows back to households, taking into account transfers and taxes.

Expansionary policies: policy actions that lead to increases in output

Contractionary policies: policy actions that lead to decreases in output.

Budget deficit: the difference between a government's spending and its taxation.

Permanent income: an estimate of a household's average level of income.

Automatic stabilizers: economic institutions that reduce economic fluctuations without any explicit action being taken.

Marginal propensity to import: the fraction of additional income that is spent on imports.

IV. PERFORMANCE ENHANCING TIPS (PETS)

PET #1

In the Keynesian model with prices and the price level fixed, output is also a measure of income. Thus, the two terms "output" and "income" may be used interchangeably.

PET #2

In the Keynesian cross diagram, the purpose of the 45 degree line is to permit you to read output (income) off of the vertical axis to more easily compare it to the level of total spending that occurs at that income level.

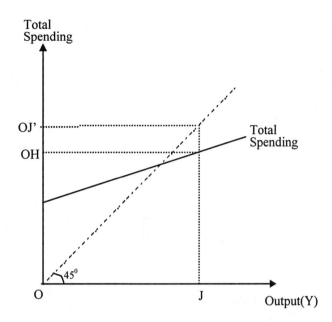

To understand this, look at the graph above.

A comparison of total spending to income (output) at income (output) level OJ may at first appear difficult to do since spending is measured on the vertical axis but income is measured on the horizontal axis. However, you can measure income on the vertical axis by drawing a line from income level OJ up to the 45 degree line and over to the vertical axis. Mark this as OJ'. This is a measure of income read off of the vertical axis. Since total spending at income level OJ is read by taking that income level up to the spending graph and over to the vertical axis (marked OH), you can see that income and output (OJ') exceed total spending (OH). Thus, you could conclude that businesses' inventories will be building up since too much has been produced relative to how much is in total being purchased by the economy.

PET #3

The difference between consumption spending (C) and imports (M) is defined to be spending by households on domestic goods and services.

In a model with exports and imports, consumption spending is defined as spending by households on domestic and foreign-produced goods and services. If consumption figures reported for the U.S. are $45 billion, part of that $45 billion is spending on U.S. made goods and services and part on foreign-made goods and services. If imports are reported to be $5 billion, then the difference between consumption and imports will define the amount of spending by U.S. households on U.S. made goods and services only. In this case, the amount would be $40 billion.

PET #4

The relationship between changes in spending, output, and the multiplier is given by the formula:

$$\Delta y = \textbf{multiplier X initial } \Delta \textbf{ in spending}$$

Given any two of these three pieces of the formula, you should be able to figure out the third.

For example, suppose you are told that the multiplier is 2.5 and that income and output have decreased by $100 billion. What might be the cause? A change in spending of $100/2.5 = $40 billion might be the cause. It may be that government spending declined by $40 billion or that investment spending declined by $40 billion, etc.

Suppose you are told that the marginal propensity to consume is 0.9 and the marginal propensity to import is 0.3. Further, you are told that investment spending has increased by $20 billion. What will be the effect on income and output? Since you know the marginal propensity to consume and the marginal propensity to import, you can compute the multiplier as 1/1-(0.9-0.3) = 1/0.4 = 2.5. With the increase in investment spending of $20 billion, you can compute the change in income and output as 2.5 X $20 billion = $50 billion.

Suppose you are told that government spending has increased by $10 billion and that income and output increased by $20 billion. What must the multiplier's value be? Using the formula in bold above, the multiplier would be $20 billion/$10 billion = 2.

PET #5

Autonomous consumption, investment spending, government spending, exports, and autonomous imports are components of total spending in an economy that do not depend on the level of income. This means that changes in income (output) will not cause changes in these spending components. However, changes in these spending components can cause changes in income (output).

For example, suppose you are given the following information:

$$C = 100 + 0.9 \text{ X } (y - T)$$
$$I = 150$$
$$G = 200$$
$$X = 20$$
$$M = 50 + 0.1 \text{ X } y$$

Based on this information, the multiplier for the economy is 1/1-(0.9-0.1) = 1/0.2 = 5. Suppose you are told that government spending increases by $20 billion. Based on multiplier analysis, income and output will rise by 5 X $20 billion = $100 billion. While the increase in government spending leads to an increase in income and output, the increase in income will not affect the Ca, I, G, X or Ma (which is autonomous imports that your textbook has set to zero by writing M = m X y). However, overall consumption (C) and overall imports (M) will be affected because they depend on the level of income. The extent to which they depend on the level of income is given by the marginal propensity to consume (0.9) and the marginal propensity to import (0.1). If income increases by $100 billion, since the marginal propensity to consume is 0.9, consumption spending will increase by 0.9 X 100 = $90 billion. Also, since the marginal propensity to import is 0.1, imports will increase by 0.1 X 100=$10 billion. The $90 billion increase in consumption spending is spending by households on domestic and foreign goods. Since imports (spending on foreign goods) have increased by $10 billion, the increase in spending on domestic goods is $80 billion ($90 - $10).

PET #6

There are several formulas for the multiplier. Each formula depends on the variables are assumed to be functions of income.

The simplest formula that your book introduces is a multiplier formula of 1/(1-b) where b is the marginal propensity to consume. This formula applies to a model in which there are either no taxes and no imports or taxes and imports are autonomous (i.e. do not depend on the level of income). For example, if b = 0.8, then the multiplier is 1/0.2 = 5.

The next multiplier formula your book introduces is one in which taxes depend on the level of income so T = t X y. In this case, the multiplier's formula is 1/[1-b X (1-t)]. For example, if b = 0.8 and the tax rate is 0.1, the multiplier is 1/1-0.72 = 1/0.38 = 2.63

Then, your book introduces a multiplier formula where taxes are autonomous (i.e. do not depend on the level of income) but there are imports which do depend on the level of income so M = m X y. In this case, the multiplier's formula is 1/1-(b-m). For example, if b = 0.85 and m = 0.10, the multiplier is 1/1-0.75 = 1/0.25 = 4.

PET #7

The magnitude of the multiplier depends on the marginal propensity to consume (b), the marginal propensity to import (m), and the tax rate (t).

A bigger marginal propensity to consume will increase the magnitude of the multiplier and vice-versa. A bigger marginal propensity to import will decrease the magnitude of the multiplier and vice-versa. A bigger tax rate will decrease the magnitude of the multiplier and vice-versa.

For example, suppose b = 0.9 and m = 0.1, and that the tax rate is zero. The multiplier will be 1/1-(0.9 -0.1) = 1/0.2 = 5. Now, suppose marginal propensity to consume decreases to 0.85. What will the multiplier's value be? The multiplier will be 1/1 - (0.85-0.1)= 1/0.25 = 4.

Now, suppose that the marginal propensity to import decreases to 0.05 while the marginal propensity to consume remains at 0.9. The multiplier will be 1/1 - (0.9-0.05) = 1/0.15 = 6.67.

Now, suppose that the tax rate is no longer zero but 10% (i.e. t = 0.10). Also, for simplicity, assume that the marginal propensity to import is zero. When taxes do not depend on income, the multiplier would be 1/1-0.8 = 1/0.2 = 5. When taxes depend on income, the multiplier will be 1/1-0.8 X (1-0.1) = 1/1-0.72 = 1/0.38 = 2.63.

PET #8

A change in government spending of $X will have a bigger impact on income and output than a change in taxes of $X because government spending works directly on total spending whereas taxes work indirectly on total spending through consumption spending.

Remember that in the Keynesian model, the level of output an economy produces depends on total spending. An increase in government spending will thus increase the level of output. The amount that output will increase depends on the size of the multiplier.

For example, suppose the marginal propensity to consume is 0.75 and the marginal propensity to import is 0. The multiplier is 1/1 - (b-m) = 1/1 - (0.75-0) = 1/0.25 = 4. Now, suppose government spending increases by $25 billion. The increase in income and output will be 4 X 25 = $100.

Compare this increase in income and output to a cut in taxes of $25 billion (the same amount by which government spending has increased). You know that the cut in taxes will increase consumption spending. The amount by which consumption spending will increase is NOT $25 billion. The reason is that the marginal propensity to consume is 0.75. In this case, consumption spending will increase by 0.75 X $25 billion = $18.75 billion. The remainder of the tax cut will be saved (25 - 18.75 = 6.25). Income and output will increase by the multiplier times the change in consumer spending. Thus, income and output will increase by 4 X $18.75 = $75 billion. As you can see, the cut in taxes is not as expansionary on spending and thus on output as is an equivalent increase in government spending.

V. PRACTICE EXAM: MULTIPLE CHOICE QUESTIONS

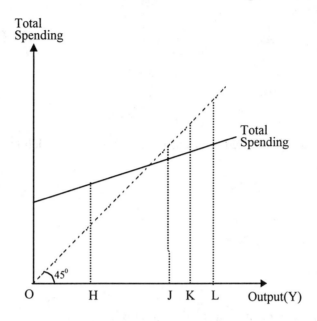

1. Which one of the following statements is true of the graph above?

    a) at output level OH, inventories are accumulating.

    b) at output level OK, total spending exceeds output.

    c) output level OJ is the equilibrium level of output.

    d) at output level OL, inventories are accumulating.

    e) at output level OH, consumption equals saving.

2. Which one of the following statements is true about the consumption function below?

    C = 20 + 0.75 X (y - T)

    a) the marginal propensity to save must be 1.75.

    b) if income is 250 and taxes are 50, then consumption is 150.

    c) if income is 400 and taxes are 120, then saving must be 50.

    d) the slope of the consumption function is 0.25.

    e) the autonomous level of consumption cannot be determined without information on income and taxes.

3. Which one of the following would cause the consumption function to shift down?

   a) an increase in stock prices.

   b) a decrease in income.

   c) a decrease in wealth.

   d) a fall in interest rates.

   e) (b) and (c).

4. Which one of the following is true of equilibrium in an economy in which there is no government and no foreign sector?

   a) I = S.

   b) C = S.

   c) C = I.

   d) Y = C.

   e) Y = I.

5. Which one of the following statements is true of the multiplier?

   a) it is greater than 1.0.

   b) it will increase with an increase in the marginal propensity to consume.

   c) it will increase with a decrease in the marginal propensity to import.

   d) it gives the multiple by which output will change in response to a change in, e.g. investment spending.

   e) all of the above are true.

6. Assume the marginal propensity to consume is 0.90 and that there are no imports. Based on this, the marginal propensity to save is ___ and the multiplier is ____.

   a) 0.10; 1.11.

   b) 0.10; 10.

   c) 1.9; 1.11.

   d) 1.9; 10.

   e) cannot be determined; 10.

7. Given a multiplier of 2, a decrease in investment spending of $40 billion will:

   a) increase equilibrium output by $80 billion.

   b) decrease equilibrium output by $80 billion.

   c) increase equilibrium output by $20 billion.

   d) decrease equilibrium output by $20 billion.

   e) decrease equilibrium output by $40 billion.

8. An increase in investment spending of $16 billion will cause output to rise by _____ assuming the multiplier is 2.5:
   a) $16 billion.
   b) $6.4 billion.
   c) $64 billion.
   d) $40 billion.
   e) $12 billion.

9. If an increase in government spending of $50 billion creates an increase in output of $200 billion, then the multiplier must be:
   a) 4.
   b) 2.5.
   c) 1.4
   d) 4.44.
   e) 0.25.

10. Suppose the President would like to increase the level of output an economy produces by $100 billion, no more and no less. Further, suppose the multiplier is 3. Which one of the following policy options would work?
   a) increase government spending by $33.33 billion.
   b) increase taxes by $33.33 billion.
   c) increase government spending by $300 billion.
   d) increase government spending by $100 billion.
   e) increase government spending by $33.33 billion and reduces taxes by $33.33 billion.

11. Suppose Congress decides to cut taxes by $25 billion. Further assume the marginal propensity to consume is 0.80. Also assume that this is a closed economy with no imports. Based on this information, consumption spending will initially change by _____ and output will change by _____.
   a) +$20 billion; +$100 billion.
   b) -$20 billion; -$100 billion.
   c) +$25 billion; +$125 billion.
   d) +$125 billion; +$625 billion.
   e) +31.25 billion; +$39.06 billion.

12. A fiscal policy of increasing government spending by $50 billion and increasing taxes by $50 billion will (assuming the marginal propensity to consume is 0.5 and the marginal propensity to import is 0):

    a) decrease autonomous consumption by $25 billion.

    b) raise output by $100 billion.

    c) create a budget deficit.

    d) raise output by $50 billion.

    e) (a) and (d).

13. Which one of the following statements is true:

    a) Keynesian fiscal policy was actively used during the Great Depression.

    b) President Kennedy applied Keynesian economics to the U.S. economy through a tax cut.

    c) a tax surcharge was imposed during the late 1960s to combat high unemployment.

    d) the tax cuts introduced by President Reagan in the early 1980s were proposed as part of a Keynesian fiscal policy prescription.

    e) all of the above are true.

14. A temporary tax cut is:

    a) expected to be very expansionary.

    b) not expected to have much affect on spending and output.

    c) will raise permanent income.

    d) an example of an automatic stabilizer.

    e) none of the above.

15. Automatic stabilizers:

    a) are part of the tax and transfer payment system.

    b) work without enacting any laws.

    c) help stabilize the business cycle.

    d) tend to reduce spending during economic expansions and raise spending during economic contractions.

    e) all of the above.

16. Which one of the following statements is true?

    a) an increase in income will reduce imports.

    b) if the multiplier is 2 and exports increase by $10 billion, output will increase by $20 billion.

    c) an increase in the marginal propensity to import will increase the multiplier.

    d) a cut in tax rates will reduce the slope of the consumption function.

    e) (b) and (c).

VI. PRACTICE EXAM: ESSAY QUESTIONS

1. Explain why an initial increase in spending leads to a multiple expansion in output. What role does the magnitude of the marginal propensity play? Use a simple model with a government but no foreign sector.

2. Suppose that you are chair of the Council of Economic Advisors and must make a recommendation to the President about what policy actions may need to be taken given that the economy is suffering a severe recession. What might you recommend and why?

VII. ANSWER KEY: MULTIPLE CHOICE QUESTIONS

1. Correct answer: d.

Discussion: At output (income) level OL, the amount the economy produces, OL, is greater than the amount of output in total purchased at that income level. Total spending at income level OL is read off the vertical axis and is OM, as shown below.

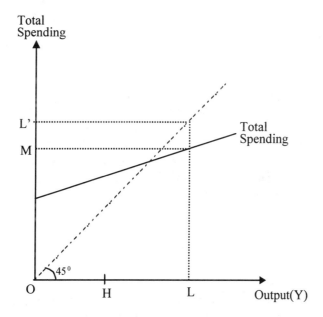

To compare this spending level to the output level, use the 45 degree line to measure the OL output level on the horizontal axis. The output level read off of the vertical axis is OL'. Since OL' is greater than OM, output exceeds total spending which means that businesses inventories will be piling up (accumulating).

Statement a is not correct because at output level OH, spending exceeds current output and so inventories are being depleted. Statement b is not correct because output is greater than total spending. Statement c is not correct. The equilibrium level of output occurs where the 45 degree line and the total spending line intersect. Statement e is not correct. There is not enough information in the graph provided to say anything about the relationship between consumption and saving.

2. Correct answer: c.

Discussion: If income is $400 and taxes are $120, then disposable income is $280. The consumption function shows that the marginal propensity to consume is 0.75. Thus, 0.75 X $280 of disposable income will be used by households to buy goods and services (consume). This amount is $210. Since autonomous consumption is $20, then total consumption based on a before-tax income level of $400 is $230. Since income is $400 and $230 is spent on goods and services and $120 is spent on taxes, the remainder is saved. Thus saving is ($400 - $230 - $120) = $50.

Statement a is not correct. The marginal propensity to save (MPS) is 1 minus the marginal propensity to consume. Thus, the MPS is 0.25. Statement b is not correct based on the discussion above. Statement d is not correct. The slope of the consumption function is 0.75 as is given in the equation for consumption. Statement e is not correct because the autonomous level of consumption is given in the equation. It is equal to the value of consumption that would occur even if income were zero and in this case is $20.

3. Correct answer: c.

Discussion: A shift down in the consumption function means that for every level of income, consumer spending is now lower. That is, autonomous consumption spending has declined. A decrease in wealth could cause consumers to be more frugal and thus spend less at every level of income than they had been willing to spend before.

Statement a is not correct. An increase in stock prices would increase wealth and thus lead to an increase in autonomous consumption, which would shift the consumption function up. Statement b is not correct because a decrease in income would be represented by a movement down along the consumption function, not by a shift in it. Remember that since income is graphed on the axis, changes will cause movements along the consumption function but not shifts in it. You may wish to review PET #1 of Chapter 1 of the practicum. Statement d is not correct. A fall in interest rates makes it less costly for households to borrow in order to buy a new car or a new home. Thus, lower interest rates will lead to an increase in autonomous consumption, which would be represented by an upward shift in the consumption function. Statement e is not correct because statement b is not correct.

4. Correct answer: a.

Discussion: macroequilibrium occurs where total output (y) is equal to total spending. Total spending in an economy where there is no government and no foreign sector is just the sum of spending by households (C) and businesses (I). Thus, y = C + I. Furthermore, since output equals income and since there is no government, there are also no taxes. Thus, income can be either spent (C) or saved (S). Thus, y = C + S. By substitution in the equilibrium condition, C + S = C + I which means S = I.

5. Correct answer: e.

Discussion: The multiplier is greater than 1.0. This means that some initial change in spending will have a bigger impact on output than the initial change in spending. For example, if spending increases by $20 billion, output and income will increase in the first round by $20 billion but will then continue to increase as more spending and hence more production and income are generated. Thus, output will increase by more than the initial $20 billion increase in spending. The multiplier's value depends on the marginal propensity to consume and import (and on the tax rate). A bigger marginal propensity to consume means that after the first-round increase in income of $20 billion, more consumption will occur than with a lower marginal propensity to consume. With more consumption occurring, more output and income will be generated in the second, third, fourth....spending rounds. This can be described by saying that the multiplier will be bigger for a bigger marginal propensity to consume. A bigger marginal propensity to import means that after the first round increase in income of $20 billion, more imports will be purchased than with a lower marginal propensity to import. With more income being used to buy foreign-made goods and services, less income is left available to buy domestic-made goods and services. Thus, with less spending on domestic goods and services, less domestic production and income will be generated. That is, the multiplier will decrease as the marginal propensity to import increases.

6. Correct answer: b.

Discussion: Since you know the marginal propensity to consume is 0.9, the marginal propensity to save must be 0.1. That is because the marginal propensity to consume and the marginal propensity to save sum to 1.0 (MPC + MPS = 1). Next, the multiplier is 10 based on the formula for the multiplier which is [1/(1-MPC)] = 1/(1-0.90) = 1/0.10 = 10. Notice that the multiplier can also be determined from the formula 1/MPS. In this question, the formula would be 1/0.10 = 10. Both methods of calculating the multiplier give you the same information. But, make sure you remember that the denominator is either (1-MPC) or just the MPS. Don't confuse the denominator as 1/MPC and (1-MPS) or you could end up with the wrong answers!

Statement a gets the MPS correct but gives the wrong multiplier. You would have gotten a multiplier of 1.11 if you had incorrectly calculated it as 1/MPC, i.e. 1/0.9. Statement c gets the multiplier and the MPS wrong. Statement d gets the MPS wrong but the multiplier correct. And statement e is not true because you can figure out the MPS by knowing what the MPC is.

7. Correct answer: b.

Discussion: First, you should be able to rule out answers a and c since a decrease in investment spending will lead to a decrease in output, not an increase. Next, you should be able to rule out answer e since the multiplier is a number that is not equal to 1. Given that the multiplier is 2, the $40 billion reduction in investment spending will circulate through the economy with multiplier effects leading to a reduction in output and income of $80 billion. You may wish to review PET #4 of this chapter to see how to use the formula.

8. Correct answer: d.

Discussion. Since you know the multiplier is 2.5 and you are told that investment spending increases by $16 billion, you can use formula (see PET #4) to figure out the change in output. The change in output will be

2.5 X $16 billion = $40 billion. In this type of question, you should always look for an answer about the change in output to be greater than the change in initial spending (in this case, investment spending). Thus, you could narrow the answers down to statements that give a change in output greater than $16 billion. That is, statements a, b, and e will not be correct.

Warning: In questions where there is an increase in government spending and an increase in taxes by the same amount, the change in output will be the same amount as the fiscal policy move. That is, if government spending and taxes both increase by $10 billion, then output will rise by $10 billion. The same holds true if the question gives equal decreases in government spending and taxes. That is, if government spending and taxes both decrease by $26 billion, then output will decrease by $26 billion. However, if government spending increases and taxes decrease (or vice-versa), you cannot answer that output will change by the same amount as the policy move.

9. Correct answer: a.

Discussion: The multiplier is figured out by using the formula from PET #4. In this question, you know that the change in output is $200 billion and that the change in spending is $50 billion. That is, by plugging these numbers into the formula you would have:

$200 billion = multiplier X $50 billion.

From this, you can calculate that the multiplier must be $200 billion/$50 billion = 4.

10. Correct answer: a.

Discussion: Since you are given the multiplier and the desired change in output, all you need to do is to apply the formula reviewed in PET #4. With a multiplier of 3, any spending increase of $33.33 billion will lead to an increase in output of $100 billion.

Statement b cannot be correct because an increase in taxes would reduce spending and thus would decrease output, not increase it. Statement c is not correct because an increase in government spending of $300 billion will lead to an increase in output of $900 billion. Statement d is not correct because an increase in government spending of $100 billion will lead to an increase in output of $300 billion. Statement e is not correct. The increase in government spending of $33.33 billion will increase output by $100 billion and the cut in taxes of $33.33 billion will raise consumption spending by the MPC times $33.33 billion. In total, output would rise by more than $100 billion since more than $33.33 billion worth of initial spending will take place.

11. Correct answer: a.

Discussion: A tax cut works initially to affect consumption spending. However, consumption spending doesn't change by the full amount of the tax cut since part of the tax cut (refund, if you prefer to think of it that way) will be saved. Since you know the marginal propensity to consume is 0.80, then 0.8 of the $25 billion tax cut will be spent. Thus, there will initially be an increase in consumption spending of 0.80 X $25 billion = $20 billion. The remaining $5 billion will be saved (0.20 X $25 billion). Now, since you know that the change in consumption spending initially is $20 billion, you can figure out the effect on output. But, you need the multiplier. Fortunately, you are told the MPC is 0.80. Thus, the multiplier will be $1/(1-0.8)$ = $1/0.2 = 5$. The change in output, using the formula from PET #4 will be 5 X $20 billion = $100 billion.

12. Correct answer: e.

Discussion: The increase in taxes of $50 billion will cause consumers to cut back on their spending. Thus, autonomous consumption will decline. By how much? Since the marginal propensity to consume is 0.5, autonomous consumption spending will decline by 0.5 X $50 billion = $25 billion. This reduction in consumption will have a multiplier effect on output. Since the MPC is 0.5 (and the marginal propensity to import and the tax rate is zero), the multiplier is $1/(1-0.5) = 2$. Thus, the fall in consumption spending of $25 billion will lead to a $50 billion fall in output. However, government spending has increased at the same time that taxes have been increased. The increase in government spending will work to raise output. By how much? Since the multiplier is 2, the increase in government spending of $50 billion will lead to an increase in output of $100 billion. On net, with output rising by $100 billion but declining by $50 billion (via the tax increase), output will increase by $50 billion. This is an example of the balanced budget multiplier. The balanced budget multiplier is 1 which means that any increase in spending of $X will lead to an $X increase in output.

Since taxes and government spending increase by the same amount, the budget will not go to a deficit (or surplus, either) but will remain in balance.

13. Correct answer: b.

Discussion: President Kennedy applied a tax cut to the U.S. economy on the advice of Walter Heller, then chair of the Council of Economic Advisors. The belief was that the U.S. economy could be doing better than it currently was and that a tax cut would help get the economy to grow and thus bring the unemployment rate down.

Statement a is not correct. While Keynes wrote during the Great Depression, his views were not put into practice in the U.S. until the 1960s. Statement c is not correct. A tax surcharge (increase) was imposed by President Nixon to combat inflation. The objective of the tax increase was to reduce spending and thus the demand for goods and services in an effort to take the pressure off of prices. Statement d is not correct. The tax cuts introduced by President Reagan were billed as part of the "supply-side" prescription for the U.S. economy. Undeniably, they would carry demand side effects. But, the view was that the tax cuts would promote work effort and additions to the capital stock, which would thereby enhance the growth of the U.S. economy.

14. Correct answer: b.

Discussion: A temporary tax cut is recognized by people to be temporary and thus is not expected to have a lasting impact on their income. Thus, people do not alter their spending behavior much in response to the tax cut. In fact, some studies suggest that people tend to save most of a temporary tax cut. Thus, the temporary tax cut has little effect on spending and consequently little effect (through the multiplier) on output.

Statement a is not correct because the policy is not likely to be very expansionary as discussed above. Statement c is not correct; a temporary tax cut raises temporary income. Statement d is not correct; an automatic stabilizer does not require legislative action as a temporary tax cut would.

15. Correct answer: e.

16. Correct answer: b.

Discussion: Exports are an autonomous component of spending and constitute spending by foreigners on goods produced by another country. Thus, if our exports increase by $10 billion, that means there is more spending on our goods. With a multiplier of 2, output will increase by $20 billion.

Statement a is not correct. Imports depend on income. Since the marginal propensity to import is positive, it means that increases in income will lead to increases in imports and decreases in income will lead to decreases in imports. Statement c is not correct; an increase in the marginal propensity to import will reduce the multiplier, not raise it. (See the answer to question 5 for more detail). Statement d is not correct. A cut in tax rates raises the slope of the consumption function. A lower tax rate means that, effectively, there is more income available for consumers to spend.

VIII. ANSWER KEY: ESSAY QUESTIONS

1. An initial increase in spending of say, $30 billion dollars, will initially lead to an increase in output and income of $30 billion. (With more output being produced, more income is generated). This is not the end of the effects on the economy of the initial increase in spending. Since income has now increased by $30 billion, consumers (households) will go out and spend more. Just how much more they spend depends on the magnitude of the marginal propensity to consume (MPC). If the MPC is 0.9, households will spend an additional $0.9 \times 30 = \$27$ billion. Their spending, of course, generates production and income in an amount equal to $27 billion. At this point, output has now increased by $57 billion which is more than the initial $30 billion increase in spending. The multiplier effect continues because the additional $27 billion worth of income propels more spending in an amount equal to $0.9 \times 27 = \$24.3$ billion which further activates production and income by $24.3 billion. At this point, output has now increased by $81.3 billion in total. This is the multiplier effect in action and is dependent on how much consumers like to spend of additional income they receive. In the end, the multiplier formula dictates that the initial $30 billion increase in spending, given an MPC of 0.9, will lead to a $300 billion increase in output. This is because the multiplier is $1/1-0.9 = 1/0.1 = 10$. If the MPC had been 0.6, then less spending would occur for each increase in income. For example, after the initial increase in output and income of $30 billion, only $0.6 \times 30 = \$18$ billion in spending and hence output and income would be generated. This is $9 billion less (27 - 18) than is generated when the MPC is 0.9. Thus, a smaller MPC creates a smaller multiplier effect, which shows up in a smaller multiplier. In this case, with an MPC of 0.6, the multiplier would be $1/1-0.6 = 1/0.4 = 2.5$. For an extreme, if the MPC was 0 (which means that when consumers receive additional income they do not spend any of it), the multiplier would be 1 and the total increase in output coming from the initial $30 billion increase in spending would be $30 billion. There would be no multiplier effect.

2. As chair of the Council of Economic Advisors and having a knowledge of economics confined to material that I've learned up through this chapter, I would be inclined to advise expansionary fiscal policy. Expansionary fiscal policy can be carried out in two ways -- through increases in government spending and/or permanent cuts in taxes. An increase in government spending works directly on spending and in comparison to an equal dollar tax cut is more stimulative to output. For example, a $50 billion increase in government spending will raise output by more than a $50 billion cut in taxes. This is because the $50 billion tax cut does not generate $50 billion worth of spending; it generates less than $50 billion worth of spending. If the marginal propensity to consume is 0.8, a $50 billion tax cut will increase spending by $40 billion which is $10 billion less than if government spending is used instead. Thus, the initial spending stimulus to the economy is smaller and for a given multiplier, its effects on output will also be smaller.

However, this is not to say that a tax cut is inferior to government spending as a tool of policymakers. If my Council deems it necessary to unleash $50 billion worth of spending into the economy, we could cut taxes by more than $50 billion. In fact, if we cut taxes by $62.5 billion, we will generate the desired $50 billion increase in spending (0.8 X $62.5). One difference with the tax cut policy compared to an increase in government spending is that it is the private sector that is doing the spending and not the government. Some people may find this preferable. On the other hand, a tax cut (holding government spending constant) will increase the budget deficit by $62.5 billion whereas an increase in government spending (without cutting taxes) will increase the budget deficit by $50 billion. In any case, I'd let the President make the choice -- that's what he's been elected to do anyway.

I would warn the President that the effects of the expansionary fiscal policy may not turn out to be what my staff and I have estimated. The reason is that the budget deficit that is created in an effort to get the economy out of the recession may have some bad side effects on the economy that are not considered in the simple Keynesian model that I am using to formulate policy. For example, if the budget deficit makes people more worried about the economy and therefore more cautious about spending, then the multiplier may not be as big as assumed.

Take It to the Net

We invite you to visit the O'Sullivan/Sheffrin page on the Prentice Hall Web site at:

http://www.prenhall.com/osullivan/

for this chapter's World Wide Web exercise.

CHAPTER 15
MONEY, THE BANKING SYSTEM,
AND THE FEDERAL RESERVE

I.   OVERVIEW

In this chapter, you will learn what money is, what the functions of money are, and how the money supply can be influenced by a central bank and the banking system. You will learn about different measures of money. You will learn how the banking system works and how it can influence the money supply through making loans to businesses and households. You will learn that the U.S. banking system operates under a fractional reserve system and it is this system that enables banks, through loan creation, to influence the money supply. You will learn how the U.S. central bank (the Federal Reserve) can act to control the banking system's ability to extend loans to businesses and households. You will be introduced to another multiplier concept -- the money multiplier. You will also learn about the structure of the Federal Reserve System and what its primary functions are.

II.   CHECKLIST

By the end of this chapter, you should be able to:

√   Define money.

√   Explain the three properties of money.

√   Describe a barter system.

√   Explain how money solves the problem of a "double coincidence of wants."

√   Compare and contrast M1 and M2.

√   Define assets, liabilities, and net worth.

√   List some items that would be considered an asset of a bank; list some items that would be considered a liability of a bank.

√   Define required reserves and excess reserves.

√   Discuss how banks make loans, i.e. discuss the process of money creation.

√   Explain how the creation of a loan by one bank can lead to a multiple expansion in the money supply.

√   Define the money multiplier and use it to compute changes in the money supply.

√   Explain why the money multiplier may be smaller than the simple formula suggests.

√   Describe how open market operations work and how they may influence the money supply.

√   Describe how changes in the required reserve ratio can affect the money supply.

√   Define the discount rate and the federal funds rate.

√   Describe how changes in the discount rate can affect the money supply.

√   Discuss the primary functions of the Federal Reserve.

√   Define the Board of Governors and the Federal Open Market Committee.

√   Discuss the role of the Chairman of the Federal Reserve System.

III. KEY TERMS

Money: anything that is regularly used in exchange.

Barter: trading goods directly for goods.

Double coincidence of wants: the problem in a system of barter that one individual may not have what the other desires.

Medium of exchange: the property of money that exchanges are made using money.

Unit of account: the property of money that prices are quoted in terms of money.

Store of value: the property of money that value is preserved between transactions.

M1: the sum of currency in the hands of the public, demand deposits, and other checkable deposits

M2: M1 plus other assets including deposits in savings and loans and money market mutual funds.

Balance sheet: an account for a bank which shows the sources of its funds (liabilities) as well as the uses for the funds (assets).

Assets: the uses of the funds of a financial institution.

Liabilities: the sources of external funds of a financial intermediary.

Net worth: the difference between assets and liabilities.

Reserves: the fraction of their deposits that banks set aside in either vault cash or as deposits at the Federal Reserve.

Required reserves: the reserves that banks are required to hold by law against their deposits.

Excess reserves: any additional reserves that a bank holds above required reserves.

Reserve ratio: the ratio of reserves to deposits.

Money multiplier: an initial deposit leads to a multiple expansion of deposits. In the simplified case:
        increase in deposits = [initial deposit] X [1/reserve ratio].

Open market purchases: the purchase of government bonds by the Fed, which increases the money supply.

Open market sales: sales of government bonds to the public, which decreases the money supply.

Discount rate: the interest rate at which banks can borrow from the Fed.

Federal funds market: the market in which banks borrow and lend reserves to one another.

Central bank: a banker's bank; an official bank, which controls the supply of money in a country.

Lender of last resort: a name given to policies of central banks that provide loans to banks in emergency situations.

Federal Reserve Banks: one of twelve regional banks that are an official part of the Federal Reserve System.

Board of Governors of the Federal Reserve: the seven-person governing body of the Federal Reserve System in Washington, DC.

Federal Open Market Committee: the group that decides on monetary policy and consists of the seven members of the Board of Governors plus five of twelve regional bank presidents on a rotating basis.

IV. PERFORMANCE ENHANCING TIPS (PETS)

PET #1

When you withdraw money from your checking account to hold as cash, you have not increased the money supply. You have simply converted one form of money into another form.

Remember that the most liquid components of money are coin and currency and demand deposits (checking account balances). That is, both are components of the money supply. Thus, when you withdraw money from your checking account as cash, you have simply exchanged one form of money for another. The reverse also holds. If you deposit $100 in cash into your checking account, you have not decreased the money supply.

PET #2

Money and income do not measure the same thing in economics. Money is what you hold as cash and in your checking account and income is what you earn.

For example, you may earn $1,000 a week and keep $700 a week in your checking account and $100 as cash. The remaining $200 you may put into, e.g, a mutual fund or stock fund. The cash money and that in your checking account is "money" and is what you primarily use to make payments with. At any given point in time, the amount of money you have may not correspond to the amount of income you earn.

PET #3

The required reserve ratio is the ratio (or fraction or percentage) of demand deposits that a bank must legally hold on reserve, either in its vault or with the Federal Reserve Bank.

PET #4

The required reserve ratio applies to a bank's demand deposits and not to it's total reserves.

Suppose a bank has $250,000 in reserves and $1,000,000 in demand deposits. If the required reserve ratio is 10%, then the bank must by law hold $100,000 as required reserves. Since the bank is currently holding $250,000 in reserves, the other $150,000 is referred to as "excess reserves." Do not make the mistake of applying the required reserve ratio to the bank's total reserves. That is, it is not correct to conclude that the bank's required reserves are 10% of $250,000 or $25,000.

PET #5

When a bank makes a loan, it effectively gives the borrower a check or checking account for the amount of the loan. Thus, loans add to the money supply.

V. PRACTICE EXAM: MULTIPLE CHOICE QUESTIONS

1. The defining property of money is that:
    a) it is accepted as a means of payment.
    b) it is easy to carry around.
    c) its value depends on gold.
    d) it can be saved.
    e) it is countable.

2. Which one of the following is NOT true of money?
    a) it serves as a store of value.
    b) it serves as a unit of account.
    c) it serves as a medium of exchange.
    d) it is equal to income.
    e) all of the above are true.

3. Suppose after the semester ends, you take a trip to the Bahamas. Upon arriving at the island, you make a stop at one of the markets and notice that everyone is carrying around jars full of little turtles. And, you notice the person in line in front of you just paid for a bottle of rum with 6 turtles. Someone else just bought a straw hat for two turtles. Thinking back to your economics class (as painful as that may be), you would conclude that:
    a) this is a barter economy.
    b) Egad, those little turtles are serving the function of money!
    c) turtles are valueless.
    d) turtle soup is a delicacy.
    e) there is a problem of double coincidence of wants.

4. Mr. Potatohead has recently obtained a bank card from Idaho National Bank. Excited about the concept of using a little plastic card to get money from a machine, he quickly runs down to the nearest Automatic Teller Machine and withdraws $1000. This action has:

   a) increased the money supply by $1000.

   b) reduced the money supply by $1000.

   c) reduced the bank's required reserves by $100 assuming the required reserve ratio is 10%.

   d) not changed the money supply.

   e) (c) and (d).

5. Which one of the following would lead to a change in the total money supply?

   a) a customer's cash withdrawal from an ATM.

   b) a bank loan to a customer.

   c) interest payments by the Treasury on its debt.

   d) depositing a paycheck in a bank.

   e) none of the above.

6. Which one of the following statements is true?

   a) approximately one-fourth of M1 is checking account balances (demand deposits plus other checkable deposits).

   b) M2 is a narrower definition of money than M1.

   c) M2 is used by economists to measure the amount of money that is regularly used in transactions.

   d) a country for which cash bribes are an everyday part of business will have a higher cash (currency) holding per capita than countries where bribes are not standard practice.

   e) the citizens of Argentina use only Argentinean currency to make economic exchanges.

7. Which one of the following would NOT be considered an asset of a bank?

   a) a loan to a corporation.

   b) required reserves.

   c) holdings of treasury securities.

   d) deposits of its customers.

   e) all of the above.

8. Which one of the following statements is true?

   a) demand deposits are assets of a bank.

   b) assets + liabilities = net worth.

   c) a bank's reserves can either be kept in a bank's vault or held on deposit with a Federal Reserve bank.

   d) if a bank is holding $500 as required reserves and has $2,000 in deposits, then the required reserve ratio must be 40%.

   e) liabilities generate income for a bank.

9. By law, banks are required:
   a) to hold 100% of customer deposits on reserve.
   b) to hold a fraction of their reserves at the Federal Reserve Bank.
   c) to hold a fraction of demand deposits on reserve.
   d) to lend out no more than the amount of their required reserves.
   e) keep their discount rate at 5% or less.

10. The money multiplier is:
    a) 1/required reserve ratio.
    b) 1/(1-required reserve ratio).
    c) 1/marginal propensity to save.
    d) 1/excess reserves.
    e) required reserves/demand deposits.

11. Suppose that while vacationing in Monaco, you won 25,000 French francs, which is the equivalent of $5,000. When you return to the U.S., you deposit the $5,000 into your checking account. The effect is to (assuming the required reserve ratio is 20%):
    a) increase your bank's liabilities by $5,000.
    b) increase your bank's excess reserves by $4,000.
    c) lead to a multiple expansion in the money supply (checking account balances) by $25,000.
    d) increase your bank's required reserves by $1,000.
    e) all of the above.

12. The money multiplier will be smaller when:
    a) bank customers prefer to hold a bigger amount of their money as cash (instead of in their checking account).
    b) banks prefer to lend out 95% of their excess reserves instead of 100%.
    c) when the marginal propensity to save declines.
    d) when the marginal propensity to consume increases.
    e) (a) and (b).

13. The most commonly used tool in monetary policy is:
    a) changes in required reserve ratios.
    b) changes in the discount rate.
    c) open market operations.
    d) express lending transactions.
    e) loan extension.

14. The federal funds rate is the interest rate that:
    a) banks charge on loans to each other.
    b) the Federal Reserve charges on loans to banks.
    c) banks charge their most creditworthy customers.
    d) banks pay on demand deposits.
    e) the U.S. government pays it on 30-year treasury bonds.

15. Which set of actions could the Fed use to increase the money supply?
    a) discount rate cut and an open market sale.
    b) reduction in the required reserve ratio and an open market purchase.
    c) a tax cut and a reduction in the required reserve ratio.
    d) an open market purchase and a tax cut.
    e) an open market sale and a reduction in the required reserve ratio.

16. The group responsible for deciding on monetary policy is:
    a) the Federal Open Market Committee.
    b) the Board of Governors.
    c) the Federal Advisory Council.
    d) the group of 12 Federal Reserve Bank presidents.
    e) the Federal Monetary Control committee.

17. The purpose of having governors of the Federal Reserve serve fourteen-year terms is to:
    a) ensure that the governors become well-experienced at policymaking.
    b) insulate the governors' policy decisions from the influence of presidential elections and politics.
    c) promote unity of opinion from shared time together.
    d) establish long-standing ties with high-level officials of other nations' central banks.
    e) ensure that price stability is achieved.

VI. PRACTICE EXAM: ESSAY QUESTIONS

1. Suppose the banking system's required reserve ratio is 25% and that an elderly customer who has kept all of their savings, totaling $8,000, under a mattress has finally decided to deposit it in the bank. Explain the effects this action has on the bank's balance sheet and the money supply.

2. Explain how an open market purchase of $2 million will affect the money supply assuming the required reserve ratio is 10%. How does a country's preference for holding cash (as opposed to checking accounts) affect the size of the money multiplier?

VII. ANSWER KEY: MULTIPLE CHOICE QUESTIONS

1. Correct answer: a.

Discussion: Money is anything that is generally accepted as a means of payment. In other words, it is used to carry out transactions or economic exchanges. At one time, gold served as money since it was accepted as a means of payment. In some foreign countries, U.S. dollars fulfill the role of "money" since they are accepted as a means of payment.

While money is typically easy to carry around, it is not the defining property of money. Today, money's value does not depend on gold -- our money is thus referred to as "fiat" money. While money can be saved (the store of value function), that is not the defining characteristic of it. Also, while money is countable, it is not the defining characteristic of it.

2. Correct answer: d.

Discussion: See PET #2 above.

Statement a means that money can be saved (stored) and used to make future transactions (i.e. paying for college education, etc). Statement b means that money serves as a measuring rod for the value of goods and services. That is, if we had to compare the value of an apple to an orange, we could compare their values by expressing them in terms of a common denominator -- money or the dollar. Suppose an apple costs $0.35 and an orange costs $0.50, money has thus served as a unit of account. We would say that an orange is more valuable than an apple. Statement c means that money is used to pay for transactions -- buying food, paying rent, going to the movies, etc.

3. Correct answer: b.

Discussion: This is an example where turtles are serving as the medium of exchange. That is, they are accepted by the seller as a method of payment and used by the buyer as a method of payment.

A barter economy is one in which there is no "money." That is, there is no commodity that is universally accepted as a means of payment. In a barter economy, a double coincidence of wants problem exists. Money would help to eliminate the problem. The fact that turtles are used as a means of payment means that turtles must be valuable, not valueless. In this case, turtle soup may be a delicacy since eating turtle soup would be like eating money. However, statement d is more of a "for fun" answer than the correct answer.

4. Correct answer: e.

Discussion: Mr. Potatohead has simply converted one form of money (demand deposits) to another form (cash). Since both demand deposits and cash are part of the money supply, the money supply has not changed. (See PET #1 for review). However, since Mr. Potatohead as withdrawn $1,000 from the bank, the bank finds that its demand deposits decline by $1,000. With a required reserve ratio of 10%, the bank is now permitted to hold $100 less as required reserves (10% of $1,000).

5. Correct answer: b.

Discussion: When a bank makes a loan to a customer, it effectively gives the customer a check or checking account for the amount of the loan. This action increases the money supply.

Statement a is incorrect because a customer's cash withdrawal from an ATM simply converts one form of money (demand deposits) to another (cash). There is not change in the money supply from this action. Statement c is not correct. Interest payments by the Treasury on its debt simply transfer money from government bank accounts to the bank accounts of holders of the Treasury's debt (households, businesses, etc). Statement d is not correct. If you deposit a paycheck into your bank account, your "money supply" will increase but the "money supply" in the bank account of the business that pays you will decrease by the same amount. On net, there is no change in the money supply, just a transfer of ownership.

6. Correct answer: d.

Discussion: In a country where cash (or currency) is used in everyday business, the people of the country must carry a lot of cash around with them to get anything done -- as simple as getting a taxi, getting into a restaurant, or getting a haircut. India is a good example of a country where bribes are prevalent.

Statement a is not true; two-thirds of M1 is checking account balances (demand deposits plus other checkable deposits). Statement b is not true; M2 is a broader definition of money than M1. Statement c is not true; M1 is used by economists to measure the amount of money that is regularly used in transactions. Remember that M2 includes money held in money market mutual funds and other investments that may be used to pay for transactions, but typically not regular transactions. Statement e is not true; in developing countries like Argentina, the U.S. dollar is commonly accepted as a means of payment and often used as a store of value, too.

7. Correct answer: d.

Discussion: Demand deposits are liabilities of a bank. They are owed to customers (on demand). That is, demand deposits (checking accounts) are an item that a bank doesn't own. Assets are items of value that a bank owns -- just like assets are items of value that we own. Thus, loans to households and businesses are an asset of a bank since the loans are items that are owed to the bank (by its customers). A bank's reserves are also an asset since they are owned by the bank (not owed by the bank). A bank's reserves are like a checking account for the bank. A bank's holdings of treasury securities (or even stock) are an asset since they are owned by the bank (not owed by the bank).

8. Correct answer: c.

Discussion: A bank's reserves can be kept either in a bank's vault or held on deposit with a Federal Reserve bank (which is referred to as a reserve account with the Fed).

Statement a is not correct. Demand deposits are a liability of a bank. Statement b is not correct. Assets minus liabilities equal net worth. Statement d is not correct. If the bank is holding $500 as required reserves and has $2,000 in demand deposits, the required reserve ratio must be 25% ($500/$2,000). Statement e is not correct. Assets generate income for a bank. Liabilities are items that a bank owes.

9. Correct answer: c.

Discussion: The required reserve ratio is the fraction or percentage of demand deposits that the bank is legally obligated to hold on reserve. (See PET #3 and #4 for review).

Statement a is not correct. The U.S. banking system operates under a fractional reserve system, which means that banks are legally permitted to hold only a fraction (i.e. less than 100%) of their deposits as reserves. Statement b is not correct; by law, banks must hold a fraction of their demand deposits as required reserves, not a fraction of their reserves. Statement d is not correct; banks can lend out the maximum amount of their excess reserves (an amount which typically exceeds their required reserves). By law, they cannot lend out any of their required reserves. Statement e is not correct; there is no stipulation on what interest rate banks are permitted to charge on loans to customers.

10. Correct answer: a.

Discussion: None necessary.

11. Correct answer: e.

Discussion: Your deposit of $5,000 into the bank increases the liabilities of the bank. That is, your checking account balance has increased by $5,000, which means that the bank is responsible to pay you, on demand, your $5,000 should you wish to withdraw it. Since the required reserve ratio is 20%, the bank is legally obligated to hold 20% of $5,000 as required reserves, i.e. $1,000. The remaining $4,000 of your deposits, the bank is permitted to lend out (or use in other ways). The $4,000 is referred to as excess reserves. If the bank lends out the $4,000 in excess reserves, the money supply will increase by $4,000, which will in turn end up in some other bank whose excess reserves will increase by $3,600. This bank will in turn lend out the $3,600. This process continues until the money supply will ultimately expand by [1/0.20] X $5,000 = $25,000. If you add the $5,000 you brought into the country to the money supply, the money supply will have in total increased by $30,000.

12. Correct answer: e.

Discussion: The money multiplier process assumes that banks lend out all of their excess reserves and that customers do not choose to hold any of the newly created money as cash (currency) but prefer to keep it in their checking accounts. If customers prefer to hold a larger amount of their money as cash instead of in their checking accounts, banks will have fewer demand deposits and thus fewer reserves and thus a reduced ability to extend loans to customers. Remember that a bank's excess reserves serve as the base from which it is able to make loans. Thus, the money multiplier process will not go as far. Furthermore, if banks prefer to lend out a smaller amount of their excess reserves, then they will not be creating as many loans and thereby not allowing the money multiplier process to go as far.

The marginal propensity to save and consume have not been related to the money multiplier process.

13. Correct answer: c.

Discussion: None necessary.

14. Correct answer: a.

Discussion: Banks can borrow money from each other. The interest rate that they charge each other for the loans is called the federal funds rate. Statement b is a definition of the discount rate. Statement c is a definition of the prime rate. Statement d is a definition of the interest rate paid on checking account. Statement e is a definition of the 30-year treasury bond rate.

15. Correct answer: b.

Discussion: The Fed has three tools that it can use to influence the money supply: open market operations, changes in the required reserve ratio, and changes in the discount rate. An open market purchase of government treasury securities from individuals and businesses that hold the treasury securities is an exchange of securities for money. In this case, individuals and businesses receive checks from the Fed and give up their securities to the Fed (which is what the Fed is purchasing). The money supply directly increases from this action. Also, since individuals and businesses will be likely to deposit at least some, if not all, of their checks into banks, banks demand deposits and thus reserves will increase. With an increase in reserves, banks will find that they are able to make more loans. The enhanced ability of banks to make loans further adds to the money supply. A reduction in the required reserve ratio frees up some of a bank's required reserves from which banks can then lend. For example, if the required reserve ratio is 20% and a bank's deposits are $1 million, the bank must hold $200,000 as required reserves. The remaining $800,000 in excess it is permitted to lend out. Now, if the required reserve ratio is reduced to 10%, the bank must now legally hold only $100,000, which means it has $900,000 to lend out. The reduction in the required reserve ratio thus enhances a bank's ability to extend loans (and thereby increase the money supply). Open market sales and increases in the required reserve ratio work in the opposite direction.

Statement a is only partially correct. A discount rate cut makes it less costly for banks to borrow money from the Fed, which they can in turn lend out. Thus, a discount rate cut may increase the money supply (and vice-versa). However, an open market sale acts to reduce the money supply. Statement e is also only partially correct. A reduction in the required reserve ratio acts to increase the money supply but again, an open market sale acts to reduce the money supply.

Statements c and d cannot be correct because a tax cut simply transfers money from government bank accounts back to households and businesses. Thus, a tax cut does not affect the money supply but it does affect who is holding the money. (The same is true of a tax increase).

16. Correct answer: a.

Discussion: The Federal Open Market Committee (FOMC) consists of the seven governors of the Board of the Federal Reserve and five Federal Reserve Bank presidents. Four of the Federal Reserve bank presidents spend two-year rotating positions on the FOMC while the president of the New York Fed has a permanent seat on the FOMC.

17. Correct answer: b.

Discussion: The central bank of the U.S. was designed to be independent of the government so that it would not conduct policy in a way that was driven by politics or who was running for president of the U.S. Some research shows that central banks that have greater independence from their governments and their presidents are able to achieve lower rates of inflation.

VIII. ANSWER KEY: ESSAY QUESTIONS

1. When the elderly customer deposits the $8,000 cash into the bank, the bank will find that it now has $8,000 more in demand deposits and $8,000 more in reserves. However, the $8,000 in reserves must be broken up into two components -- required reserves and excess reserves. Since the required reserve ratio is 25%, the bank must by law hold 25% of $8,000 as required reserves. Thus, the bank must hold $2,000 as required reserves. The remaining $6,000 is referred to as "excess reserves" and are what the bank is permitted to lend out (or use in other ways). Since the money multiplier is 1/required reserve ratio, the value of it is 1/0.25 = 4. Thus, the potential maximum increase in the checking account balance money supply is 4 X $8,000 = $32,000. Since $8,000 of the $32,000 was simply the transfer of cash to a checking account, the banking system will, in effect, be able to generate $24,000 ($32,000 - $8,000) in loans. Another way to calculate the loan expansion part of the money multiplier process is to use the formula [1/required reserve ratio] X (initial change in excess reserves) which in this case would be 4 X $6,000 = $24,000.

2. An open market purchase is when the Fed purchases U.S. government treasury securities from individuals and businesses that currently own them. If the Fed purchases a total of $2 million in government treasury securities, it effectively writes a check totaling $2 million, which it gives to individuals and businesses. For example, if the Fed purchases 200,000 treasury securities and paid $1,000 for each one, then the total open market purchase is $2,000,000. If each seller of the treasury security deposits his check for $1,000 into a bank, the banking system will find that it has $2 million more in demand deposits and consequently $2 million more in reserves. With a required reserve ratio of 10%, the banking system must hold $200,000 (0.10 X $2,000,000) as required reserves. The banking system can then lend out the remaining $1,800,000. Thus, the money supply increases directly through the open market purchase and then indirectly through influencing the banking systems ability to make loans. The money multiplier process dictates that the potential maximum increase in the money supply is (1/0.10) X $2,000,000 = 10 X $2,000,000 = $20,000,000. Of the $20 million, $2 million is a direct result of the open market purchase and $18 million is a result of banks making loans. (To figure out the effect of the loan expansion process, use (1/required reserve ratio) X (initial change in excess reserves) = 1/0.10 X $1,800,000 = $18,000,000 i.e. $18 million).

The simple money multiplier used above assumes that all of the money generated is re-deposited in other banks. Nobody holds any of it as cash. If the public preferred to hold some of the money as cash, then the money multiplier would be smaller than 10. The public's preference for holding money as cash instead of in checking accounts reduces the reserves of the banking system and thereby reduces their reserves and their ability to make loans.

Take It to the Net

We invite you to visit the O'Sullivan/Sheffrin page on the Prentice Hall Web site at:

http://www.prenhall.com/osullivan/

for this chapter's World Wide Web exercise.

CHAPTER 16
MONETARY POLICY AND INFLATION

I. OVERVIEW

In this chapter, you will learn about the factors that affect investment in an economy. You will be given a broader definition of investment than that used in GDP accounts. You will see how the interest rate, the inflation rate, taxes, a firm's stock price, and the current state of the economy can affect how much investment and individual or business may be willing to undertake. You will re-encounter the reality principle and see how it affects the costs of borrowing and lending. You will see how investment spending moves with the business cycle. In this chapter, you will also learn how the Fed, through monetary policy, is able to influence interest rates thus aggregate spending and thus output (GDP). The context in which you will examine monetary policy is the short run in which prices are temporarily fixed. In this setting, monetary policy actions are not directed at inflation nor do monetary policy actions affect inflation. You will learn that monetary policy works through its effects on interest rates, which in turn determines spending in an economy. You will use a supply and demand model of the money market to see how changes in money supply and money demand influence the price of money, i.e. the interest rate.

You will learn about the role expectations of future inflation play in preferences for holding money, wage setting, real interest rates, and the determination of inflation and unemployment. You will learn how expectations of future inflation can be influenced by the stance of monetary policy and the commitment of central bankers to maintaining low inflation. You will learn that central banks that are credibly committed to low inflation often have an easier time securing low inflation. You will use an expectations Phillips curve to explore the relationship between the unemployment rate relative to the natural rate of unemployment and unanticipated inflation.

II. CHECKLIST

By the end of this chapter, you should be able to:

√   Explain why investment is volatile.

√   Discuss what percentage of GDP is investment spending.

√   Explain the multiplier-accelerator model of investment spending.

√   Explain the difference between nominal and real interest rates/returns.

√   Calculate nominal and real interest rates.

√   Explain why savers may be hurt by inflation and why borrowers may benefit by inflation.

√   Define the expected real interest rate/return.

√   Explain why investment spending and the interest rate are negatively related.

√   Explain how lower (higher) interest rates affect investment spending and output.

√ Discuss actions that could be taken by the Fed to lower (raise) interest rates. Use a money supply/money demand model to illustrate the effects.

√ Give several reasons for why people hold money.

√ Explain why money demand is negatively sloped when graphed against the interest rate.

√ Discuss how expectations of inflation affect individual and business decision-making.

√ Explain why countries with higher money growth rates typically have higher nominal interest rates.

√ Recite the reality principle and explain money illusion.

√ Explain how money growth that exceeds the public's expected rate of inflation will increase money demand and the real interest rate, and vice-versa.

√ Define the expectations Phillips curve.

√ Discuss what happens to inflation when the unemployment rate is above the natural rate and when it is below the natural rate.

III. KEY TERMS

Nominal interest rates: interest rates that are quoted in the market.

Real interest rate: the nominal interest rate minus the actual inflation rate.

Expected real interest rate: the nominal interest rate minus the expected inflation rate.

Accelerator theory: the theory of investment that emphasizes that current investment spending depends positively on the expected future growth of real GDP.

Pro-cyclical: a component of GDP is pro-cyclical if it rises and falls with the overall level of GDP.

Multiplier-accelerator model: a model in which a downturn in real GDP leads to a sharp fall in investment which, in turn, triggers further reductions in GDP through the multiplier.

Transactions demand for money: the demand for money based on the desire to facilitate transactions.

Liquidity demand for money: the demand for money that arises so that individuals or firms can make purchases on short notice without incurring excessive costs.

Speculative demand for money: the demand for money that arises because holding money over short periods is less risky than holdings stocks or bonds.

Monetary policy: the range of actions taken by the Federal Reserve actions to influence the level of GDP or inflation.

Exchange rate: the rate at which one currency trades for another in the market.

Depreciation: a fall in the exchange rate or a decrease in the value of a currency.

Appreciation: a rise in the exchange rate or an increase in the value of a currency.

Expectations of inflation: the beliefs held by the public about the likely path of inflation for the future.

Nominal wages: wages in dollars.

Real wages: nominal or dollar wages adjusted for inflation.

Money illusion: confusion of real and nominal magnitudes.

Expectations Phillips curve: the term that describes the relationship between inflation and unemployment taking into account expectations of inflation.

IV. PERFORMANCE ENHANCING TIPS (PETS)

PET #1

Remember that in economics, investment spending is largely spending on plant and equipment. It is NOT the purchase of stocks and bonds and other financial assets (which economists would refer to as saving).

PET #2

The investment schedule will shift when factors other than the interest rate that are relevant to investment spending change. Changes in the interest rate will cause movements along the investment schedule.

For example, consider the investment schedule below:

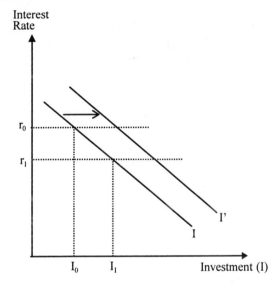

Suppose that the government enacts a tax credit for investment spending on plant and equipment. The tax credit makes it less costly for businesses to purchase plant and equipment. The tax credit will increase the level of investment spending at every interest rate as before. We would represent this by shifting the investment schedule out, to the right. Since the investment schedule is negatively sloped, it shows that an increase in the interest rate will reduce the quantity of investment spending and a decrease in the interest rate will increase the quantity of investment spending.

PET #3

Investors are borrowers.

An investor is an individual or business who borrows funds from savers (either directly or indirectly). The investor uses the borrowed funds to undertake an investment project for which the borrower expects the payoff from the project to be large enough to not only pay back the saver but to also have made a profit.

PET #4

The real interest rate is equal to the nominal interest rate minus the rate of inflation. You can equivalently say that the nominal interest rate is equal to the real interest rate plus the rate of inflation.

For example, suppose you are told that the nominal interest rate is 7% and that the inflation rate is 3%. The real interest rate is 4%. Likewise, if you are told that the real interest rate is 4% and the inflation rate is 3%, the nominal interest rate must be 7%.

PET #5

The real interest rate determines the level of investment spending, not the nominal interest rate.

For example, compare two cases: (1) a nominal interest rate of 15% when the inflation rate is 10%; and (2) a nominal interest rate of 8% when inflation is 2%. In case (1), the real interest rate is 5% and in case (2), the real interest rate is 6%. Thus, even though in case (1), the nominal interest rate is higher, the real cost of borrowing is lower. Thus, the real interest rate is a better indicator of the true cost of borrowing funds for investment spending.

PET #6

The accelerator model of investment spending assumes that investment spending depends on expected output (income), much like the consumption spending is assumed to depend on income.

An accelerator model of investment spending could be represented by writing out an investment function:

$$I = g + h \times Ey$$

where h > 0, g is autonomous Investment, and Ey is expected output. Since h is greater than zero, it means that expected increases in output and income (y) lead to increases in investment spending. The amount by which a $1 increase in expected output changes investment spending is given by h. You should recognize that "h" plays the same role that "b" plays in the consumption function of Chapter 25. You could say that "h" is the marginal propensity to invest. For example, if h = 0.25, every $1 increase in expected output (income) will generate $0.25 worth of investment spending.

PET #7

As real income (or real GDP) increases, the demand for money increases. As real income (or real GDP) decreases, the demand for money decreases.

Sometimes this point is confusing to students who will state, "If I make more money (i.e. earn more income), I won't demand as much of it. Thus, the PET #7 seems backwards." The proper way to think about the relationship between money and income is this: at higher income levels, people typically make more transactions and thus need to have more money on hand (as cash or in checking accounts). That is, at higher income levels, people typically demand more money, not less (and vice-versa).

For example, consider what your average checking account balance is right now and how much you hold in your wallet. Also, consider what your income level is right now. Given that you are a student, your income is probably pretty low. Since your income is low, you probably don't buy steak and lobster every week, or go out to expensive restaurants very frequently, or take trips very frequently, or buy expensive clothing. Thus, your checking account balance plus what you hold as cash is probably low, too. However, after you graduate and start earning the big bucks, you will probably begin to undertake more transactions (money is fun to spend when you have it!). You may start buying more expensive clothing and buying it more frequently. You may decide to take some weekend visits to the beach or to some far away island. Maybe you'll even start taking tennis lessons and buying expensive art to decorate your apartment. This just means that you will need to hold more money in your checking account and in your wallet. So, we'd say that your demand for money has increased as your income has gone up.

PET #8

Factors relevant to the demand for money will cause the demand for money to shift. Changes in the interest rate will cause a movement along the money demand curve.

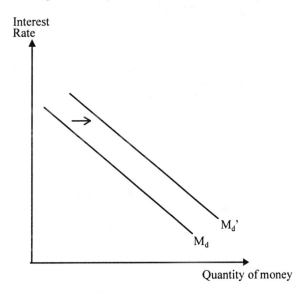

Your book suggests several other factors besides the interest rate that affect the demand for money. They are the price level and income. As the price level rises, the demand for money increases since economic transactions become more expensive and people need more money to carry out those transactions (vice-versa for a decrease in the price level). This would be represented by a rightward shift in the demand curve above. Secondly, as PET #1 above suggests, changes in income also affect the demand for money. An increase in real income will increase the demand for money (shift right) and vice-versa.

Changes in the interest rate are represented as movements along the money demand curve. Higher interest rates reduce the quantity of money demanded and lower interest rates raise the quantity of money demanded.

PET #9

The unanticipated rate of inflation is the difference between the actual rate of inflation and the expected rate of inflation. Unanticipated inflation will be greater than zero when the unemployment rate is less than the natural rate of unemployment. Unanticipated inflation will be less than zero when the unemployment rate is greater than the natural rate of unemployment.

For example, suppose that the natural rate of unemployment is 5% and the actual unemployment rate is 4.6%. Then, the actual inflation rate will exceed the rate of inflation that was expected. That is, the public may have expected inflation to be 6% when it turns out that inflation is actually 7.5%.

For another example, suppose that the actual unemployment rate is 8%. Since the actual unemployment rate is above the natural unemployment rate, the actual inflation rate will be less than the rate that was expected by the public. That is, the public may have expected 4% inflation when the actual inflation rate turns out to be 3%.

PET #10

In the long run, the rate of inflation will equal the growth rate of money, holding other factors constant.

This is just a special case of PET #1 above where other factors constant mean that velocity and real GDP are not growing (percentage change = 0). So, if the money supply is growing at 3% a year, other factors constant, the rate of inflation will also be 3% per year.

PET #11

When expected inflation exceeds the rate of growth of the money supply, money demand will be increasing more than money supply will be increasing. Thus, nominal and real interest rates will rise. When expected inflation is less than the rate of growth of the money supply, money demand will be increasing more than money supply will be increasing. Thus, nominal and real interest rates will fall.

Remember from the previous chapter that increases in the price level act to increase the demand for money (and vice-versa). Similarly, when the price level is expected to increase (i.e. expected inflation is greater than zero), the demand for money will increase and at a rate equal to the expected inflation rate. Using a money supply/money demand diagram, you would represent this with a rightward shift in money demand. If expected inflation exceeds the rate of growth of the money supply, then the rightward shift in money demand will be greater than the rightward shift in money supply. As a consequence, the nominal interest rate will increase. With expectations of inflation unchanged, the real interest rate rises, too. The reverse is true when the expected rate of inflation is less than the growth rate of the money supply.

V. PRACTICE EXAM: MULTIPLE CHOICE QUESTIONS

1. Which one of the following statements is NOT true of investment?

   a) the payoff is typically uncertain or unknown.

   b) an increase in the real interest rate raises investment spending.

   c) according to the accelerator model, expected growth and investment spending are positively related.

   d) investment spending is procyclical.

   e) investment spending is a volatile component of GDP.

2. The multiplier-accelerator model:

   a) emphasizes how increases in investment spending can plunge the economy into a recession.

   b) is that acceleration in the growth of the economy can trigger increases in interest rates which lead to reductions in investment spending.

   c) is that investment spending is a function of "animal spirits."

   d) explains how a downturn in real GDP can lead to a sharp fall in investment, which will in turn trigger further reductions in GDP.

   e) none of the above.

3. Interest rates quoted by banks and that appear in the newspaper are:

   a) nominal interest rates.

   b) real interest rates.

   c) inflation-adjusted interest rates.

   d) official interest rates.

   e) federal funds rates.

4. If you put $1,000 of your savings into a one-year certificate of deposit that offers a nominal interest rate of 5.31%, then:

   a) your real return will be 7.31% if the inflation rate was -2% that year.

   b) your real return will be 3.31% if the inflation rate was -2% that year.

   c) your real return will be -10.62% if the inflation rate was -2% that year.

   d) your real return will be 10.62% if the inflation rate was -2% that year.

   e) your real return will be 2.655% if the inflation rate was -2% that year.

5. Which one of the following statements is correct?

    a) nominal interest rate = real interest rate + inflation rate.

    b) nominal interest rate = real interest rate - inflation rate.

    c) real interest rate = nominal interest rate + inflation rate.

    d) real interest rate = nominal interest rate/inflation rate.

    e) inflation rate = real interest rate - nominal interest rate.

6. Based on the investment schedule below, how many of the projects would be undertaken assuming an interest rate of 6%?

Investment	Cost	Return
A	$1,000	$1,030
B	$2,000	$2,100
C	$500	$550
D	$5,000	$5,250
E	$300	$306

    a) one project would be undertaken.

    b) two projects would be undertaken.

    c) three projects would be undertaken.

    d) four projects would be undertaken.

    e) five projects would be undertaken.

7. Which one of the following statements is NOT true of money?

    a) it is a component of wealth.

    b) people hold money primarily to conduct transactions.

    c) the opportunity cost of holding money is foregone interest earnings on other financial assets.

    d) as interest rates rise, the quantity of money demanded increases.

    e) all of the above are true.

8. Which one of the following would explain the liquidity motive for holding money?

    a) stock prices are very variable and their rate of return risky compared to money.

    b) bond prices are very variable and their rate of return risky compared to money.

    c) a need to pay for an unexpected, big expense -- like when your car breaks down.

    d) a need to pay for daily transactions like lunch.

    e) it takes time to go to the bank and withdrawal cash from your checking account.

9. Which one of the following statements is correct?

    a) an increase in the price level will increase money demand and lower interest rates.

    b) a decrease in the price level will increase money demand and lower interest rates.

    c) an increase in real income (GDP) will increase money demand and raise interest rates.

    d) a decrease in real income (GDP) will increase money demand and raise interest rates.

    e) an increase in real income (GDP) will decrease money demand and lower interest rates.

10. Which one of the following statements is correct?

    a) an increase in the money supply will shift the money supply curve to the right, lower interest rates, and reduce investment spending.

    b) an increase in the money supply will shift the money supply curve to the right, lower interest rates, and raise output.

    c) a decrease in the money supply will shift the money supply curve to the left, lower interest rates, and raise output.

    d) a decrease in money demand will lower interest rates and raise investment spending.

    e) (b) and (d).

11. Which one of the following statements is correct?

    a) an open market purchase will raise interest rates.

    b) a reduction in the required reserve ratio will lower interest rates.

    c) a reduction in the discount rate will raise interest rates.

    d) a cut in the tax rate will lower interest rates.

    e) (a) and (b).

12. If the Fed decreases the money supply, in the short run:

    a) investment spending and output (GDP) will fall.

    b) investment spending and output (GDP) will rise.

    c) investment spending will fall and output (GDP) will rise.

    d) investment spending will rise and output (GDP) will fall.

    e) investment spending will not respond to changes in the money supply.

13. Which one of the following statements is true?

    a) the expected real rate of interest = nominal rate + expected rate of inflation.

    b) money illusion is the confusion of nominal and real magnitudes.

    c) if two countries had the same real rate of interest but one had a higher inflation rate, it would have a lower nominal interest rate.

    d) if money demand and money supply each grow by 3% per year, the real interest rate will rise by 3% per year.

    e) Milton Friedman is the father of the rational expectations school of thought.

14. If the public currently expected the inflation rate to be 8% and the Fed increased the money supply by 5%, then:
    a) real interest rates would increase in the short run.
    b) money demand would decline by 8%.
    c) money demand would decline by 5%.
    d) money demand would increase by 8%.
    e) (a) and (d).

15. If the Fed increased the money supply by 10% and the public expected inflation to be 6%, then:
    a) the nominal and real interest rates will drop in the short run.
    b) in the long run, inflation will be 10%, other factors constant.
    c) real GDP will rise and unemployment will fall in the short run.
    d) in the long run, the real interest rate will remain constant.
    e) all of the above.

16. The expectations Phillips curve shows:
    a) that if the actual unemployment rate is below the natural rate of unemployment, inflation will be higher than anticipated.
    b) that the unemployment rate varies with anticipated inflation.
    c) can be used to calculate the misery index.
    d) that the natural rate of unemployment can be defined as the unemployment rate associated with a zero percent inflation rate.
    e) that there is a permanent, negative relationship between the inflation rate and the unemployment rate.

17. Which one of the following is a factor that could cause the natural rate of unemployment to change?
    a) more teenagers entering the workforce.
    b) a prolonged recession which causes some workers' skills to become outdated.
    c) a change in the power of unions.
    d) a change in the dollar amount of unemployment compensation that is granted.
    e) all of the above.

VI. PRACTICE EXAM: ESSAY QUESTION

1. Explain why real interest rates are more closely related to investment spending than nominal interest rates are. Also, explain how high real interest rates affect investment spending and output.

VII. ANSWER KEY: MULTIPLE CHOICE QUESTIONS

1. Correct answer: b.

Discussion: Statement b is incorrect because an increase in real interest rates reduces, not raises, investment spending.

Statements a is correct and means that investment spending is risky. It also means that when savers lend their funds to investors (borrowers), their savings are subject to risk, as well. Statement c is correct. The accelerator model suggests that when businesses expect the economy to boom, investment spending will increase now and when they expect the economy to go into a recession, they will reduce investment spending now. Statement d means that when output (real GDP) increases, investment spending increases and vice-versa. Statement e means that investment spending fluctuates a lot more than some of the other spending components of GDP.

2. Correct answer: d.

Discussion: The multiplier-accelerator model links investment spending to changes in output through the multiplier (as discussed in the previous chapter) and further adds that when output changes, investment spending, in turn, changes again setting off further changes in output.

Statement a is not correct; increases in investment spending would help to push the economy up, i.e. to do better. Statement b is not correct because the multiplier-accelerator model does not address the role of interest rates. Statement c is not correct. Keynes coined the term "animal spirits" which meant that sharp swings in the moods of investors could trigger sharp swings in investment spending. Statement e is not correct because statement d is correct.

3. Correct answer: a.

Discussion: Nominal interest rates are often referred to as quoted or stated rates. Real interest rates are inflation-adjusted interest rates.

4. Correct answer: a.

Discussion: The real interest rate or real return is the nominal interest rate (what is actually paid) minus the inflation rate. In this case, the inflation rate is negative meaning that the economy is experiencing deflation -- the price level is declining. Thus, the real interest rate (the purchasing power of the interest proceeds) will be greater than 5.31% because at the end of the year, prices will be, on average, 2% lower and so the saver will find that the interest proceeds stretch farther in terms of what they can be used to purchase. Thus, the real return is 7.31% = (5.31% - (-2%)).

5. Correct answer: a.

Discussion: The nominal interest rate is the sum of the real interest rate plus the inflation rate. Statement a can also be re-written to say that the real interest rate is equal to the nominal interest rate minus the rate of inflation (as discussed in the answer to #5). All of the other statements are thus incorrect.

6. Correct answer: a.

Discussion: Since the interest rate is 6%, only those investment projects earning a return greater than 6% will be worthwhile. Otherwise, an individual could just put money in the bank and earn 6%. Investment project A's return is 3% [($1,030-$1,000)/$1,000] X 100. Investment project B's return is 5% [($2,100 - $2,000)/$2,000]X100. Investment project C's return is 10% [($550-$500)/$500] X 100. Investment project D's return is 5% [($5,250-$5,000)/$5,000] X 100. Investment project E's return is 2% [($306-$300)/$300] X 100. Thus, since only investment project C has a return greater than 6%, it will be the only project that is worthwhile to invest in. All of the other projects earn a return less than 6%.

7. Correct answer: d.

Discussion: Statement d is incorrect because as interest rates rise, the quantity of money demand decreases. That is, there is a negative relationship between the quantity of money demanded and the interest rate. This is reflected in a money demand curve that is negatively sloped when graphed against the interest rate. While there are other reasons that people hold money (for liquidity and speculative reasons), the transactions motive is the primary motive for holding money. The opportunity cost of holding money is foregone interest earnings on other financial assets. Money held as cash earns no interest whereas money held in a checking account may earn some interest but the interest rate is very low compared to other financial assets in which money could be placed.

Money is one component of wealth. An individual's holdings of stock, bonds, real estate, art, gold, etc. are other components of wealth.

8. Correct answer: c.

Discussion: Money is the most liquid component of wealth. You can easily convert it to cash to pay for things or can write a check to pay for things. Obviously, money is held to pay for daily transactions (the transactions motive as implied in Statement d), but some money is held in order to cover unexpected expenses. In other words, you never know when you may need to pay for something quickly. This is the liquidity (or "precautionary") motive for holding money.

Statements a and b are examples of the speculative motive for holding money. Statement e is not an explanation of the liquidity motive.

9. Correct answer: c.

Discussion: An increase in real income is a shift factor of money demand. At higher income levels, people undertake more transactions and thus demand more money. As the demand for money increases (shifts right) the interest rate rises, holding fixed the money supply.

Statement a is not correct; while an increase in the price level will increase money demand, interest rates will go up, not down. Statement b is not correct because a decrease in the price level will reduce money demand and reduce interest rates. Statement d is not correct because a decrease in real income will reduce money demand and reduce interest rates. Statement e is not correct because an increase in real income will increase money demand and raise interest rates.

10. Correct answer: e.

Discussion: An increase in money supply is represented by a rightward shift in the money supply curve. As the supply of money increases, the price of money (the interest rate) drops. As the interest rate drops, investment spending increases which leads to a multiple expansion in output. Thus, statement b is correct. A decrease in money demand will lower the price of money (the interest rate). At lower interest rates, investment spending (and consequently output) will increase. Thus, statement d is correct.

Statement a is not correct because investment spending will increase, not decrease. Statement c is not correct because a decrease in the money supply will raise, not lower, interest rates and thereby reduce investment spending and thus output.

11. Correct answer: b.

Discussion: A reduction in the required reserve ratio is one arm of monetary policy that can lead to an increase in the money supply. Since the reduction in the required reserve ratio increases the money supply, interest rates will decrease.

Statement a is incorrect because an open market purchase is an increase in the money supply which leads to lower interest rates, not higher interest rates. Statement c is not correct because a cut in the discount rate acts to increase the money supply and thereby lower interest rates, not raise them. Statement d is not correct because a tax cut is an example of fiscal policy and, at this point, is not assumed to have any effect on interest rates. Statement e cannot be correct because statement a is not correct.

12. Correct answer: a.

Discussion: A decrease in the money supply raises interest rates. The increase in interest rates raises the cost of borrowing and thus reduces investment spending (spending by businesses on plant and equipment). As investment spending declines, output (GDP) declines because there is less spending taking place in the economy.

Based on the answer above, none of the other statements are correct.

13. Correct answer: b.

Discussion: Money illusion occurs when an increase in, e.g. the nominal wage rate, is perceived as an increase in the real wage . In fact, an increase in the nominal wage rate only makes a worker better off if the nominal wage increase is bigger in percentage terms than the inflation rate. In this case, the real wage rate would rise. However, if the percentage increase in the nominal wage is equal to the inflation rate, then there is no change in the purchasing power of the worker's wage and thus the worker is no better off than before, despite the increased nominal wage. (The same is true for savers. They should consider their real return, not their nominal return).

Statement a is not correct. The expected real interest rate = nominal interest rate minus the expected rate of inflation. Statement c is not correct. If two countries had the same real rate of interest but one had a higher inflation rate, it would have a higher, not lower nominal interest rate. For example, if both countries had a real rate of interest of 5% and inflation was 5% in country A and 20% in country B, the nominal interest rate in country A would be 10% and that in country B would be 25%. Statement d is not correct. If money demand and money supply each grow by 3% per year, the real interest rate will not change. Statement e is not correct. Milton Friedman is the "father" of monetarism and Robert Lucas is the "father" of rational expectations.

14. Correct answer: e.

Discussion: If the public expected the inflation rate to be 8%, they would want to hold 8% in cash and/or checking account balances. That is, money demand would increase by 8%. But, money supply is not growing as fast as money demand. This would be represented by a bigger shift rightward in money demand than the rightward shift in money supply. Thus, the nominal (and real) interest rate would increase in the short run. (See PET #4 for review).

Statements b and c cannot be correct because money demand will increase, not decrease.

15. Correct answer: e.

Discussion: This question is the reverse of question (2). In this case, the money supply will shift rightward by more than money demand will shift rightward (compare 10% to 6%). Thus, the nominal and real interest rates will drop in the short run. As the real interest rate drops, spending by businesses on plant and equipment (investment) will increase and lead to an increase in real GDP. As real GDP rises, the unemployment rate will fall. This all happens in the short run. In the long run, money is neutral and so the real interest rate will return to its initial level, i.e. it remains constant in the long run. However, the 10% increase in the money supply, other factors constant, will create a 10% inflation rate.

16. Correct answer: a.

Discussion: The expectations Phillips curve shows the relationship between the unemployment rate (relative to the natural rate of unemployment) and the unanticipated rate of inflation. The relationship is negative, i.e. if the unemployment rate is below the natural rate, say 4.7% compared to 6%), then the actual inflation rate may exceed the expected inflation rate (e.g. 10% compared to an expected rate of 8%). Thus, when the unemployment rate is below the natural rate of unemployment, unanticipated inflation is greater than zero. In this example, the unanticipated rate of inflation (actual minus expected) would be 2%.

Statement b is not true since the expectations Phillips curve shows that unemployment varies with the unanticipated rate of inflation. Statement c is not correct. Moreover, you have not been introduced to the misery index (sum of inflation plus unemployment). Statement d is not correct. The expectations Phillips curve shows the natural rate of unemployment is defined where unanticipated inflation is zero, i.e. where the anticipated inflation rate is equal to the actual inflation rate. Statement e is not correct. The expectations Phillips curve will show that there is NO permanent relationship between the inflation rate and the unemployment rate. In fact, the view is that an economy will eventually always return to its natural rate of unemployment regardless of a inflation rate.

17. Correct answer: e.

Discussion: All of the above changes could cause changes in a nation's natural rate of unemployment. Europe used to have a lower natural rate of unemployment than the United States but since the 1970s, the natural rate of unemployment in Europe has exceeded that in the United States. The change in Europe's natural rate is attributed to statements c and d. Other explanations for changes in the natural rate of unemployment are offered in statements a and b.

VIII. ANSWER KEY: ESSAY QUESTIONS

1. First of all, it is the real interest rate that influences investment spending and not necessarily the nominal interest rate. For example, compare two cases: (1) a nominal interest rate of 15% when the inflation rate is 10%; and (2) a nominal interest rate of 8% when inflation is 2%. In case (1), the real interest rate is 5% and in case (2), the real interest rate is 6%. Thus, even though in case (1), the nominal interest rate is higher, the real cost of borrowing is lower. Thus, the real interest rate is a better indicator of the true cost of borrowing funds for investment spending.

At higher real interest rates, the opportunity cost of funding an investment project increases. In other words, the real rate of return necessary to be earned by the investment project must pass a higher hurdle in order for it to be considered more worthwhile than taking those funds and placing them in a bank or other interest bearing asset. For example, a firm may consider opening up a new factory or developing a new line of products. However, if the expected real payoff from funding such an investment is not as high as what could be earned by the firm simply investing those funds into an interest-bearing financial asset, then the firm may be inclined not to fund the investment project. Thus, higher real interest rates are typically associated with lower levels of investment spending. If higher real interest rates lead to lower levels of investment spending and lower levels of investment spending, through the multiplier, lead to lower levels of output (at least in the short run), then higher interest rates may be associated with lower levels of output (i.e. a stagnating economy). From the previous chapter, a reduction in investment spending of say $10 billion, caused by higher real interest rates, would lead to a reduction in output of say $20 billion if the multiplier is 2. Now, if the $20 billion decline in output influences investment spending as well, then investment spending may decline further (even without a change in real interest rates). That is, investment spending may decline by $2 billion more, and thus lead to a further drop in output of $4 billion (2 X $2 billion). This is an example of the multiplier-accelerator model at work.

Take It to the Net

We invite you to visit the O'Sullivan/Sheffrin page on the Prentice Hall Web site at:

http://www.prenhall.com/osullivan/

for this chapter's World Wide Web exercise.

CHAPTER 17
INTERNATIONAL TRADE AND FINANCE

I.   OVERVIEW

In this chapter, you will learn markets exist because individuals can gain from specialization and exchange. You will learn the concept of comparative advantage and specialization, or dividing production to minimize opportunity costs, which shows why individuals gain through specialization and exchange. You will learn why trade among countries is based on the same principles of trade between individuals. You will learn that specialization based on comparative advantage results in gains for all participants. In this chapter, you will also learn the rationale for various types of protectionist policies, and look at various trade agreements between countries. You will learn that exchange rates are determined by the desire of economic agents to purchase goods and assets in other countries. You will study the main determinants of supply and demand for a country's currency, and analyze the impact of shifts in supply and demand on the level of the exchange rate. You will learn the concept of the real exchange rate, or the exchange rate that expresses the prices in one country in terms of foreign currency and then compares those prices to foreign prices. In this chapter you will also learn about the global financial system today. You will learn the advantages and shortcomings of fixed and flexible exchange rate systems. You will also learn that, in today's global economy, nations have become increasingly interdependent through both product and financial market linkages, creating efficiency but also vulnerabilities.

II.   CHECK LIST

By the end of this chapter, you should be able to do the following:

√   Explain why specialization and exchange can benefit all participating parties.

√   Determine comparative advantage by comparing opportunity costs of production.

√   Explain what exports and imports are.

√   Define an exchange rate and use it to convert the dollar price of a good or service to a foreign currency price, and vice-versa.

√   List different types of trade protection and define what they are.

√   List the different types of protectionist trade policies.

√   Explain how the different protectionist trade policies work and their effects on import prices.

√   Discuss some arguments (or rationales) for protectionist trade policies.

√   Discuss why trade policy and environmental issues have become linked.

√   Explain how trade might cause income inequality to widen.

√   Discuss some recent trade agreements.

√   Explain a currency appreciation and depreciation.

√ Explain how a currency appreciation or depreciation might affect exports and imports.

√ Use an exchange rate to convert the foreign currency price of a good to an equivalent price in U.S. dollars (or another currency besides the U.S. dollar).

√ Use an exchange rate to convert the U.S. dollar price of a good to an equivalent price in foreign currency.

√ Use demand and supply analysis to show how changes in the demand and supply of a currency affect its price (the exchange rate).

√ Explain how an increase in the prices and interest rates of a country may affect the price of its currency. Use demand and supply analysis to illustrate.

√ Describe what actions a country would have to take to keep its currency's value from increasing or decreasing.

√ Explain what actions a government must take to keep its exchange rate fixed if it has a balance of payments deficit or surplus.

√ Explain what actions besides foreign exchange market intervention a country may need to take in order to eliminate a persistent balance of payments deficit or surplus under a fixed exchange rate system.

√ Discuss the U.S. experience with fixed and floating (flexible) exchange rates.

√ Discuss the Mexican financial crisis of 1994.

√ Discuss the Asian financial crisis of 1997.

III. KEY TERMS

Absolute advantage: the ability of one person or nation to produce a particular good at a lower absolute cost than another person or nation.

Comparative advantage: the ability of one person or nation to produce a good at an opportunity cost that is lower than the opportunity cost of another person or nation.

Export: a good produced in the "home" country (for example, the U.S.) and sold in another country.

Import: a good produced in a foreign country and purchased by residents of the "home" country (for example, the U.S.).

Exchange rate: the price at which currencies trade for one another.

Foreign exchange market: a market in which people exchange one currency for another.

Protectionist policies: rules that restrict the free flow of goods between nations, including tariffs (taxes on imports), quotas (limits on total imports), voluntary export restraints (agreements between governments to limit imports), and non-tariff trade barriers (subtle practices that hinder trade).

Import quota: a limit on the amount of a good that can be imported.

Voluntary export restraint (VER): a scheme under which an exporting country "voluntarily" decreases its exports.

Tariff: a tax on an imported good.

Learning by doing: the knowledge gained during production that increases productivity.

Infant industry: a new industry that is protected from foreign competitors.

Exchange rate: the rate at which we can exchange one currency for another.

Appreciation: an increase in the value of a currency.

Depreciation: a decrease in the value of a currency.

Foreign exchange market intervention: the purchase or sale of currencies by governments to influence the market exchange rate.

Flexible exchange rates: a currency system in which exchange rates are determined by free markets.

Fixed exchange rates: a system in which governments peg exchange rates.

Euro: the currency that members of the European Union will begin using as their own currency.

Balance of payments deficit: under a fixed exchange rate system, a situation in which the supply of a country's currency exceeds the demand for the currency at the current exchange rate.

Balance of payments surplus: under a fixed exchange rate system, a situation in which the demand of a country's currency exceeds the supply for the currency at the current exchange rate.

Devaluation: a decrease in the exchange rate to which a currency is pegged in a fixed rate system.

Revaluation: an increase in the exchange rate to which a currency is pegged.

IV. PERFORMANCE ENHANCING TIPS (PETS)

PET #1

Opportunity cost calculations used to determine comparative advantage should be based on a per unit comparison.

Suppose you are given the following information:

	Country A	Country B
Wood Products	10/hour	8/hour
High-tech products	15/hour	4/hour

The information in the table tells you that Country A can produce 10 units of wood products in one hour (with its resources) and 15 units of high-tech products in one hour. Country B can produce 8 units of wood products in one hour (with its resources) and 4 units of high-tech products in one hour. How can this information be used to determine which country has a comparative advantage in wood production and which country has a comparative advantage in high-tech production?

As a side point, you may wish to note that Country A has an absolute advantage in the production of both wood and high-tech products since it can produce more per hour of either good than can Country B. But, absolute advantage does NOT determine the basis for trade.

The easiest way to compute comparative advantage is to determine what the opportunity cost of production is for each good for each country, on a per unit basis. To do this, you must first answer how much Country A must give up if it were to specialize in the production of wood. For every additional hour of effort devoted to producing wood products, Country A would give up the production of 15 units of high-tech products. (Of course, it is then able to produce 10 more units of wood products). On a per unit basis, Country A must give up 1.5 units of high-tech products for each 1 unit of wood products = (15 high-tech products/hour)/(10 wood products/hour) = 1.5 high tech products/1 wood product. You would read this as "for Country A, the opportunity cost of 1 wood product is 1.5 high-tech products." For Country B, for every additional hour of effort devoted to producing wood products, it must give up 4 units of high tech products. (Of course, it is then able to produce 8 more units of wood products). On a per unit basis, Country B must give up 0.5 units of high-tech products for each 1 unit of wood products = (4 high-tech products/hour)/(8 wood products/hour). You would read this as "for Country B, the opportunity cost of 1 wood product is 0.5 high-tech products." Thus, Country B has the lower opportunity cost of producing wood products since it has to give up fewer high-tech products.

Since Country B has the lower opportunity cost of wood production, it should specialize in wood production. (Wood production is "less costly" in Country B than in Country A). If this is true, then it must also be true that Country A has the lower opportunity cost of high-tech production and thus should specialize in producing high-tech goods.

Let's see if this is true using the numbers from the table above. For Country A, the opportunity cost of producing more high-tech products is that for every additional hour of producing high-tech products, it must give up producing 10 units of wood products. (Of course, it is then able to produce 15 more units of high-tech products). On a per unit basis, Country A must give up 0.67 wood products for every 1 high-tech product = (10 wood products/hour)/(15 high-tech products per hour). You would read this as "for Country A, the opportunity cost of 1 high-tech product is 0.67 wood products." For Country B, the opportunity cost of producing more high-tech products is that for every additional hour of producing high-tech products, it must give up producing 8 units of wood products. (Of course, it is then able to produce 4 more units of high-tech products). On a per unit basis, Country B must give up 2 wood products for every one unit of high-tech products = (8 wood products/hour)/(4 high-tech products/hour). Thus, Country A has the lower opportunity cost of producing high-tech products since it has to give up fewer wood products. (High-tech production is "less costly" in Country A than in Country B).

PET #2

Trade protection increases the price a country pays for goods it imports from other countries.

Your textbook mentions different types of trade protection -- tariffs, quotas, and non-tariff barriers, all of which act to raise the price of the goods and services that a country imports from other countries.

PET #3

The exchange rate is the price of one currency in terms of another. It can be thought of just like the price of any good or service.

Think about the price of any good or service, say a painting priced at $200, i.e. $200/painting. The item in the denominator is what is being priced. So too for an exchange rate. Suppose the exchange rate is expressed as 0.50 U.S. dollars/1 German mark. In this case, the currency that is being priced is the mark.

Its price is 50 cents. The inverse of this exchange rate would be 2 German marks/$1 U.S. dollar. Now, the currency that is being priced is the dollar. One dollar is priced at (or costs) 2 German marks.

If the price of a painting rises, we would say the painting has appreciated in value. If the price of a painting falls, we would say the painting has depreciated in value. So too for an exchange rate. If the exchange rate decreased from 0.50 U.S. dollars/1 German mark to 0.40 U.S. dollars/1 German mark, we would say that the mark has depreciated since it now worth 40 cents instead of 50 cents. If the German mark has depreciated against the dollar, then it must be true that the U.S. dollar has appreciated. To see this, the inverse of 0.40 US dollars/1 German mark is 2.5 German marks/1 U.S. dollar. Thus, the dollar has appreciated in value since it is now worth 2.5 marks instead of 2 marks.

PET #4

Trade protection reduces the total supply of a good in a country. The reduced supply will increase the price a country pays for the protected good.

Your textbook mentions different types of trade protection -- import bans, import quotas, voluntary export restraints, and tariffs -- all of which act to raise the price of the goods and services that a country imports from other countries. Protectionist trade policies effectively reduce the total supply of a good (where the total supply comes from domestic production plus foreign imports) by restricting the amount of foreign imports. Thus, in terms of supply and demand analysis, protectionist trade policies shift the supply curve to the left. A leftward shift in the supply curve raises the price of a good. (See the box in PET #7 in Chapter 4 for review.)

PET #5

The exchange rate is the price of one currency in terms of another. It can be thought of just like the price of any good or service.

Think about the price of any good or service, say a painting priced at $200, i.e. $200/painting. The item in the denominator is what is being priced. So too for an exchange rate. Suppose the exchange rate is expressed as 0.50 U.S. dollars/1 German mark. In this case, the currency that is being priced is the mark. Its price is 50 cents. The inverse of this exchange rate would be 2 German marks/$1 U.S. dollar. Now, the currency that is being priced is the dollar. One dollar is priced at (or costs) 2 German marks.

If the price of a painting rises, we would say the painting has appreciated in value. If the price of a painting falls, we would say the painting has depreciated in value. So too for an exchange rate. If the exchange rate decreased from 0.50 U.S. dollars/1 German mark to 0.40 U.S. dollars/1 German mark, we would say that the mark has depreciated since it now worth 40 cents instead of 50 cents. If the German mark has depreciated against the dollar, then it must be true that the U.S. dollar has appreciated. To see this, the inverse of 0.40 US dollars/1 German mark is 2.5 German marks/1 U.S. dollar. Thus, the dollar has appreciated in value since it is now worth 2.5 marks instead of 2 marks.

PET #6

You can think of the terms "U.S. assets" and "foreign assets" as referring largely to U.S. financial assets and to foreign financial assets.

Financial assets include stocks, mutual funds, corporate bonds, and government bonds (securities, bills). For example, suppose a U.S. resident purchases a Treasury bond issued by the British government. We would say that the U.S. resident has acquired a foreign asset. Alternatively, if a German resident purchases a U.S. corporate bond, we would say that the German resident has acquired a U.S. asset.

PET #7

A U.S. resident's purchase of a foreign asset means that the U.S. resident is lending his saving to the foreign country. A foreign resident's purchase of a U.S. asset means that the foreign resident is lending his saving to the U.S.

PET #8

If the price of a currency (i.e. the exchange rate) is fixed below its equilibrium value, there will be an excess demand for the currency. If the price of a currency is fixed above its equilibrium value, there will be an excess supply of the currency.

For example, suppose the exchange rate is $0.50/German mark at which it is fixed. First of all, the currency that is being priced is the German mark. Its price is $0.50. Thus, the demand and supply curves drawn below represent the demand and supply of German marks.

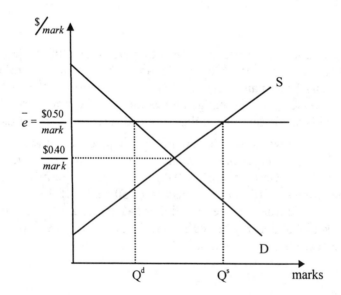

Since the equilibrium price of a mark is $0.40/German mark, the quantity of marks supplied must exceed the quantity of marks demanded at the fixed rate. That is, there will be an excess supply of German marks. This also means that there must be an excess demand for dollars.

The reverse happens when the exchange rate is fixed below the equilibrium price. If the exchange rate is fixed at $0.30/mark, the quantity of marks demanded will exceed the quantity of marks supplied. That is, there will be an excess demand for German marks. This also means that there must be an excess supply of dollars.

V. PRACTICE EXAM: MULTIPLE CHOICE QUESTIONS

1. Which one of the following statements is true of markets?
   a) they exist because we are not self-sufficient.
   b) they are places where money is exchanged for goods.
   c) the factor market is where labor services are bought and sold.
   d) they allow us to exchange what we have for what we want.
   e) all of the above.

2. Use the information below to determine which answer is correct.

	Lena	J. Martin
Brownies produced per week	4	5
Pictures painted per week	2	10

   a) the opportunity cost of one picture for Lena is 1/2 a brownie.
   b) the opportunity cost of one picture for J. Martin is 2 brownies.
   c) Lena has a comparative advantage in brownies production.
   d) Lena's opportunity cost of brownies is greater than J. Martin's.
   e) (c) and (d).

3. Which one of the following statements is NOT correct?
   a) comparative advantage arises when a nation has a lower opportunity cost in the production of X than another nation.
   b) a nation that is more productive in producing all goods will not benefit from trading with less productive nations.
   c) about three-fourths of income earned by households comes from wages and salaries.
   d) household saving is used by firms to fund purchases of factories, equipment, etc.
   e) none of the above are correct.

Use the table below to answer the following question.

	Country A	Country B
Toys	50 per day	20 per day
Ships	2 per day	1 per day

4. Which country has the comparative advantage in producing toys and which country has the comparative advantage in producing ships?

   a) Country A has the comparative advantage in producing both toys and ships.

   b) Country B has the comparative advantage in producing both toys and ships.

   c) Country A has the comparative advantage in producing toys and Country B has the comparative advantage in producing ships.

   d) Country B has the comparative advantage in producing toys and Country A has the comparative advantage in producing ships.

   e) Need information on exchange rates to answer the question.

5. Suppose that you are going to buy a cuckoo clock from Germany and the German mark price for the clock is 250 marks. If the current exchange rate is 2 marks/U.S. dollar, you will pay $_____. If the exchange rate changes to 1.8 marks/U.S. dollar, the _____ will have depreciated.

   a) $125; dollar.

   b) $125; mark.

   c) $500; dollar.

   d) $500; mark.

   e) $250; dollar.

6. Which one of the following is NOT an example of trade barrier?

   a) tariffs.

   b) quotas.

   c) health and safety laws.

   d) the General Agreement on Tariffs and Trade.

   e) slow and inefficient customs systems.

7. Which one of the following is NOT an example of a protectionist trade policy?

   a) ban on imports.

   b) voluntary export restraint.

   c) tariff.

   d) import quota.

   e) all of the above are protectionist trade policies.

8. Which one of the following would NOT be a result of a tariff imposed by the U.S. on footwear imported from Brazil?

   a) U.S. footwear firms will be winners.

   b) employment in the U.S. footwear industry will be higher than compared to a situation of free trade.

   c) the price that U.S. consumers pay for footwear produced in the U.S. will be lower than compared to a situation of free trade.

   d) U.S. citizens should prefer a tariff on footwear to an import quota.

   e) all of the above would result from the tariff on Brazilian footwear.

9. Which one of the following statements is true?

   a) under an import quota, if the government sells import licenses to importers, then importers may not make money from the quota.

   b) Japan's agreement to a voluntary export restraint on its automobile exports to the U.S. resulted in a decrease in the price of U.S.-made automobiles.

   c) the threat of retaliation may persuade a country to impose harsher protectionist trade policies on its trading partners.

   d) the Smoot-Hawley Tariff bill was designed to gradually lead to the removal of tariffs around the world.

   e) the NAFTA agreement turned a U.S. trade surplus with Mexico into a U.S. trade deficit.

10. Which one of the following statements is true?

   a) attempt to shield workers from foreign competition.

   b) the infant industry argument for trade protection is that it promotes learning by doing and thus can enable a new industry to be able to compete with other producers from around the world.

   c) a problem with granting trade protection to an infant industry is that the protection is not likely to be removed as the industry matures.

   d) by protecting infant industries from foreign competition, trade protection may lead to inefficient production by the protected industries.

   e) all of the above are true.

11. Which one of the following is a problem with a government subsidizing an industry in the hope of establishing a world-wide monopoly?

   a) the taxpayers ultimately pay for the government subsidy.

   b) there is no guarantee that country will be able to profit from securing the monopoly.

   c) another country may also grant a subsidy to the same industry.

   d) the government may end up subsidizing an industry in which there are not economies of scale.

   e) all of the above are problems.

12. Suppose the current franc/deutschemark rate is 4.1. If this rate changed to 3.80, we would say that:
    a) the deutschemark has depreciated.
    b) the franc is now worth fewer deutschemarks.
    c) the demand for francs must have decreased.
    d) the supply of deutschemarks must have decreased.
    e) (b) and (c).

13. Suppose the price of a Swedish crystal vase is 80 Swedish krona and the current exchange rate is 6 Swedish krona per U.S. dollar. Which one of the following statements would be true?
    a) an increase in Swedish interest rates will reduce the dollar price of the crystal vase.
    b) an increase in U.S. interest rates will reduce the dollar price of the crystal vase.
    c) the current dollar price of a Swedish crystal vase is $480.
    d) if the price of a U.S. crystal vase is $30, then Swedish crystal vases cost more than U.S. crystal vases.
    e) none of the above.

14. A decrease in interest rates in Japan will:
    a) reduce the demand for yen.
    b) cause a depreciation of the yen.
    c) raise the demand for yen and appreciate the yen.
    d) reduce the supply of yen and depreciate the yen.
    e) (a) and (b).

15. Suppose that prices in Austria fall relative to those in the U.S. Which one of the following would be expected to happen?
    a) the shilling/dollar exchange rate will fall.
    b) the demand for shillings will fall.
    c) the supply of dollars will fall.
    d) Austria's net exports will increase.
    e) (a) and (d).

16. Which one of the following transactions would give rise to a supply of foreign currency from the U.S perspective?
    a) income earnings from foreign investments in the U.S.
    b) U.S. imports.
    c) a foreigner's purchase of a U.S. asset.
    d) U.S. aid to a foreign country.
    e) none of the above.

17. Which one of the following transactions would give rise to a demand for foreign currency from the U.S perspective?

    a) income earnings from U.S. investments in foreign countries.

    b) sale of a U.S. telephone system to an Indonesian business.

    c) a U.S. resident's purchases of a government bond issued by Switzerland.

    d) sale of U.S. financial services to a Mexican government.

    e) none of the above.

18. If the current yen/$ exchange rate is 135 and the U.S. government believed that the exchange rate was too high, the U.S. government:

    a) might sell dollars to the private market.

    b) might buy dollars from the private market.

    c) might buy yen from the private market.

    d) fix the exchange rate.

    e) (a) and (c).

19. Which one of the following statements is true of the foreign exchange market?

    a) the Federal Reserve has official responsibility for conducting foreign exchange market intervention.

    b) when a country runs a balance of payments surplus under a fixed exchange rate system, its holdings of foreign exchange will decrease.

    c) Europe has plans to issue a new common currency named the "European currency unit" or "ecu."

    d) foreign exchange intervention may not be successful at changing a currency's value because the dollar amount of intervention is very small relative to the trillions of dollars traded on the foreign exchange market by private market participants.

    e) today, all countries participate in flexible exchange rate systems.

VI. PRACTICE EXAM: ESSAY QUESTIONS

1. Discuss the different methods of trade protection and some of the newer organizations aimed at reducing trade protection.

2. Suppose the U.S. initially has no trade restrictions on imports of copper. Explain how a tariff on copper creates winners and losers within the U.S. Where might resources (labor and capital) move after the tariff is imposed? Be sure to address the government's use of the tax revenues earned by the tariff. Use demand and supply analysis to show the effects of the tariff.

3. Discuss some of the arguments made in favor of trade protection.

4a. Suppose you have $1,000 to invest and are considering buying either a 1-year U.S. Treasury bond, which has an interest rate of 7% per year, or a German treasury bond, which has an interest rate of 10% per year. The current exchange rate is 1.60 marks/dollar. If you expect the mark/dollar rate to be 1.68 in one year, where might you invest and why?

4b. Suppose that one year from now, the mark/dollar rate is 1.62, did your decision based on your expectation in part (4a) turn out to be a good decision? Explain.

5a. Consider the market for French francs (Ffr) where the current equilibrium exchange rate is $0.20/Ffr. What will happen to the exchange rate if the price of French goods declined relative to the price of U.S. goods? Use supply and demand analysis to answer the question.

5b. Suppose that the U.S. and France wanted to prevent any change in the exchange rate, i.e. they want to keep it fixed at $0.20/Ffr. What will happen to France's balance of payments given your answer to 5a? What will the U.S. and French governments have to do?

VII. ANSWER KEY: MULTIPLE CHOICE QUESTIONS

1. Correct answer: e.

Discussion: All of the above are correct statements about why markets exist.

2. Correct answer: c.

Discussion: For Lena, the opportunity cost of producing one picture is the two brownies that must be given up (4 brownies/2 pictures) = (2 brownies/1 picture). For J. Martin, the opportunity cost of producing one picture is 1/2 brownie (5 brownies/10 pictures) = (1/2 brownie/1 picture). Since Lena must give up more brownies to produce one picture, the opportunity cost of producing pictures is higher for Lena than it is for J. Martin. This also means that for Lena, the opportunity cost of producing one brownie must be lower than it is for J. Martin. To see this, invert the ratios above. From this you'll see that so that for Lena, the opportunity cost of one brownie is 1/2 picture and for J. Martin, the opportunity cost of one brownie is two pictures. Since the opportunity cost of brownie production is lower for Lena than for J. Martin, Lena has a comparative advantage in brownie production. Statements a and b are wrong since these statements have the numbers reversed for Lena and J. Martin. Statement d is wrong since Lena's opportunity cost of pictures, not brownies, is greater than J. Martin's.

3. Correct answer: b.

Discussion: Absolute advantage (i.e. being more productive -- producing more per hour or day) in the production of two or more goods does not establish the basis for mutually beneficial trade. Comparative advantage is what determines the basis for trade. For example, the United States may be more productive at producing clothing and airplanes than China is. But, if China has a lower opportunity cost of producing clothes than the United States, even though they may not be able to produce as many clothes per hour, they can specialize in (i.e. put more of their resources in) clothing production and the United States can specialize in airplane production and then trade with each other. The net result of the trade is that the United States will be able to get back more clothing in exchange for one airplane than if it instead had cut back airplane production and devoted its own resources to clothing production. The same is true for China. China will be able to get back more airplanes from trading clothes with the United States than if it had cut back clothing production in its own country and devoted those freed up resources to airplane production.

Statements a, c, and d are all correct statements.

4. Correct answer: c.

Discussion: Country A must give up 50 toys to produce 2 ships. On a per unit basis, Country A must give up 25 toys to produce 1 ship. On the other hand, Country B must give up 20 toys to produce 1 ship. Since Country B has to give up fewer toys to produce 1 ship, Country B incurs a smaller opportunity cost of building one more ship. That is, it is less costly to produce a ship in Country B than in country A. So, Country B should produce ships which means Country A should produce toys. The two countries will be able to acquire more of both goods by trading or exchanging toys for ships and vice-versa.

Statement a is not correct. It would be correct if the question had been "which country has an absolute advantage in toy production and which in ship production?" The table shows that Country A can produce more toys and more ships per day than can Country B. However, this is not the concept of comparative advantage. Statement b is not correct for similar reasons just mentioned. Statement d is not correct because it is the other way around -- Country A has a comparative advantage in toy production and Country B in ship building. Statement e is not correct because comparative advantage can be computed using the table of numbers given.

5. Correct answer: a.

Discussion: To figure out the dollar price of the clock, the mark price must be converted to dollars using the exchange rate. Since the exchange rate is expressed as marks/dollar, you can determine the dollar price by multiplying 250 marks X (1 dollar/2 marks) = $125. (The marks in the numerator and denominator cancel each other out). Since the exchange rate is expressed as marks/dollar, it is best to think of the exchange rate as the price of a dollar. Since the exchange rate has changed from 2 marks/dollar to 1.8 marks/dollar, the price of a dollar has decreased (See PET #5), i.e. the dollar has depreciated (which also means that the mark must have appreciated).

Statement b is not correct because the mark appreciated, not depreciated. Statement c is not correct because the conversion of the mark price of the clock to a dollar price leads to a price of $125, not $500. Statement d is not correct for the reasons mentioned for b and c. Statement e is not correct because the dollar price of the clock is $125, not $250.

6. Correct answer: d.

Discussion: The General Agreement on Tariffs and Trade (GATT) is an agreement between countries to work together to reduce tariff rates amongst themselves.

A tariff is a tax on an imported good which raises the price that a country must pay to buy it from another country. This acts as a trade barrier. A quota is a restriction on the quantity of imports of a particular good that a country may purchase from another country. It is also a trade barrier and acts to raise the price of the imported good. Health and safety laws are non-tariff trade barriers. These laws may effectively make it more difficult for a country to import a product from another country. For example, the health and safety laws of European countries restrict them from importing hormone-fed beef. This meant that they could not buy hormone-fed beef from the U.S. Slow and inefficient customs laws also act as a trade barrier. For example, if a product must pass through several layers of administration and paperwork before being admitted into the importing country, this raises the cost of the good and thus its price. This effectively makes it harder and more expensive for the importing country to buy the good and more of a hassle for the exporting country to deliver its products to another country.

7. Correct answer: e.

Discussion: None necessary.

8. Correct answer: c.

Discussion: Statement c is not correct. A tariff on footwear from Brazil will raise the price to U.S. consumers of footwear, regardless of whether the footwear is produced in Brazil or the U.S.

Statement a is correct. U.S. footwear firms will be winners in the sense that they will be able to get a higher price for the footwear that they sell to U.S. consumers. Statement b is correct. In free trade, there would be less production of footwear by U.S. producers and more by foreign producers. Thus, under free trade, employment in the U.S. footwear industry would be lower than when footwear is subject to a tariff, which is to say employment in the U.S. footwear industry would be higher with the tariff than in free trade. Statement d is correct. A tariff raises the price of the protected good (footwear in this case) less than does an import quota. Moreover, the government collects tariff revenue that the government could then use to fund government programs that benefit consumers (or to even give them tax refunds!).

9. Correct answer: a.

Discussion: When the government establishes an import quota, it gives licenses to importers which dictate how much of a good they are permitted to import. Naturally, importers are aware that they can profit by having an import license because they can buy the good from the foreign Country At the unrestricted price and sell in the home Country At the quota-induced price which is higher. However, if importers have to pay for the import licenses, then some of the profit that they expect to make from the import quota will be "eaten up" by the cost of the import license. That is, paying for the import license is a cost that an importer would have to consider in determining how profitable it would be to have the license.

Statement b is not true. Japan's agreement to a voluntary export restraint (VER) on its automobile exports to the U.S. resulted in a higher, not lower price of U.S.-made automobiles. U.S. consumers paid approximately $660 more for a U.S.-made automobile after the VER. Statement c is not true. The threat of retaliation may persuade a country to impose less harsh (i.e., less restrictive) protectionist trade policies on its trading partners, not harsher policies. Statement d is not correct. The Smoot-Hawley Tariff bill raised U.S. tariffs by an average of 59% and is pointed to as a policy that may have worsened the U.S. depression of the 1930s.

Statement e is not correct. The devaluation of the peso is much more likely to have turned the U.S. trade surplus with Mexico into a U.S. trade deficit. The devaluation of the peso effectively made Mexican products much cheaper than U.S.-made products.

10. Correct answer: e.

Discussion: None necessary.

11. Correct answer: e.

Discussion: When a government subsidizes an industry, it gives money to the industry. The money the government has to give to the industry is ultimately provided by taxpayers. There is no guarantee that a country will be able to profit from securing a monopoly in a particular industry since other governments, may have, at the same time, chosen to subsidize the same industry. In this case, one or both countries may end up earning losses. The government also may choose to subsidize an industry thinking that the industry has large economies of scale (low average cost of production at very large levels of output) and thus is much more likely to exist as a monopoly (single producer). However, if it turns out that the industry is actually able to exist with more than one producer, the government-subsidized industry may find itself having to compete with producers from other firms around the world. In this case, monopoly profits anticipated by the government may not materialize.

12. Correct answer: a.

Discussion: Since the exchange rate is expressed as francs/deutschemarks, the currency that is priced is the deutschemark; its price is 4.1 francs. If the exchange rate changes to 3.80, we would say that the price of a deutschemark has declined. It is now worth only 3.80 francs. That is, the deutschemark has depreciated in value.

A depreciation in the value of the deutschemark means that the franc has appreciated in value. To see this, invert the exchange rate. In this case, the initial price of a franc would be 1 deutschemark/4.1 francs = 0.24 deutschemarks/franc and the new price would be 1/3.8 = 0.26 deutschemarks/franc. Thus, the franc is now worth more deutschemarks, not fewer deutschemarks. Thus, statement b is not correct. We could also say that the franc has appreciated in value. Statement c cannot be correct. A decrease in demand for francs would mean that the price of a franc would decline, i.e. it would depreciate in value. However, the change in the exchange rate implies that the franc has appreciated in value. Statement d cannot be correct. A decrease in the supply of deutschemarks would increase the price of a deutschemark, i.e. the deutschemark would appreciate in value. However, the change in the exchange rate implies that the deutschemark has depreciated in value.

13. Correct answer: b.

Discussion: Statement b is correct and requires that you understand that the increase in U.S. interest rates will increase the value of the U.S. dollar, say from 6 krona/dollar to 8 krona/dollar. At the current exchange rate, a Swedish vase costing 80 krona will, in terms of dollars, cost 80 krona/(6 krona/dollar) = $13.33. Since the increase in U.S. interest rates increases the value of the U.S. dollar, the dollar price of the Swedish vase will be reduced. If the exchange rate changes to 8 krona/dollar, the Swedish vase will cost, in terms of dollars, $10 (= 80 krona/(8 krona/dollar)).

Statement a is not correct. An increase in Swedish interest rates will increase the value of a krona (appreciate the krona) and decrease the value (depreciate) the dollar. That is, the exchange rate may change from 6 krona/dollar to 4 krona/dollar. In this case, the dollar price of the Swedish vase will increase from $13.33 to $20, not decrease. Statement c is not correct. The current dollar price of a Swedish vase is $13.33. Statement d is not correct. If a U.S. crystal vase costs $30 and the current dollar price of a Swedish crystal vase is $13.33, then Swedish crystal vases are less expensive than U.S. crystal vases, not more expensive.

14. Correct answer: e.

Discussion: A reduction in Japanese interest rates will reduce the attractiveness of Japanese financial assets to investors in the United States (and other countries, too). Consequently, the demand for Japanese financial assets (Japanese government and corporate bonds) by foreign investors will be reduced. If foreigners do not want to buy as many Japanese financial assets, the demand for yen, which is necessary to pay for the Japanese assets, will also be reduced. Thus, statement a is correct. In terms of demand and supply analysis, this can be represented by a leftward shift in the demand for yen. A decline in the demand for yen reduces the price of yen. A decrease in the price of yen is also referred to as a depreciation of the yen's value. Thus, statement b is correct.

Statement c is not correct because the demand for yen decreases, not increases. Statement d is not correct. In fact, the supply of yen would increase since residents of Japan would seek to invest in financial assets outside of their country given the now reduced interest rates in their own country. Thus, Japanese residents, by increasing their demand for foreign (say, U.S.) financial assets would supply yen and demand dollars in exchange so as to be able to pay for the U.S. assets. Statement d is also not correct for the reason that a decrease in the supply of yen (assuming you thought that was correct) would actually increase the price of yen and appreciate it, not depreciate it.

15. Correct answer: e.

Discussion: If prices in Austria fall relative to those in the U.S, Austrian-made goods become relatively less expensive than U.S-made goods. This will increase the demand for Austrian-made goods and reduce the demand for U.S-made goods. Thus, Austria's net exports will increase and so statement d is correct. (Also, a decrease in the price of Austrian-made goods reduces Austria's real exchange rate. A lower real exchange rate is associated with an increase in net exports). To buy the goods, U.S. consumers must convert their dollars to Austrian shillings. That is, U.S. consumers will demand Austrian shillings (and correspondingly supply their dollars in exchange). Thus, statements c and d are not correct. The increase in demand for Austrian shillings will increase the price of a shilling (appreciate the shilling) and correspondingly decrease the price of the dollar (depreciate the dollar). That is, the shilling/dollar exchange rate will decline. Thus, statement a is correct.

16. Correct answer: c.

Discussion: When a foreigner wants to purchase any U.S. item, be it a computer, airplane, tobacco, or financial assets, will require that the foreigner convert their currency to U.S. dollars. That is, the foreigner will supply foreign currency to the international market and demand, in exchange, U.S. dollars.

Statements a, b, and d are all examples of transactions that would create a demand for foreign currency (and so too, a supply of U.S. dollars). For statement a, when we pay foreigners interest from U.S. financial assets they have acquired, foreigners will take the interest earnings in dollars and convert them to their own currency. That is, they will demand their (foreign) currency and supply (sell) dollars to pay for the foreign currency. For statement b, when we purchase a foreign good or service (an "import"), we must pay for it with foreign currency, not dollars. Thus, we will demand foreign currency and supply (sell) dollars to pay for the foreign currency. For statement d, when the U.S. provides aid to foreign countries, we convert dollars to foreign currency and then give the foreign currency to the country. Thus, U.S. aid to foreign countries creates a demand for foreign currency and a supply of dollars.

17. Correct answer: c.

Discussion: When a foreigner purchases a U.S. asset, he must buy the U.S. asset with U.S. dollars. Thus, the foreigner must convert his foreign currency to U.S. dollars before purchasing the asset. Thus, the foreigner supplies foreign currency (and correspondingly demands U.S. dollars).

Statement a is not correct. If a foreign resident has made an investment in the U.S. (i.e. purchased a U.S. asset), the investment income will be paid in terms of U.S. dollars (since it is a U.S. asset). The foreign resident, of course, will want to convert the U.S. dollar proceeds into foreign currency. Thus, U.S. dollars will be supplied and foreign currency demanded. Statement b is not correct. When a U.S. resident imports goods from a foreign country, the goods must be paid for with foreign currency. The U.S. resident must convert dollars to foreign currency to make the payment. Thus, imports into the U.S. create a demand for foreign currency and a supply of U.S. dollars. Statement d is not correct. When the U.S. gives foreign aid to another country, it gives the country aid in terms of the foreign country's currency. Thus, the U.S. government must convert U.S. dollars to foreign currency. That is, the U.S. supplies dollars and demands foreign currency.

18. Correct answer: e.

Discussion: If the U.S. government believed that 135 yen/$ was too high, the government would take action to push down the exchange rate, i.e. reduce the (yen) price of a dollar say to 125 yen/$. A decrease in the price of a dollar could be accomplished by increasing the supply of U.S. dollars on the private market. That is, the government would sell dollars to the private market. At the same time, a decrease in the price of a dollar (which means an increase in the price of a yen) could be accomplished by increasing the demand for yen (i.e. buying yen). Thus, statements a and c will both work to reduce the exchange rate (i.e. reduce the yen price of a dollar).

19. Correct answer: d.

Discussion: Statement d is true; there is limited evidence that foreign exchange market intervention can actually alter, in any substantial way, the value of one currency against another.

Statement a is not true. The U.S. Treasury has official responsibility for conducting foreign exchange market intervention although it may act in concert with the Fed. Statement b is not true. A country that runs a balance of payments surplus (sum of current account plus capital account) is on net earning foreign exchange. That is, the country's foreign reserves will increase, not decrease. Statement c is not true. While Europe does have plans to issue a common currency, the name of the currency is to be the "euro." Statement e is not correct. Some countries participate in fixed exchange rate systems. Many countries in Europe currently participate in a fixed exchange rate system known as the "exchange rate mechanism."

VIII. ANSWER KEY: ESSAY QUESTIONS

1. Trade protection comes in a variety of forms. The most common form of trade protection is a tariff, which is a tax on an imported good. Tariffs effectively raise the price of a foreign good from the importing country's perspective. Quotas also raise the price of an imported good but do so by restricting the supply of the imported good into the country. Quotas are physical limitations on the quantity of imported good coming into a country. Voluntary export restraints are agreements between the importing and exporting country for the exporting country to limit the quantity of goods it exports. Voluntary export restraints are similar to quotas but are imposed by the exporter on itself rather than by the importing country on the exporting country. There are other, more subtle ways that countries have developed for the purpose of reducing imports from other countries. Anything from stiffer health and safety standards on imported products to more paperwork and checkpoints to pass through can effectively reduce the availability of imported goods into another country. Many of the recent trade agreements across country groups are aimed at completely eliminating tariff and quotas on each other's goods. NAFTA is a free-trade agreement between the United States, Canada, and Mexico. The European Union has essentially created a free-trade zone amongst the participating countries. However, the less overt forms of trade protection (like health and safety standards or environmental standards) can be problematic since they may be used to re-introduce trade protection while enabling a country to appear as if it is adhering to the free trade agreement.

2. First of all, one might wonder why the U.S. decided to institute a tariff on a previously freely traded good. There are a few explanations. One explanation might be that the U.S. imposed the tariff as a retaliatory action to its trading partner's decision to impose a tariff on a U.S. good(s). The retaliation may be used as a device to prompt the trading partner to remove their tariff on a U.S. good(s). An alternative explanation might be that workers in the U.S. copper industry felt threatened by the competition from copper producers in foreign countries. Fearing that the competition might mean that U.S. copper producers would lose their market to foreign producers (and thus jobs and profits), workers/management in the U.S. copper industry may have lobbied Congress for trade protection.

When a tariff is introduced on foreign imports of copper, there will be winners and losers in the U.S. The winners will be the copper producers and workers in the copper industry. The price at which producers can sell copper will increase (as the graph below shows) and thus their profits may increase as well.

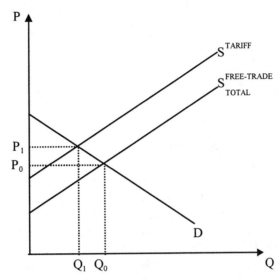

More workers and capital may now be needed in the copper industry, so resources may be taken out of other industries and moved into copper production. Thus, workers with skills in the copper industry will benefit. However, since the tariff raises the price of copper, users (buyers) of copper will lose.

Since the tariff generates tariff revenue for the government, the government may be able to use the revenue to offset some of the higher costs to copper users (i.e., subsidize copper users). Alternatively, the government may be able to use the tariff revenue to reduce income taxes on all workers, i.e., all workers might be given a tax refund. Or, the government could use the tariff revenue to help pay for other government programs that the citizens of the country feel are worth supporting.

3. There are several arguments made in favor of trade protection. One argument is that trade protection should be granted to industries that are just starting out -- so-called "infant industries." The argument is that the infant industries need protection from international competition in the early stages of development so that they become competitive themselves. Without the protection, the industry may not be successful, so the country loses out on establishing an industry that it may want. Another argument made in favor of trade protection is that trade protection "keeps jobs at home." Here, the argument is that without trade protection, the industry will be unable to compete against foreign competitors and so the domestic industry will go out of business. Thus, by granting protection to a domestic industry, a government can prevent the industry from going out of business and thereby prevent any attendant job losses that would result. Another argument made in favor of protection is that monopoly profits may be obtained. In this case, protection would be granted to industries which are likely to survive as monopolies. By granting protection to a monopoly industry, the country becomes the sole producer of the industry output and may thus be able to extract monopoly profits from sales around the world. The government may encourage this if it is able to share in the profits with the producer. Another argument that can be made in favor of protection is that it can be used to get trading partners to loosen their trade restrictions. For example, a country may threaten to or actually impose stiff tariffs against a good or set of goods imported from another country to prompt the country to reduce its tariffs. The U.S. used this type of threat against Japan and was successful in getting Japan to loosen some of its trade restrictions against the U.S. Another

argument made in favor of protection is that it will "level the playing field." This is a tit-for-tat application of protectionism. For example, if one country's government subsidizes a particular industry, then its production costs are unfairly low relative to the production costs of the same industry in other country that is not subsidizing the industry. Thus, to compete on a level ground, trade protection is considered to be a fair response.

This discussion provides arguments made in favor of trade protection. To be sure, there are many arguments that can be made against trade protection.

4a. While the 10% interest rate on the German bond makes it seem a more appealing investment than the U.S. bond, I must take into account any losses (or gains) on currency conversions required to purchase (and then redeem) the German treasury bond. To purchase the German treasury bond, I must convert my $1,000 to marks. Since the current exchange rate is 1.60 marks/dollar, I will be able to exchange $1,000 for 1,600 marks. Then, I will invest the 1,600 marks in the German bond, where I will earn a 10% return, i.e. 0.10 X 1,600 = 160 marks. At the end of the year, I will thus receive 1,760 marks. Since I expect the exchange rate to be 1.68 marks/dollar (dollar appreciation/mark depreciation), I expect to convert the 1,760 marks to dollars at 1,760 X ($1/1.68 marks) = $1,047.62. So, I expect $1,000 investment to yield $1.047.62, which is less than I could earn if I used my $1,000 to buy the U.S. bond. In one year, the U.S. bond will yield $1,070 ($1,000 X 1.07). It would thus be wiser to invest in the U.S. bond since I expect it to earn more than the German bond.

4b. My decision in (4a) to invest in the U.S. bond was based on what my expectation of the exchange rate would be in one year (which may turn out to be wrong). If the exchange rate one year later is 1.62 marks/dollar, then had I invested in the German bond, I would have converted 1,760 marks back to dollars at this exchange rate. That is, I would have gotten back $1086.14 = (1760 marks X $1/1.62marks). If I had known that the exchange rate would be 1.62 marks/dollar in one year, then I would have invested in the German bond since I could have earned a higher return ($1,070 versus $1,086.14). Hindsight is always accurate!

5a. A decrease in the price of French goods relative to U.S. goods will increase the demand for French goods (from both French and U.S. residents). The increased demand for French goods by U.S. residents translates into an increase in the demand for French francs (and correspondingly, an increase in supply of U.S. dollars on the foreign exchange market) since U.S. residents need the French francs in order to purchase the French goods. The increase in demand for French francs will increase the price of the French franc, i.e. the exchange rate expressed as $/Ffr will increase above, say, $0.20/Ffr. That is, the French franc will appreciate (and the dollar will depreciate). For example, the French franc may rise in value to $0.25/Ffr.

The demand and supply diagram for French francs below shows how the increase in demand for French francs raises the price of the franc.

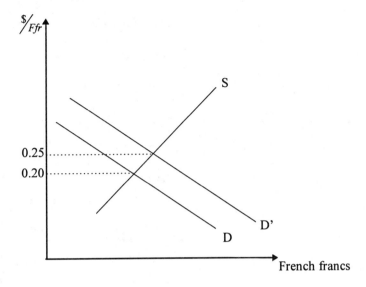

5b. France's balance of payments will (assuming it started at zero) move toward a surplus. The increase in demand for French francs with the exchange rate fixed will create a situation of an excess demand for French francs at the $0.20 price. (See diagram below). An excess demand for French francs corresponds to a balance of payment surplus for France.

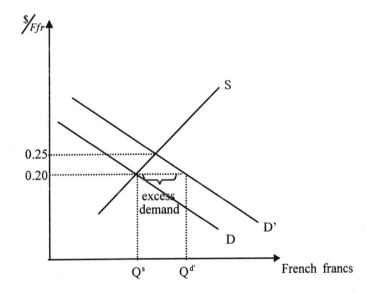

The governments must intervene in the foreign exchange market to prevent the French franc from appreciating to $0.25/Ffr. They must take action to keep the exchange rate fixed at $0.20/Ffr. Since the demand for French francs has increased (and correspondingly, the supply of dollars has increased), the governments must supply the market with the French francs they desire (and buy up the supply of dollars, i.e. take dollars off of the market). Thus, the U.S. government will lose French francs (since the U.S. government will be supplying them to the foreign exchange market (and taking in U.S.

Take It to the Net

We invite you to visit the O'Sullivan/Sheffrin page on the Prentice Hall Web site at:

http://www.prenhall.com/osullivan/

for this chapter's World Wide Web exercise.